ADDITIONAL PRAISE FOR *THE CRAFT BEER REVOLUTION*

"A lively, entertaining history by an insider. Steve Hindy portrays colorfully and knowledgeably the people who created the new breweries and the new beers. It's a compelling story of the craft beer revolution, a phenomenal flowering of American entrepreneurship."

—*Jerry Steinman, Founder,* Beer Marketer's Insights

"Steve's position in the craft industry puts him in a unique position—he both grew alongside it as an owner of Brooklyn Brewery and helped steer its course as an active Brewers Association member. He very accurately depicts the craft revolution's highs and lows and the camaraderie, challenging to maintain at times, that underlies it all."

—*Ken Grossman, Cofounder and CEO, Sierra Nevada*

"Balance. It's a desired trait in the brewing world. That perfectly comforting zone created through the interplay of hops and barley. Steve Hindy has found the equivalent space as a beer-journalist-slash-brewing-pioneer in his book *The Craft Beer Revolution*. Combining entertaining doses of craft brewing history with approachable descriptions of the brewers' art and fearless exploration of these entrepreneurs who changed the face of American brewing. A delicious and session-able read."

—*Sam Calagione, Founder and President, Dogfish Head*

"Steve Hindy weaves a vivid mix of passionate advocacy and cold hard journalism to describe the disruption which occurred first to large brewers, and now to small brewers grown big. *The Craft Beer Revolution* is a fascinating and entertaining read, revealing the idiosyncrasies and passion of the players who built the movement. If you love beer, you have to read it!"

—*Tom Long, CEO, MillerCoors*

"The rise of the American craft beer movement is one of the greatest business stories of all time. As a founding father and one hell of a writer, Steve weaves an amazing story of innovation and imagination that is truly unique to the world."

—*Dolf Vandenbrink, CEO, Heineken USA*

"With great passion and creativity, a generation of new American brewers is elevating the status of beer in the culinary world. *The Craft Beer Revolution* is the compelling inside story of their rise."

—*Dr. Tim Ryan, CEO, The Culinary Institute of America*

"The Craft Beer Revolution has captivated the imagination of the media, Wall Street, and Big Beer, as well as the attention, minds, and hearts of the consumer. Hindy's history, research, real-life experience, and story-telling ability paint an accurate picture of how this movement got started and what propelled it to its current heights. It's been a great ride for craft brewers, and this is a great read!"

—*Gary Fish, Founder and CEO, Deschutes Brewery, and Chairman, Brewers Association*

"The craft beer revolution, the most exciting development in the beer industry since the birth of lager beer in the nineteenth century, now has its chronicler. Steve Hindy tells the story as only a skilled journalist and an important player in the revolution could tell it. For decades going forward, this will be an important book for those who want to understand this transformative business story."

—*Daniel Bradford, Publisher,* All About Beer Magazine

"Steve Hindy brings a war-tested reporter's journalistic skill and a veteran insider's perspective to the good beer story, making his new book, *The Craft Beer Revolution,* compelling. This book is an essential resource and a great read, not only for those of us who participated in the craft beer renaissance, but also for a new generation of brewers and beer enthusiasts thirsting for the real story."

—*Tom Dalldorf, Publisher,* Celebrator Beer News

"*The Craft Beer Revolution* is a great American success story, told from the front row seat of Brooklyn Brewery cofounder Steve Hindy. The book shows an industry of brewers and distributors that is great because of the goodness of its people. Hindy entertains the reader with wonderful portraits of the people involved. The book is part high school yearbook and part Tom Wolfe's *The Right Stuff.* It shows us an industry that is being transformed and still works well for all involved, most importantly the consumer."

—*Craig Purser, President and CEO,*
National Beer Wholesalers Association

"Steve Hindy is a pioneer, visionary, and tireless advocate for the craft beer industry. His extensive background as a journalist coupled with his experience and passion for the craft beer industry result in a fascinating and most interesting perspective of the last six decades of a dynamic and colorful industry. Steve captures both the makings of the craft beer revolution and more recent evolution of the industry as a whole. I applaud Steve for this great work, his tireless commitment to this wonderful industry, and congratulate all those that make this such a great and unique business."

—*Bill Hackett, President, Crown Imports LLC*

"This book serves as a great history lesson about how craft brewing has changed the beer industry and captivated consumers. Through innovation and meeting customers' demands, craft brewers have grown far beyond their niche and now own a sizeable piece of the beer market once controlled by a select group of larger breweries. As this trend has grown, it's consumers that have been the real winners as unique craft beers are now an important part of any culinary experience. Steve has written a book drawing from his incredible expertise as a true trail blazer in the industry, focused on how to not only make great beer, but how to gain respect and notoriety when brewing."

—*Scott Crawford, Executive Coordinator of Purchasing,*
Whole Foods Market Northeast Region

THE CRAFT BEER REVOLUTION

HOW A BAND OF MICROBREWERS IS TRANSFORMING THE WORLD'S FAVORITE DRINK

STEVE HINDY

FOREWORD BY JOHN HICKENLOOPER

palgrave
macmillan

Dedicated to all brewers

THE CRAFT BEER REVOLUTION
Copyright © Steve Hindy, 2014, 2015.
All rights reserved.

First published in hardcover in 2014 by PALGRAVE MACMILLAN TRADE®
in the United States—a division of St. Martin's Press LLC, 175 Fifth Avenue, New
York, NY 10010.

Palgrave® and Macmillan® are registered trademarks in the United States, the
United Kingdom, Europe and other countries.

ISBN 978-1-137-28012-1 (paperback)

The Library of Congress has cataloged the hardcover edition as follows:

Hindy, Steve, 1949–
    The craft beer revolution : how a band of microbrewers transforming the
world's favorite drink / Steve Hindy.
        pages   cm
    ISBN 978-1-137-27876-0 (alk. paper)
    1. Brewing industry—United States—History. 2. Beer industry—United
States—History. 3. Microbreweries—United States—History. I. Title.
HD9397.U52H56   2014
338.4'7663420973—dc23

                                                                    2013036500

Design by Letra Libre, Inc.

First Palgrave Macmillan Trade paperback edition: May 2015

10 9 8 7 6 5 4 3 2 1

Printed in the United States of America.

CONTENTS

FOREWORD

THE CRAFT BEER REVOLUTION IS AN EXCITING ACCOUNT OF THE REBIRTH OF THE American brewing industry that has unfolded over the last four decades. In the mid-1970s, there were fewer than forty breweries in America; today, there are more than 2,500, and another thousand are in the works. According to the Brewers Association (BA), almost all Americans live within ten miles of a brewery.

Steve Hindy is the right guy to tell this remarkable story of American entrepreneurship and renewal. A journalist for 15 years before founding Brooklyn Brewery with his partner Tom Potter, Steve has been intimately involved in the evolution of the industry while serving on the board of directors of the BA, the trade association of small brewers, and the Beer Institute, the large brewer dominated trade association.

I got to know Steve in the early 1990s, while he was working to establish Brooklyn Brewery in a blighted part of Brooklyn and I was growing the Wynkoop Brewery in Denver's run-down Lower Downtown (LoDo) neighborhood.

When Jerry Williams and I, along with Russ Schehrer and Mark Schiffler, signed a lease for an abandoned warehouse in historic LoDo in 1987, the rent was a dollar per square foot per year. It took us 18 months to open the doors to Wynkoop Brewing Company. It takes a long time to raise money for something people have never seen before.

We were the first brewpub in the Rocky Mountains, and the first restaurant to open in LoDo in five years. Like Steve's business half a continent away and dozens of others around the country, we tried to build relationships with our neighbors. And through those relationships, rebuild neighborhoods.

Today, LoDo is one of Denver's most vibrant entertainment neighborhoods, and Brooklyn's Williamsburg neighborhood is one of the most dynamic in New York City. As detailed in *The Craft Beer Revolution,* this sort

Governor John Hickenlooper. Class of '88. Photograph courtesy of Evan Semón.

of urban renewal has taken hold in cities where small breweries have been established across America; from San Diego to Portland, from Kansas City to Atlanta, and from Abita Springs to Cleveland.

The Craft Beer Revolution tells the story of pioneering visionaries like Fritz Maytag of Anchor Brewing Company, Ken Grossman of Sierra Nevada Brewing Co., Matthew Reich of Old New York Brewing Co., Jim Koch of Boston Beer Company and innovative brewers like Wynkoop's Russell Scherer, Brooklyn's Garrett Oliver, Russian River's Vinnie Cilurzo, Allagash Brewing's Rob Tod, Dogfish Head's Sam Calagione, and New Belgium's Jeff Lebesch.

Many of the craft brewer entrepreneurs were homebrewers before they started their companies. Many were inspired by a little paperback book called *The Complete Joy of Homebrewing,* written by Charlie Papazian, a former schoolteacher who now leads the BA. And, by the way, still makes Colorado his home.

The pioneers of the movement introduced Americans to amber ales, lagers, porters, and stouts. The next generations of brewers started brewing Belgian style beers and inventing new styles and processes. These craft brewers were inspired by the great brewing nations of Europe—Belgium, Britain, Germany, and the Czech Republic—but now European brewers are looking to their American counterparts for inspiration. American craft beer has become a significant export.

Overall beer consumption in America is declining, but the craft beer segment is exploding with growth. People seem to be drinking less beer, but drinking more "good beer."

I am honored to have been a part of the craft beer revolution, and I salute all those entrepreneurs, brewers, distributors, and retailers who have made it happen.

John Hickenlooper
Denver, Colorado
August 2013

AUTHOR'S NOTE

History will be kind to me for I intend to write it.

—Winston Churchill

THE STORY OF THE CRAFT BEER REVOLUTION IS A RICH ONE. IT IS A GREAT BUSINESS story and the sum of many wonderful human stories. And it is still unfolding. I interviewed many of the main characters in this book. I pulled many quotations from newspapers, magazines, books, and speeches, particularly the *New Brewer* magazine, which is a treasure. I used the meeting minutes and position papers from the Brewers' Association of America archive. Some of the events were told from my personal recollections. I have tried to be fair to all involved in this great venture. I have great respect for my colleagues in the Brewers Association, the Beer Institute, and the National Beer Wholesalers Association. I am particularly grateful to Benj Steinman, the scrupulous publisher of *Beer Marketer's Insights,* and Bob Pease, the Chief Operating Officer of the Brewers Association, for reading the manuscript and correcting errors. I also thank my agent Ed Claflin, my editors at Palgrave Macmillan, Emily Carleton and Katie Haigler, and my editor at home, Ellen Foote.

It is an honor to work in this great industry. I hope I have done justice to the story of the craft beer revolution.

Steve Hindy
Brooklyn, New York,
October 2013

PROLOGUE

THE CRAFT BREWING INDUSTRY HAS EVOLVED FROM A RAGGEDY BUNCH OF HOME-brewers and dreamers to a bonafide 10 percent segment of the $100 billion American beer industry. For a few decades, it has been the most dynamic segment of the US beer industry, and the craft brewing revolution is spreading around the world.

In 2013 America had more than 2,700 craft breweries and 1,500 more were in the planning stages. Paul Gatza, a spokesman for the Brewers Association (BA), says that 48.4 percent of brewery-restaurants that have opened since 1980 are still in business, and 66.2 percent of the production brewery startups are still brewing. That is an amazing record of success, a much higher winning percentage than the average business startup can claim.

American-style craft breweries can now be found all over the world, in Asia, Africa, Latin America, and in the great brewing nations of Europe, whose traditions originally inspired American brewers.

The new brewers believe they are restoring beer to its rightful place as a local business and a product that says something about its hometown and region. Their capacity for innovation is huge. They are taking beer back from the mass-producing multinational brewers who make beer the way Kraft makes cheese or Hershey makes chocolate. The craft brewers are taking beer back to its artisanal roots, the way many local bakers are making bread and cheese makers are making cheese.

At its heart, the craft beer movement is a quest by a band of Davids to bring down the Goliaths. Brooklyn Brewery's brewmaster Garrett Oliver, the multi-talented man who creates the recipes for our beers and also writes books, captures the zeitgeist of the craft beer revolution in a tongue-in-cheek piece he wrote to explain a beer he created for the opening party of New York Comic Con 2012, an annual convention of comic book writers. The beer was called the Brooklyn Defender, and the call to arms went like this:

Once, a long time ago, benevolent Beer Gods bestrode the lands of the world, bringing wonderful beer and great happiness to the People. Collaborating joyously among themselves, the Beer Gods defended the pleasures of the table and promulgated the virtues of Flavor, Variety, Deliciousness, Versatility and Honesty in beer. And the People loved them for it.

But the Beer Gods were far too trusting—in truth, they were not without enemies. Out of the stygian depths of the Earth's crust rose a cabal of anti-Beer Gods, the Megaliths. Taking the peaceful Beer Gods by surprise, the warlike Megaliths cast a powerful spell that drove the Beer Gods down into the shadows. Flavorful beer vanished from the land, and the People wept. Their victory complete, the Megaliths sent among us the ghostly pale, thin tasteless beers known colloquially as "foam jobs." Blandness led to mediocrity, mediocrity led to hate, and hate led to suffering. And O, how the People suffered! They forgot the true taste of beer, the soft rustle of barley, the smell of hops.

And then, just as it seemed that the darkness had stamped out all good things, a new dawn rose . . . [wielding] the rich power of caramel malts, the sharpest unbreakable blade of pure hop bitterness and an incredible focused blast of hop aroma to shatter the Megalith's [sic] spell. The Beer Gods awoke to find themselves forever shielded within the hearts of the People, and once again the great virtues of true beer spread through the land.

The craft beer revolution is a story involving hundreds of entrepreneurs in hundreds of towns across America. They fought the battles over taste buds to gain acceptance of their quirky, tasty beers. They persuaded jaded beer distributors, who took orders for mass-produced, mass-advertised beers, to take a chance on obscure but lovingly crafted beers. The entrepreneurs taught these distributors that the ingredients and processes that produce these special local beers matter and that the stories behind these companies matter, too. And slowly but surely these distributors, many of whom had grown rich selling the light lager beers of the national and international giants, began to appreciate the spirit and drive of the craft brewers. The distributors hired beer-savvy sales and marketing people and learned how to sell these small brands that did not have million-dollar ad budgets.

Like the craft brewers, most of these distributors were relatively small, community-based businesses. Initially the obvious natural alliance—craft brewers and community-oriented distributors—faced some barriers, but they have begun to come down, and the strength of the alliance has grown.

This is also a story about how the craft brewers have dealt with internecine battles, resolved their differences, and developed a community that supports the efforts of all. While butting heads with each other in markets from coast to coast, craft brewers have learned much from each other in the process. Together they founded BA, an organization that could stand up to the international conglomerates.

Their unlikely leader is Charlie Papazian, a nuclear engineer with a gentle handshake and a passion for homebrewing. Papazian wrote *The Complete Joy of Homebrewing,* a how-to book that taught generations of beer nuts how to brew their own beer. Papazian nurtured a small gathering of homebrewers in Boulder, Colorado, in the late 1970s, then known as the Association of Brewers, as it evolved into the BA in the early twenty-first century, a $16 million-a-year trade association that has challenged the international conglomerates in surprising ways.

Another part of the story is the legislative battles waged by the craft brewers association. They lobbied to overturn Prohibition-era bans on homebrewing in all 50 states. The BA has nurtured state brewers' associations in most of the country. And, as a result of their campaign, elected officials in Washington, state capitols, and city councils across the country now recognize the important role that craft breweries play in their communities.

Not the least of the craft brewing industry's challenges has been to educate Americans about beer—its history and its place in our culture and at our dinner table. Among those who have taken up that challenge are the pioneering British beer writer Michael Jackson, Ray Daniels, the man behind the "Cicerone" beer education curriculum that has trained 30,000 people as of December 2013, and Garrett Oliver, editor-in-chief of *The Oxford Companion to Beer,* the first encyclopedia dedicated to beer.[1]

But no one has told the whole story until now. *The Craft Beer Revolution* will tell you how the founding brewers and their successors built 2,700 breweries across America and got your favorite artisanal suds into your mug at your local pub, and how these craft brewers developed a community that sparked a worldwide revolution.

CHAPTER ONE

THE PIONEERS

1965-1984

1965: 1 microbrewery
182 national and regional breweries[1]
1984: 18 microbreweries
76 noncraft national and regional breweries

IN THE BEGINNING THERE WAS FRITZ MAYTAG. AND FOR MORE THAN A DECADE, HE stood alone. He was *the* pioneer. Others followed—in the West, there was Jack McAuliffe, Jane Zimmerman, and Suzy Denison of New Albion Brewing Company, the first home-built microbrewery; Ken Grossman and Paul Camusi of Sierra Nevada Brewing Co.; Randolph Ware and David Hummer of the Boulder Beer Company; the Cartwright Brewing Company; Bert Grant of Yakima Brewing and Malting Co.; and the Independent Ale Brewery (Redhook) in Seattle, Washington. In the East, there was Matthew Reich of the Old New York Brewing Co., the pioneer of contract brewing, and Bill Newman of Wm. S. Newman Brewing Co. But Fritz Maytag started it all.

According to the *Oxford English Dictionary* a *pioneer* is "one of a body of foot-soldiers who march with or in advance of an army or regiment, having spades, pickaxes, etc. to dig trenches, repair roads, and perform other labours in clearing and preparing the way for the main body."

I am quite sure that Fritz Maytag and the others did not think of themselves as "preparing the way for the main body," but that's what they did in the 1960s and 1970s. They built the foundation for the craft brewing movement, which, as I write, includes more than 2,700 breweries and accounts for a rich 6.5 percent of the US beer market by volume and more than 10 percent by dollar.[2] They laid down the enduring principles of smallness, independence, and all malt beers (as opposed to the rice and corn additives favored by the national brewers). They figured out how they had to price their beer to make their companies viable. Maytag was generous with his time, advice, and even ingredients when others came to visit his brewery in San Francisco.

Almost all of us in the movement think of ourselves as pioneers in our home markets. And we were. The breweries that opened subsequently played important roles in building a market for craft beer in America. All of us knew what it was like to confront a barroom full of Bud/Miller/Coors drinkers who turned up their noses at our dark and flavorful beers, our hoppy beers, our strong beers.

But it must have been even more difficult in 1965 when Maytag bought the failing Anchor Brewing Company in San Francisco. At the time micro-brewed beers, or craft beers, did not exist. There were no domestic beers competing with the foreign imports. The import segment itself was growing in the United States, but that was because sophisticated drinkers already rec-ognized it as "better beer." Fritz Maytag and his cohorts had to make it all up, the same way the early settlers did when they pushed their wagons across the Allegheny Mountains.

First off, I have a confession to make. In my early days in the craft brew-ing industry, I did not understand the adoration afforded Fritz Maytag. I guess it was a class thing. After all, he was the grandson of Frederick Louis Maytag, founder of the Maytag Washing Machine Company, the gold stan-dard of washing machines in the United States, known everywhere for its TV ads with a dozing Maytag repairman who had nothing to do because Maytag washing machines were so darn sturdy and reliable. Fritz's father, Frederick Louis Maytag II, developed Maytag Blue Cheese, an American original based on the French Roquefort style.

Fritz Louis Maytag III was educated at Deerfield Academy in Massachu-setts and then got a degree in American literature from Stanford. He dressed in tweedy jackets and button-down shirts. He wore wire-rimmed glasses and spoke with a mellifluous baritone that commanded attention. And he was a Maytag.

I remember saying to my colleagues, "I don't see what the fuss about Fritz Maytag is. He is an heir to the Maytag Washing Machine Company. He is playing with different sheet music than the rest of us."

How wrong I was. I apologize, Fritz. Those of us in the "main body," as I'll call the band of brewers that followed the pioneers, are so fortunate to have had Maytag out in front. Over the years he gave spellbinding speeches at Craft Brewers' Conferences. He elevated our passion for brewing. He quoted Euripides and Aeschylus speaking of the honor of being a brewer. He chided the contract brewers for being fake brewers because they contracted with other breweries to produce their beer, but he applauded them for educating the public about good beer. When we bitched about beer distributors, he reminded us that the three-tier legal system—which in many states prevents brewers from owning distributors and retail outlets—protects the independence of distributors and impedes big brewers' ability to create monopolies, allowing independent brewers to cut into the market.

Years later I got to know Maytag better when we both served on the board of the BAA. Fritz was a treasure for the craft brewing movement. And he arguably was the forerunner not just for microbrewing, but the entire DIY movement that includes cheese making, winemaking, and distilling.

But back to the story.

In the early 1960s Maytag spent some time in Japan after he graduated from college, but he soon moved to San Francisco, the ultraliberal city that was the epicenter of the hippie movement. Haight-Ashbury was ground zero for the "tune in, turn on, drop out" culture of the LSD advocate Dr. Timothy Leary. I didn't know Maytag at that time, but I doubt LSD drew him to San Francisco. He did have a full beard, but he declined to talk to me about the '60s.

Maytag, seventy-four, shared his story with fifty-seven-year-old Grossman, cofounder of Sierra Nevada, at the 2011 Craft Brewers Conference in San Francisco. Grossman was a student of Maytag's early work, but the two deserve equal credit for founding the craft brewing industry. The interview provides important insights into the early brewing experience of both men.

"I actually got into brewing before I got into the wine world, just barely but a little before," Maytag said, sitting in a comfortable easy chair before the audience of small brewers. "I used to hang out at an old place in San Francisco called the Old Spaghetti Factory—those who knew it remember it well. It was a charming place. And it was the equivalent of my local, as they would say in England. I would go there in the evening for a few beers before bed, meet with friends most every night. And one day the owner, Fred Kuh, asked me if I had ever been to the Anchor brewery and said they were closing down that next weekend, and he thought I should go see it before it was closed because it was the kind of thing I would like.

"And I later realized he was hoping I would either loan them some money or buy in or something, and that's what happened. I went down. I sat in the taproom with the owner-manager guy, Lawrence Steese, lovely man, and I just fell in love. I've often said you don't get up in the morning and think you are going to fall in love today. I had no idea I would buy the brewery when I went. But before the day was out, we had done a deal."[3]

Not too many people could fall in love and buy a piece of a brewery just like that. But Maytag could.

Grossman quickly followed with the question: "Your family think you were nuts?"

Maytag replied: "Yeah, but they thought I was kind of goofy anyway. . . . My father had actually died a very young man in 1962, so he was not there. I think if he had been around, he would have realized any business is better than no business at all."

Eleven years after Maytag bought Anchor, Grossman started running a bicycle shop in Chico, California. He said he could have bought the shop, but he thought he would be bored for the rest of his life. So instead he started a home-brew shop, selling equipment and ingredients, "which wasn't a great way to make a livelihood either. . . . Getting into the brewing business sounded like an exciting career. I'm sure that has been an inspiration for a lot of people here. Brewing beer is a great thing to do with your life."

Maytag asked what Grossman's family thought about his building a brewery.

"They thought I was nuts," Grossman said, "They just stopped thinking that a few years ago." Sierra Nevada expected to pass the million-barrel sales mark in 2013 (a barrel of beer is thirty-one gallons, or about fourteen cases of twenty-four twelve-ounce bottles of beer) and is building a $120 million state-of-the-art brewery in Ashville, North Carolina.

Maytag recalled brewing about a thousand barrels of beer that first year. Anchor was the smallest brewery in America. The Anchor brewhouse was fifty-five barrels, and the company only brewed one or two brews a month. "We brewed more than we sold because it turned sour before we could sell it sometimes," he said.

"Well, I invested in the Anchor brewery," he said. "I was the majority owner, not the sole owner. And I was absolutely amazed at the idea of owning a brewery. And I knew about the Brewers' Association of America [BAA], and I knew they had a convention, and I was in Chicago at that time for another reason. I actually snuck into the convention. I never told anyone who I was, and there were all these big important guys in double-breasted suits and badges and I don't know what-all, and there were exhibits of beer signs, and I just snuck around thinking, 'Wow, I am part of this, I guess,' and then I left. But I then did next year go to the convention, which was the first year they held it in Fort Lauderdale. It had been in Chicago for many years. . . .

"We went one year to Florida, and the Budweiser distributors were having their convention nearby, and I went over there and some of their yachts were bigger than my brewery."[4]

The BAA was the trade association for small US brewers. It was started in 1942, when the government started rationing commodities like tin for World War II, by Bill O'Shea, owner of a printing company that made labels for many breweries. Small brewers came together to demand their share of the metal to make bottle caps. After the war, the BAA continued to represent small brewers' interests in Washington, DC.[5]

When Fritz Maytag invested in Anchor, the United States had fewer than fifty breweries, and the family-run breweries were losing out to large breweries like Anheuser-Busch (AB) and Miller that were shipping and advertising their beers nationally. The Adolph Coors Company brewery was stubbornly regional at the time, but it too would go national in the 1980s. The large national breweries had a huge advantage of scale. They could use their size to buy large quantities of raw materials at lower prices. They could also use mass marketing budgets to sell the idea that their beer was better than the local stuff over TV and radio ads: "Our beer is so special we ship it all the way from St. Louis and Milwaukee to you." The use of corn and rice additives—a cheaper alternative to malted barley adjuncts that also extended the beer's shelf life—was ubiquitous even among family-run breweries. Anchor was the only brewery making all-malt beer.

Grossman asked Maytag about his first experience selling Anchor Steam Beer, a rich malty brew that was completely different from what most Americans drank at the time.

"Well, yeah, it was a tough row to hoe," said Maytag. "All the small American brewers, the small family brewers, were making very mild, light lager beers, and so the idea of having an all-malt, hoppy brew as a domestic was just unheard of. But the imports, bless their hearts—that was the category, that was the umbrella that I used to think of. Price-wise, we would be at the import price, or just below, and in terms of character and flavor, and styles, some of [the imports] were dark. Some of them were flavorful. Most of them were not. Most of them were very, very mild. If you think about it, the imports were all lagers, but there was the Mackeson Stout, the Guinness Stout, even the Dos Equis, and that was the story we told—'Look, there are different beers for different times, and if you are going to sit by the fire and read a book, you want something you can chew on, like we did.'"[6]

I think it safe to say most San Franciscans stuck with their Budweiser or Miller or Hamm's or Bergy or Lucky Lager. But some fell in love with Anchor Steam. My neighbor in Brooklyn, Charley Ryan, is the co-owner of Brooklyn Bowl, a bowling alley with a stage and performance space that serves great food and only carries beer from Brooklyn breweries. Charley was living in San Francisco in 1972, and he recalls buying kegs of Anchor Steam Beer for his parties.

"That beer was so rich, so fresh, so different," he recalled. "There was nothing else like it. The flavors were so vivid. It still colors my memory of San Francisco." Charley became a lifelong advocate of microbrewed and, later, craft brewed beer, thanks to Fritz Maytag and Anchor Steam beer.[7]

Maytag, meanwhile, longed to bottle his beer. For years, he only sold his beer in kegs.

"As I look back on my earliest days in the brewing business, I used to eat dinner at a place called the Brighton Express, and they had a beautiful, beautiful black stout, Mackeson Stout. I used to sit—I'd come in from the brewery late in the evening, and I'd sit there at the communal table, and I'd have a Mackeson Stout, in a bottle, with a label, and I'd dream of the day our little brewery would be successful. And I loved those beers."

Grossman met Maytag in 1978 when Maytag did a tour of the Anchor Brewery for participants in the first wine and craft beer trade show, held in San Francisco. In those early days, Maytag encouraged Grossman to attend a BAA meeting.

"I remember encouraging you to come, and the one reason was, a small English brewer once said to me, 'The big guys come by every now and then and have a giggle.' No doubt they snickered a little behind our backs. But in fact, to our faces, and very genuinely, they welcomed us. And it was thrilling to feel welcomed to a trade. I'm sure you had the same experience."

Fritz recalled meeting many of the family brewers, including Warren Marti of August Schell Brewing Company; F. X. Matt of the Matt Brewing Company; Bill Leinenkugel of the Jacob Leinenkugel Brewing Co. Their regionally focused companies were under siege from the big national brewers, but he recalled a "cheerful camaraderie" among them.

"I mean, these were grand old brewing families, they loved getting together," Maytag said.

Grossman was just beginning to think of starting a brewery when he attended his first BAA meeting in the early 1980s.

"I was just a home brewer, so for me it was a whole new experience to meet and hang out with people who had run breweries for generations. I remember being a bit—feeling an outsider and also a little bit concerned because [industry analyst] Bob Weinberg had come out with some statement saying by the year 2000 there would only be two or three breweries left in America, and here he is the smartest brewing industry analyst. He got his PhD when he was nineteen. He's predicting my demise, and I'd go to that convention every year, and there would be a few less breweries, and everyone is talking about how terrible the industry is. I was a bit concerned the first few years." (Weinberg was partly right: by 2013 AB-InBev and MillerCoors would control about 74 percent of the US beer market.[8])

Both Grossman and Maytag recalled that small and large brewers were helpful to them during their early days.

Maytag said he believed they were collegial because these brewers were not directly competing with each other.

"Each had survived because it was in a rural area, often with a German population, significant German element, German oriented, and in general they didn't compete with each other. . . . So there was a sense of brotherhood without the competitive aspect. And that was part of it there. Among the big brewers, I always remember when we called Miller in Los Angeles and asked if we could come and see something, and they said no. I was absolutely horrified, and it had started when Budweiser and Miller went after each other, dueling to the death. . . . I don't remember what year it was, probably the early eighties or late seventies. That was the first time any brewer ever said no."

He was referring to the 1970s when AB and Miller Brewing Company bitterly accused each other of using chemical additives in their beers. They fought their battles in national advertisements on television and radio—the powerful weapons of the big brewers.

Another aspect of Maytag's experience that all craft brewers can identify with, even today, is the challenge of distribution.

"We had self-distributed from the beginning," Maytag said. (In some states, there are exceptions to the three-tier system that allow brewers to distribute their own beer.) "As far as I know, Anchor had never had a distributor, and when we got involved in 1965, we certainly did all our distributing, and the markup—we could not possibly have afforded the middleman in there, so we did all the delivering and all the rest of it. In fact, when we started bottling, which was in 1971 . . . my key person, the guy who did the delivering, announced that he was going to work for the church or something. And so I did all the deliveries. And it did not take me long to understand the value of a beer distributor. We would have one account in San Jose, and one in Walnut Creek, and one in Santa Rosa, and if you drive all the way to Walnut Creek to deliver one keg of beer, it doesn't take you long to realize you need some help.

"And a remarkable man, Don Saccani, [of] Anchor Distributing, which was a coincidental name, was pestering me to get the brands, and so from a very early date, we turned the bottles over to a beer distributor."

Fritz bought out his partner, Lawrence Steese, in 1969 and in 1977 moved the brewery from its original site at Eighth Street and Brannon to a former coffee bean roaster on Potrero Hill. By then he was bottling Anchor Steam, the brewery's flagship, amber lager fermented in ale-like conditions in shallow open fermenters; Anchor Porter, a dark ale; Liberty Ale, a very hoppy ale that was the forerunner of the India pale ale style—the most popular craft-style as I write these words in 2013—and Old Foghorn, a barley wine. Maytag also brewed the first of his greatly anticipated Christmas ales, a richly spiced concoction that is brewed with a different recipe every year. By the time he moved the brewery, he was brewing 12,500 barrels annually. It was an expensive move and Maytag bet all his resources on its success.

"I borrowed every penny I could and I still didn't have enough," he recalled. "I had everything I owned pledged. [In the late 1970s] the prime rate was 21 [percent]. And my wife, bless her heart, at one point I said to her, 'You realize we may lose everything,' and it was nip and tuck, and she looked at me and she said, 'I know. I could sleep in a tent.' I always love telling that story. It was wonderful."

The financial pressure took its toll on Maytag—a familiar stressor for many craft brewers.

"We called the doctors once," Maytag said. "I collapsed. I thought I was having a heart attack from stress, I guess, and the doctors—I was lying on the floor and they checked me—and they said, 'You're fine. It must be stress.' And it was stress. That was a big day."

Many wannabe microbrewers ventured to San Francisco to meet the sage of Anchor Brewing. He advised them all not to start breweries.

"I used to advise them not to do it, because I didn't want any competition," he recalled. "But I also—and I actually, truthfully, and I've said this many times—never did it occur to me that anyone else could do what we had done. It had been so hard for me. I think it was partly because I wasn't really cut out to do that sort of thing, and without the people I had to help me, I never could have done it. I thought it was an extraordinary achievement, and I just didn't think anybody else would be able to do it, so I was surprised when they started coming."

GROSSMAN LEARNED MUCH FROM HIS FRIENDSHIP WITH MAYTAG. HE ALSO LEARNED from another, slightly later, standard-bearer, Jack McAuliffe of New Albion Brewing Company in Sonoma, California. In his book, *Beyond the Pale*, Grossman recalled visiting McAuliffe at the brewery. "We left with several cases of beer that we bought from Jack. His beers were closer to home brew in style than Fritz's, but he made a bigger impression because his operation was essentially a glorified home brewery. I came to the conclusion that I could take my passion and talent for home brewing and brew the kind of beer I wanted to drink."[9]

McAuliffe had taken up homebrewing while serving in the US Navy and repairing Polaris-class nuclear submarines at a base in Holy Loch, Scotland. He had read Dave Line's *Big Book of Brewing*, one of the first how-to books on brewing published in the United Kingdom. When McAuliffe returned to the United States, he studied physics on the GI Bill and began a career in engineering. He decided to start a brewery because US beer was a "national disgrace" compared to the rich ales of Great Britain. He wanted to brew ales, porters, and stouts like the beers he drank in Britain. Behind everything he says about his brewery's beginnings it is possible to hear his defiance of industrial brewers that was the basis for the craft beer revolution.[10]

McAuliffe started New Albion with partners Suzy Denison (later Suzy Stern) and Jane Zimmerman in 1976. Denison, a native of Harrisburg, Pennsylvania, and graduate of Vassar College, was divorced and had come to Sonoma with her three children because her son had gotten into Stanford University. She met McAuliffe and Zimmerman through the local food co-op. The two women put up $1,500 each and McAuliffe raised the rest of the $5,000 in capital they needed to start the brewery.[11]

"American beer all tastes the same, because they all try to make it as cheaply as possible," McAuliffe told the *Washington Post* in 1978. "Our beer consists of malt, hops, water and yeast. There are no enzymes, which the big companies use to speed the process of mashing and aging, or to ensure longer shelf life. There are no adjuncts—such as corn grits, corn flakes or corn syrups—which are often used as a cheaper source of starch than malt. . . . There are no heading agents or foam stabilizers to create an artificial head on your glass of beer. It's the proteins that produce the head in real beer, but these are filtered out in most commercial beer for cosmetic reasons: they make the beer hazy. And there's no carbon dioxide added. The beer is naturally fermented in the bottle."[12]

The three partners cobbled the physical brewery together from dairy and soft drink tanks they salvaged at scrap yards. They called the brewery New Albion, the name the English explorer Francis Drake gave to the West Coast of America when he arrived in the *Golden Hinde* in 1579. (Albion was an early name for Britain.) The New Albion brewery was located in a corrugated steel warehouse on a ranch owned by the Batto Fruit Co., a grape grower.

"History is important in the brewing industry," McAuliffe told John Holl, editor of *All About Beer*. "But if you don't have a history you can just make one up."[13] New Albion's label, designed by Sal Guardino, pictures the *Golden Hinde* sailing out of San Francisco Bay with the Golden Gate Bridge in the distance and Drake's Bay off the starboard quarter.

Denison, now eighty and living in Seattle, recalled that she immediately admired McAuliffe for his "gumption and brains."

"Jack was a very intrepid home brewer, a very brilliant guy, but a difficult person, to say the least," she said. "I got very interested in the idea of learning to brew beer and helping him get started with a brewery. He scrounged stainless steel drums to use as brewing vessels and did everything himself. We built the brewery from the ground up. My God, I had never had a hammer in my hand. But I learned how to weld. I learned how to hang sheetrock. It was pretty crazy. I went to the county seat in Santa Rosa with Jack repeatedly for all the various licenses. You can imagine the bureaucracy. And no one could believe us. Everyone kept saying, 'How big is your winery going to be?' and we kept saying, 'No, it's not a winery, it is a brewery.'

"Everything was difficult, and it was difficult getting ingredients in the small amounts we needed. Anchor [Brewing]—Fritz Maytag and his crew—were extremely helpful to us. Instead of getting huge amounts of hops and grain, we got ingredients in the beginning from Anchor. They were very helpful.

"We had a lot of fun, but believe me, as you well know, it was hard work," she said. "It was a 24/7 business. Jane Zimmerman and I, we brewed the beer. I mean, Jack was there to supervise, but after he felt confident we could do it, he was sometimes gone from the brewery."

Denison said she and McAuliffe lived together for a while, and Steve Denkin, a Sonoma resident, was an adviser to New Albion. "Steve used to say that Jack should be kept on a short leash at the brewery," she said. "Jack's definitely not a people person. He is a very smart guy and just a real curmudgeon."

Zimmerman left the brewery after a year to become a psychotherapist. Denison stuck it out to the bitter end in 1982, when McAuliffe failed to convince investors or banks to fund an expansion of his quixotic venture.

When we spoke, Denison had just returned from a trip to Italy with her seventeen-year-old granddaughter. Denison and Zimmerman are still friends and traveling companions. After the failure of New Albion, Denison taught English as a second language for years and then became a yoga instructor. She is amazed at the craft beer revolution that she helped launch. "I don't regret any of it, even though it ended badly, because it was an amazing experience," she said, referring to the demise of New Albion. "Jack had the idea to start a brewpub, which of course did not exist at that time. He had that vision. . . . We were just ahead of our time."[14]

"They just didn't understand what I was doing," McAuliffe said, echoing the predicament of many craft brewers of the pioneer generation. "They couldn't comprehend the idea of a small brewery. It was like I arrived from Mars and was speaking Martian."[15]

To Don Barkley, a homebrewer and later a brewer for Mendocino Brewing Company who helped McAuliffe in that first year, what happened to New Albion was no mystery.

"[It] could be put under the broad category of mismanagement," Barkley said during the 1984 Microbrewers' Conference in Colorado. "In the end, New Albion—at a barrel-and-a-half brew length—was too small to support the number of people working there. . . . To expand the facility required . . . a production team, a sales team and a management team. To bring together a team costs money."[16]

A fifty-five gallon kettle big enough to brew a barrel and a half would produce fewer than twenty cases of beer per brew. Making a profit with such a system is virtually impossible.

A wonderful photo of McAuliffe shows him leaning, with one muscled arm, on an ancient cast-iron keg-cleaning contraption that looks more like a medieval torture device, all big screws, brushes, and wheels. He is the picture of a noble pioneering craft brewer, with a square jaw, level gaze, and thick dark hair falling over his ears and across his high forehead. He's wearing a short-sleeved collared shirt and a leather apron. His jeans are splattered with what must be whitewash or paint. His smile is as enigmatic as the *Mona Lisa's*.

McAuliffe clearly had no idea that he had sparked a revolution. After New Albion failed, he lived in obscurity for thirty years, but then resurfaced in 2012 to join Grossman in brewing a barley wine-style ale to commemorate Sierra Nevada's thirtieth anniversary year. Sierra Nevada donated $10,000 to Texas Public Radio in McAuliffe's name.

Jim Koch of the Boston Beer Company claimed New Albion's trademark years ago and brewed a version of New Albion Ale in 2013. In a gesture of generosity that is not uncommon among craft brewers, Koch gave the trademark to McAuliffe when he reemerged, along with $400,000 in profits from the recreated beer. McAuliffe gave the mark and money to his long-lost daughter, Renee DeLuca. She is planning to brew New Albion under contract at the Mendocino Brewing Company.[17]

IN THE EAST WERE TWO OTHER PIONEERS WHO, LIKE MCAULIFFE, WOULD FAIL, BUT would ultimately have an outsized influence on the future of the craft brewing industry.

Bill and Marie Newman built the first microbrewery in the East in late 1980, the Wm. S. Newman Brewing Co. in Albany, New York. The couple had developed a taste for England's bitter ales while living there in the 1970s. That was when the Campaign for Real Ale—the consumer movement that sought to preserve the traditional English way of brewing and serving English bitters and best bitters—was started by a group of Fleet Street journalists lamenting the consolidation of the British beer industry and the marginalization of cask-conditioned ales, the luscious amber ales that are fermented in casks in the cellars of a pub.

The Newmans raised $250,000 from federal, state, and local job development loans and purchased a small brewery from Peter Austin, the founder of Ringwood Brewery in England. The brewery was located not far from downtown Albany and was easily identified by the red brick that enclosed the brew kettle.

"At the time, we had no idea about the brewing business, about selling beer," Newman told the *New Brewer's* Greg Giorgio in 1991. "In fact, our original plan was to make English-style draft ales, only draft. What we didn't understand was that, in England, 85 to 90 percent of the sales were on draft, but here it was just the reverse."[18] In the United States draft beer is barely 10 percent of the beer market.

I recall visiting the Newmans in 1986, when their tiny operation was, to all outward appearances, a shining success. The media wrote glowing accounts of their venture, but I wondered about its profitability. We had lunch at a rustic wood-paneled working-class saloon near the brewery. When Bill stepped away from the table, the owner of the saloon, a middle-aged woman, asked how we liked the beer, Newman's Albany Ale. We said we thought it was great.

She leaned over the table and asked us to please tell Bill that he should not insist the beer be sold at warm temperatures, as in England. "My customers won't drink warm beer," she said. Out of respect, we did not share her advice with Newman. The beer tasted pretty good to me.

Newman opened a brewing school at his Albany facility, tutoring would-be microbrewers in the business and art of brewing. Unfortunately, the volume of ink that Newman got in the mainstream press probably was greater than the volume of beer he sold. He later lamented that the $250,000 he raised was not enough to allow for proper marketing, promotion, and packaging. He sold his ales in half and quarter kegs as well as one gallon plastic jugs. The unpasteurized, unfiltered ales had a short shelf life, and sales personnel from rival distributors sabotaged his beer by twisting open the plastic lids.

Desperate to get his beer in bottles, Newman started contract brewing at Wisconsin's Hibernia Brewing Company in the mid-1980s and later closer to home at the Christian Schmidt Brewing Co. in Philadelphia. Schmidt shut down unexpectedly. Saddled with half a million dollars in debt, the Wm. S. Newman Brewing Co. declared bankruptcy and sued Schmidt Brewing for breach of contract.

Newman then moved to contract brewing at Matt Brewing Company in New York and later Catamount Brewing Co. in Vermont. With a partner he developed a Dortmunder-style beer, Saratoga Pilsner. (The German city is famous for its pilsner-style beer.) But the partners then fell into a ruinous feud, and Bill and Marie Newman were out of the beer business.

THE STORY OF THE EARLY DAYS OF THE INDEPENDENT ALE BREWERY IN SEATTLE, which became Redhook, is a fascinating tale of trial and error that is familiar to many craft brewers. Its founders were Paul Shipman, a wine seller and marketer, and Gordon Bowker, the cofounder of Starbucks. Their story is told in Peter Krebs's excellent book, *Redhook: Beer Pioneer*. After he sold Starbucks, Bowker worked in an advertising firm that represented K2 skis. He grew tired of advertising and after reading about New Albion began to mull over the idea of starting a microbrewery. He attended a seminar on microbreweries sponsored by Fritz Maytag. According to Bowker, Maytag said his dream was that someday every city in the United States would have a brewery—a dream that in 2013 is becoming a reality.[19]

Shipman and Bowker hired Charles McElevy, a former assistant brewer at Rainier Brewing Company, to be their brewmaster and set out to raise $350,000 to start their brewery. They purchased a brewhouse from the Wacker-Bräu in Germany. Instead of going to a reliable source for brewing yeast, such as the Schwarz Laboratories, the headstrong McElevy chose a yeast propagated in the microbiology lab at the University of Washington. Schwarz supplied yeast to Sierra Nevada, and McElevy feared other brewers would copy a yeast made by Schwarz. Mick McHugh, co-owner of two restaurants in Seattle, convinced Shipman and Bowker to launch their beer at his restaurant, Jake's, where other premium beers—Guinness, Henry Weinhard's, and Anchor Steam—had debuted in the Seattle market. Bowker had a theory, based on the thinking of the Nobel Prize-winning physicist Niels Bohr, that any decision to move forward was essentially irrational, and so they picked a debut date—August 11, 1982—out of thin air.

"The idea was that nobody would rationally make a decision to build a brewery," Shipman told Krebs. "So we were not pretending to be rational about it. The decision to pick a date was made with the acceptance that the decision would force a series of other decisions. You could always come up with a reason for opening later. But one day you had to actually open the doors."[20] That is certainly a rationale that any entrepreneur would appreciate.

But when the mayor of Seattle raised a glass to inaugurate the new beer and brewery on August 11, everyone at the opening ceremony was aware that the beer had the cloying off-flavor of ripe bananas—a sign of bacterial infection, a brewer's term for yeast contamination. They pressed ahead with Redhook Ale, and many bar owners bought it, even though customers complained it was undrinkable. A *Seattle Weekly* reporter dubbed it "banana beer." The British beer writer Michael Jackson came to town and tasted the beer. Jackson was a big booster of the microbrewing movement in the United States and was never known to put down a microbrewed beer. He savored Redhook Ale and pronounced it "more Belgian" than American. The partners seized on Jackson's description and changed their marketing materials to read, "An ale in the Belgian style is rare in the United States. Redhook is one of the few we know; only hops, barley malt, water and yeast are used in this hand-brewed process. It is the top-fermenting ale yeast that gives Redhook Ale its distinctive character: complex, rich with the nuances of spices, herbs, and fruits."[21]

Despite most Seattle beer drinkers' rejection of Redhook, Jackson gave Redhook "Four Stars—Highly Distinctive" in a March 1983 article in *Seattle Weekly*. "More than any of its contemporaries, Redhook displays that fruitiness that is a definitive ale characteristic. When this characterful ale was launched, its assertiveness came as a shock to some drinkers, which is testimony to the blandness that has come to pass for beer." Even with the endorsement of the man known as "the bard of beer," Seattle's home-brewing community was buzzing with rumors that Redhook's yeast was infected. Sales declined and losses piled up. The partners debated changing the yeast.[22]

They brought in Joseph Owades, the brewing chemist who lectured at Maytag's All About Beer seminars. Ironically, Owades, who held a Ph.D. in biochemistry from the Polytechnic Institute of New York, was known as the father of light beer—the antithesis of craft beer. He was a short, bespectacled, nattily dressed man with a pencil mustache and sharp opinions. As head of the technical department at the Rheingold brewery in Brooklyn, he had developed the first American "diet beer," a brew that relied on special enzymes to eat up all the sugars, creating a low-calorie beer. Unfortunately the marketing department called it "Gablingers Diet Beer," and it flopped. Years later the Miller Brewing Company would capitalize on Owades's invention with Miller Lite, a beer that launched a new and dominant category in the US beer industry. Owades would have an outsized influence on the American craft brewing movement, as adviser to Matthew Reich at Old New York Brewing Co., Jim Koch at Boston Beer, and many other craft brewers.

Owades was not one to suffer fools. He was an extremely direct, even blunt, man. According to Krebs, Owades took a sip of Redhook Ale and asked, "What is this?"

Shipman replied, "This is our marvelous Belgian-style ale."

"Who drinks it?" Owades asked. "Is it a particular ethnic group, or is it somebody with a genetic taste defect who can't taste the problem?"

He advised Shipman and Bowker to order Schwarz Laboratories' #96 ale yeast. They did so, and in the spring of 1984 they launched a new ale called Ballard Bitter with a fictitious mustachioed Captain Ballard on the label and the Scandinavian-American phrase "Ya Sure, Ya Betcha!"[23] The people of Seattle and Washington gave them a second chance.

"We inspired people to become microbrewers," Shipman claimed to Krebs, "because every home brewer who tasted our beer thought they could make better beer in their bathtub. They were thinking that if Redhook could be this successful with a beer that tasted this odd, just think what they could do with a good-tasting beer."[24]

MEANWHILE IN NEW YORK CITY MATTHEW REICH DREAMED OF DOING HIS OWN thing while working for Citibank and then Hearst Magazines. A graduate of Boston University, he was a wine enthusiast and taught wine classes at the New York Restaurant School and volunteered at the New York Wine Experience. He was a quick-witted New Yorker with a can-do attitude toward life and business. Like Grossman and McAuliffe, Reich's entree to the beer world was homebrewing.

"I always wanted to make wine," Reich said in an interview at his home in Hastings-on-Hudson, the town where he grew up in Westchester County, north of New York City. "I was a wine drinker. A friend, Robert Gartman, and I talked about making wine, but we couldn't get grapes."

They wanted to make wine the traditional way, starting with fresh grapes. But New York City had only one store for home winemakers, the Milan Laboratory on Spring Street in Manhattan, and it could supply only grape juice. Milan also sold home-brewing kits, so Reich and Gartman decided to make beer instead. Reich had read about the Campaign for Real Ale in England.

"We made a pale ale from grain," Reich said. "It created quite a mess in my kitchen, but it was delicious. We made a couple of batches and said, 'Let's open a brewery and sell this stuff.'"

It was that simple. Reich did a business plan, raised $300,000, and jetted off to San Francisco to take the brewing course offered by Owades at Anchor Brewing Company in 1982.

"I became obsessed with starting a brewery," Reich said. His wife, Karen Miller, was in medical school and encouraged him to pursue the dream. Reich named the brewery Old New York Brewing Co.

"Owades was the most influential person I met. His course was one of the only ones available," Reich said. "Joe encouraged me to start New Amsterdam. Joe said, 'We can do something unique, make a beer with real flavor and character. People are getting tired of light beers. We can make some money at this.'"

Owades suggested that Reich brew the beer at the Matt Brewing Company in Utica. With an introduction from Owades, Reich traveled to Utica and met with F. X. Matt himself, a second-generation brewer of Utica Club Beer and Matt's Premium. Times were hard in Utica, a city in the Rust Belt, and times were hard at the Matt Brewing Company, too.

F. X. could be crotchety. Reich said he had to listen to a three-hour lecture by F. X. about how he was making more money producing Billy Beer for the ne'er-do-well brother of the thirty-eighth president of the United States than he was making brewing his family's traditional beers. But F. X. was taken by the New Yorker's business plan and the name of the beer—New Amsterdam, after the name given to Manhattan by the early Dutch settlers who established the first brewery in 1632 after buying the island from Native Americans.[25]

"That is a very clever name for a beer; it's got history, but it has a nice ring to it, New Am," F. X. once told me.[26] Reich said F. X. eventually agreed to produce New Amsterdam Amber Beer for him. "He said that his grandfather struggled when he started the brewery, 'but some people in Utica helped him, so now it is my turn to help someone,'" Reich recounted. He added that he had to pay upfront for all the malt, hops, and packaging.

Reich thus became the first microbrewer to brew his beer under contract, allowing the Matt brewery to handle the complexity of brewing and packaging the beer and leaving Reich to market and sell the beer.

"Some people gave me a hard time about contract brewing," Reich said. "But in New York City it was the only way to get started. The costs of building a brewery in New York were way beyond my means. The category of microbrewed beer was nonexistent. Bars had three taps, with Budweiser, Heineken, and Beck's, maybe Miller Lite."[27] New York was, and still is, a big imported beer town.

Edward Koch, then-mayor of New York, was on hand when Reich launched Old New York in July 1982. Reich's business got a lot of attention from New York City media, which noted that the last big New York breweries, Schaefer and Rheingold, had closed in 1976. To New York reporters, contract brewing was a footnote.

"It was a very heady time," Reich said. "New Amsterdam grew like crazy. Paul Hawken, cofounder of Smith & Hawken, the gardening products company, featured me in his book, *Growing a Business,* along with the founders of Ben & Jerry's Homemade Ice Cream, Patagonia, and other startups. It became a fourteen-part PBS series. Distributors all over the country are calling me. Here I am, flying around the country, opening new markets. People recognize me in airports from the TV series."

Reich said that a banker from the New York venture firm Prospect Partners came to him and asked what he wanted to do next to grow the company.

"I want to build a brewery," he said.

"How much do you need?" the banker asked.

"Three million dollars," Reich replied.

"Great, you got it," the banker said. "Let's do it."

Soon after, Reich hired the brewing engineer John Bergman. They flew to France and had dinner at the 3 Michelin starred Auberge de Lille restaurant before renting a car and traveling around Germany for a week to look at failed breweries. Like their counterparts in the United States, many local and regional breweries in Germany were struggling as larger breweries used their marketing muscle to expand beyond their traditional bases.

"We found a defunct brewery in Ravensberg, Germany, that was owned by the Stuttgarter Hofbräu," Reich said. "I recall we paid $25,000 for it in December 1983. It was a beautiful copper-clad brewhouse." He hired Andy Bernadette, a young graduate of the brewing school at the University of California, Davis, to be brewmaster.

Meanwhile Reich's New Amsterdam was almost selling itself. He had expanded to twenty-two states and was selling 15,000 barrels annually, more than any other microbrewer except Anchor. *Inc. Magazine, Newsweek,* and *Fortune* all ran adoring articles. Mayor Koch was happy to return for the opening of the new brewery at Twenty-sixth Street and Eleventh Avenue in Manhattan.[28]

The industry press was not as impressed as the mainstream press. An article in the September–October 1982 issue of *Beer Wholesaler* bore the headline "Small Brewery Sells Snob Appeal" and reported:

New Amsterdam Amber Beer will sell for $17 per wholesale case, making it the most costly domestic beer in the New York market. New Amsterdam Amber claims to be the first beer available in the New York market brewed in the style of one of the many micro-breweries being established throughout the country. These breweries produce fewer than 25,000 barrels per year. Examples of this marketing phenomenon, which started about six years ago, include Anchor Steam Beer, brewed in San Francisco, and New Albion Beer, from Sonoma, California. These local products are limited in production, locally distributed, and differ in taste from mass-marketed American beers. . . . New Amsterdam Amber Beer will be distributed on a controlled basis to New York City restaurants and "society" saloons. These on-premise outlets will account for most of the company's first year of sales. The product will not be sold to supermarkets or neighborhood delicatessens.

Reich was relishing the wave of publicity, "but," he said, "at the same time I knew it was an illusion. We were struggling financially. We were not generating positive cash flow, and the brewery was demanding more and more investment."[29]

This irony is well known to most entrepreneurs. In the early days of any venture, the appearance of success is important. It masks the reality of the struggle. You laugh and smile and talk about your great success, all the while knowing that it isn't real. The last thing you want to do is confess that you are hemorrhaging money. You've got to keep up that confident facade in the hope that profit will eventually flow.

For Krebs's book Paul Shipman, cofounder of Independent Ale Brewery (Redhook), reflected on the angst that all entrepreneurs know from the early days of their venture:

There's no question, when I look back at the old transmission shop [Redhook's first location], that was a charming period. Sometimes when I've had a bad day dealing with the hassles of the board, or I'm having problems with investors, I think about going back to the old days. Entrepreneurs often talk about the romance of the early garage phase of their business when it was struggling to survive. But the truth of the matter is that when the entrepreneur is in the garage phase, his motivation to succeed is incredibly powerful. Because the garage phase is so painful, all you want to do is get out of it—as fast as you can. The truth of the matter is, it is hell.[30]

Reich's success was attracting other would-be entrepreneur-brewers, including my partner, Tom Potter, and me. We were envious when we observed—through twenty-foot windows behind the bar—the lovely copper brewhouse at Old New York's brewery and restaurant. It was a microbrewer's dream. Reich met with us in 1987, but he didn't tell us much, except that we would be crazy to get into this business.

"There was no brotherhood or band of brewers at that time, I can tell you," Reich said. "I was trying to sell something that did not exist in the market. There was no shelf space for microbrewed beer. There were no taps for microbreweries. There was nothing out there but yellow fizzy beer. I didn't want to share the PR I was getting. A lot of people who wanted to start a brewery wanted to see me. But my feeling was 'why should I help anyone else? Let them figure it out for themselves like I did.'"[31]

Eventually Reich started charging $100 per hour to meet with wannabes. Among those who paid were Jeff Ware, founder of Dock Street Brewing Co. and Jim Koch, founder of the Boston Beer Company. Koch, an expert in manufacturing who was working for the prestigious Boston Consulting Group, said he found $100 an hour a reasonable fee. Koch was getting $250 an hour at BCG. Koch paid Reich for a four-hour session at Reich's Manhattan office.[32]

Reich recalled Jim Koch as a "Harvard MBA type. He was all about marketing strategy. His grandfather had been a brewer. I am quite sure I gave him Owades's phone number."[33]

Reich closed his New York City brewery in 1987, less than two years after it opened. Prospect Partners, the venture firm that had funded construction of the brewery, hit the jackpot with one of its projects and then folded the venture firm, leaving Reich holding a big bank loan. He sold the trademark for New Amsterdam to F. X. Matt, who in turn sold it to a large New York-based liquor distributor. The New Amsterdam brand struggled for a few more years before disappearing.

At the time Reich regretted building the brewery. "The basic problem that exists, no matter where you're operating, is the economies of scale," he told the *New Brewer*. "The amount of resources you must put into a production facility detracts from the resources you can spend on marketing and sales."[34]

"If you want to be in the beer business, you don't have to have a production facility," Reich said, adding that he should have stuck with his contract brewing operation at Matt's. "Matt made money," he said. "I had a lot of fun. It was the most fun thing I ever did, but I wouldn't invest in the microbrewing business again."[35]

IN ADDITION TO WORKING OUT PRODUCTION, PRICING WAS ANOTHER CONUNDRUM for the pioneers. Maytag started pricing Anchor Steam at 43 cents a bottle retail, but soon realized it had to be three times that. McAuliffe sold his New

Albion Pale Ale for 95 cents a bottle. Reich started at $4.99 for a six-pack. Bill Newman talked about pricing his beer 25 cents below the $4.09 price of a six-pack of Molson, the Canadian import. It was wishful thinking. Retail pricing is determined by the retailer, not the brewer. And retailers are quick to round prices up to the nearest dollar. Getting $3.84 for a six-pack was a fantasy. But Newman didn't know that. Nor did anyone else at the time. In general the pioneers were aiming for import pricing, a far cry from twenty-first-century pricing, which sees a six-pack go for $10 and more.

The first generation of craft brewers went to school on the pioneers, particularly Reich and Newman. The pioneering period was followed by a wave of hundreds of microbreweries opening in nearly every state in the nation in the next decade. The revolution was on.

CHAPTER TWO

POLITICS, WRITERS, TEACHERS, AND COMMUNITY BUILDERS

IF FRITZ MAYTAG'S DECISION TO SAVE ANCHOR BREWING COMPANY WAS THE CRITI-cal microbrewing event of the 1960s, two pieces of federal legislation were the most influential events for artisanal brewers in the 1970s. At the time, I don't think any of the players involved imagined these measures would pave the way for the craft beer revolution. But they did.

In 1976 Congress approved a $2-per-barrel reduction in the $9-per-barrel federal excise tax for US breweries producing fewer than 60,000 barrels of beer annually.

At the time the United States had fewer than forty-five breweries, and many of the smaller regional breweries—such as Christian Schmidt Brewing Co. in Philadelphia, Haffenreffer Brewery in Boston, Olympia Brewing Company in Washington, and the Pittsburgh Brewing Company—were near declaring bankruptcy. The Brewers' Association of America (BAA) was little more than a club whose members gathered once a year at the rotating rooftop bar at Pier 66 in Fort Lauderdale to drink, dine, dance, and commiserate about the pathetic state of the small brewing industry. Nick Matt, CEO of the Matt Brewing Company has described the association as "the last man standing club."[1] Bill O'Shea, president of the BAA, was a friend of Henry King's. King was the president of the large brewers' trade association, the US Brewers Association (USBA), founded in 1862 in response to Congress's levying a beer excise tax to finance the Civil War.

Ken Grossman, who got involved with the BAA in 1982, recalls hearing how the $2 differential came to be. "Small breweries were going out of business left and right, and I think O'Shea went to Henry [King] and said, 'We've got to do something about this,'" Grossman said. "'Small brewers can't compete and it's not going to look good if there are only two companies left.' . . . Henry was very influential with August Busch's [company] and Stroh's and all the other players that had to agree to it [the differential]. They were all supportive of the two-dollar differential."[2]

The most influential voices in the USBA were those of Anheuser-Busch (AB) and Coors Brewing Co.[3] King ran the USBA from 1962–1983. The national association had 175 employees, including 57 attorneys. In a presentation at the 1995 Craft Brewers Conference, King recalled that on the day he was hired Bill Coors made clear what King's priorities should be: "We don't want you to learn how to make beer. We want you to know everything there is to know about the legislation that relates to the industry."[4]

He paid attention. When O'Shea approached King about getting help in securing a tax differential, King was able to persuade Texas congressman Jay Pickle to sponsor the legislation. Because King had also become friendly with Wilbur Mills, then chair of the House Ways and Means Committee, "we thought that our bill would fly through," King said. "We went to the maltsters, the hopsters, the glass, paper, aluminum and steel merchants—as well as the labor unions—and marshaled them to call and write their congressmen."

They wanted to pass the bill in a voice vote, so the southern legislators whose districts included many neo-prohibitionists would not face an embarrassing roll call vote. At the last minute, an Ohio congressman called for a roll call vote and the bill was "very badly, badly beaten," King recalled. Eight months later King was able to get the bill through Congress, with support from the large brewers and the Gallo winemaking family.

But President Gerald Ford was getting pressure from neo-prohibitionist groups, church groups, and the Center for Science in the Public Interest, an anti-alcoholic beverage lobbying group that is still a formidable enemy of the beer industry. To work on the bill, King enlisted Peter Stroh, a native of Ford's home state of Michigan; Bill Coors; and August Busch III, who was related to one of Ford's economic advisers. Ford had ten days to sign the bill or kill it with a pocket veto. He signed on the ninth day.[5]

Each brewery producing fewer than 2 million barrels annually could save up to $120,000 as a result of the $2 tax break. The 2 million barrel threshold came to identify a "small" brewery in America.

The second crucial piece of federal legislation passed in the 1970s addressed homebrewing, which was of singular importance to the craft brewing revolution. Three of the five pioneers profiled in Chapter 1 began as home-brewers. Ken Grossman, the most successful of the pioneers, ran a store that catered to homebrewers before starting Sierra Nevada. He studied Fred Eck-hardt's *A Treatise on Lager Beers* and Dave Line's *Big Book of Brewing*. Gross-man's signature beer, Sierra Nevada Pale Ale, a beer that defined the California pale ale style, is still bottle conditioned, like most homebrews. Bottle con-ditioning is a process in which a small amount of yeast is deposited in each bottle, allowing for a further fermentation and conditioning after bottling. Jack McAuliffe took up homebrewing while in Scotland, after reading Line's how-to book. And Matthew Reich made a couple of homebrews in his West-chester County kitchen before embarking on the Old New York Brewing Co.

But until February 1, 1979, what the homebrewers were doing was illegal, a holdover from Prohibition. Months earlier, on October 14, 1978, President Jimmy Carter had signed a federal transportation bill, HR1337, into law. The measure included Amendment 3534, which legalized the production of beer at home as of February 1979; its author was Senator Alan Cranston, the California Democrat. Homebrewers in California had complained that winemaking, but not homebrewing, had been legalized after Prohibition was lifted in 1933. The key elements of the Cranston amendment were that any household could produce beer for personal or family use without being taxed so long as production remained less than 200 gallons a year for a household with two or more adults (anyone eighteen or older) or less than 100 gallons annually for a household with one adult.

Both measures continue to influence the craft beer movement. Making homebrewing legal helped ensure the rise of a new generation of hobbyists, some of whom would turn their avocation into a vocation and provide arti-sanal beer making with a steady infusion of new blood.[6] And the $2 differ-ential took on added importance in 1991, when Congress raised the federal excise tax on beer from $9-per-barrel to $18-per-barrel and left the $7 rate in place for small brewers. This was one of the so-called luxury taxes approved by President George H. W. Bush in betrayal of his famous pledge: "Read my lips: no new taxes." It is interesting to note that all those "luxury" taxes on things like yachts and jewels have been rescinded except for the increased federal excise tax on beer, the drink of the working man, hardly a luxury.

Grossman notes that many people like to take credit for the politicking that left the $7 tax rate on small brewers in place while doubling the tax on large brewers. He said that King did not want to participate in the 1991 fight about the excise tax, but added, "I don't know what the truth is. . . .

I was at a BAA meeting, we had spun off a group called Coalition for Beverage Interests (COBI), and it was Hudelpohl [Brewing Company], Bob Pohl was involved, Ted [Marti from August Schell Brewing Company] was there. . . . There were 10 or 15 brewers maybe."[7]

Members of COBI contributed money and hired a Washington lobbyist to press the case for leaving the small brewer tax rate in place. Even so, Grossman recalled that Ted Marti suggested that COBI take the position that the small brewer rate should not change, they had little hope that the small brewers would prevail, "but that was our position, and that is how the bill got written and went through. I don't know if Henry [King] helped on that."[8]

In a 1995 speech at the Craft Brewers Conference, King said the large brewers were the key to keeping the tax differential. Stroh, Coors, Miller, AB, G. Heileman Brewing Company—all supported keeping the small brewers at $7-per-barrel. "That's one reason I get upset when I hear people denigrate these [big breweries'] beers," King said. "You can say you have the best beer in the world—I am sure all of you have great beers—but it hurts our industry when in speeches, in writing, or in any way we denigrate anyone's beer."[9] Wise words that still ring true.

FOR MANY ENTREPRENEURS, HOMEBREWING WAS A GATEWAY TO A CAREER IN THE US craft brewing industry. Their bible was *The Complete Joy of Homebrewing*, a delightful collection of home-brewing instructions, recipes, and tips by Charlie Papazian, the nuclear-engineer-turned-homebrewer. Papazian was a short, soft-spoken, bearded man. Papazian's oft-quoted motto, invoked at anxious moments during the brewing process, was "Relax, don't worry, have a homebrew."

"This book is written for the will-be homebrewer: who will be a homebrewer and will be able to relax and make good beer time after time," Papazian wrote in the introduction. "It is for you who want to jump right in and brew a batch of beer today. And why not? Stouts, ales, lagers, porters, bitters, milds, Oktoberfests, Pilsners, specialty beers and meads . . . they are all easy to make. Many of these styles are even ready to enjoy within three weeks! This book is for you, the will-be homebrewer who wants to enjoy the creative process of doing and learning what beer is all about. Relax."[10]

In his exuberant style Papazian goes on to explain to the beginner the fundamental principles of brewing. His book provides recipes for all the world's great brewing styles for readers at each level—the neophyte, who mainly brews from canned malt extract; the intermediate homebrewer, who mixes malt extract and grain; and the advanced homebrewer, who goes all the way to all grain brewing.

I still have my 1984 edition, signed when Charlie visited Brooklyn Brewery's Oktoberfest party in October 1989. He signed the book, "Relax. Don't worry, have a homebrew (and a Brooklyn Lager too)." He was on a mission to visit fledgling brewing operations like mine and enlist them in his association, then the Association of Brewers (AOB). He still is on that mission.

Papazian, now in his mid-sixties, grew up in Warren, New Jersey, about forty-five miles from New York City. He graduated from public schools in 1967 and got a Reserve Officers Training Course (ROTC) scholarship to the University of Virginia in Charlottesville. He ended up majoring in nuclear engineering and dropping out of the 5-year ROTC program, which obligated participants to serve in the military. The Vietnam War was at its peak in the late 1960s, and many of us of that generation were determined to find a way to avoid serving in that unpopular conflict. He completed his bachelor's degree in five years, taking many courses in education, art, and other subjects that were outside the core engineering curriculum.

He told me he was introduced to homebrewing by a neighborhood friend in Charlottesville. "He dropped by, was a beer drinker, liked to hang out and talk and he invited us, if we were interested, to visit his neighbor who made homebrew," he said. "So I said, well, didn't know you could do that. Sounds interesting . . . Sounds pretty good, so that was my introduction to homebrewing and he gave me a four-by-five card with a five- or six-line recipe on it, and we proceeded to try to brew beer.

"A couple of batches were dumped down the drain, and somehow we figured out there was something called beer yeast rather than bread yeast, and corn sugar versus cane sugar, and that made enough of a difference that we enjoyed the stuff. My first beer was made from Blue Ribbon malt extract with hop flavor in it, so the first couple of years of my homebrewing, I didn't even know what a hop looked like. I just knew it was hop-flavored malt."

The friend who introduced him to homebrewing also gave him a job at the pre-school he ran. He found that he enjoyed being around children and also worked at a daycare center in Charlottesville and a boy's summer camp in Maine. He graduated from the University of Virginia in 1972 in the midst of a recession that, together with the war, led President Carter to talk gloomily of a "malaise" in America, a message that Americans did not want to hear.

Papazian did not have a job and explored several possibilities. Then, on a whim, he went out to Boulder, Colorado, "because I wanted to get away from the East Coast because I had spent my life up to that point on the East Coast. A friend was coming out here, so we came out. . . . I stayed and eventually nine months later I got a job in teaching at this school in Boulder."

He started teaching pre-school but eventually taught kindergarten through third grade, including classes in geography, science, math, shop, and social studies. "I wasn't the English specialist, the reading specialist or the music specialist, but I was the math specialist and the all other," he said. He worked at the Bixby school for eight years, from 1973 to 1981. He started homebrewing in the middle of 1973 and was approached by a community free school to teach a home-brewing course.

Papazian taught homebrewing from 1973 until the early 1980s, and more than 1,000 people took his class. He charged a nominal fee, enough to pay for the ingredients and materials he needed to make homebrew. "I thought it was a pretty good deal to get all my beer paid for [by] teaching a beer class, so it was not a money maker," he said.

"Out of that class . . . a community . . . was built, and I really recognized that homebrewing brought people together as a community," he said.[11] (In 2013 the Boulder History Museum featured an exhibit, "Beer and Boulder," chronicling the impact of homebrewing on Boulder: Papazian loaned the museum his early home-brewing vessels for the exhibit.) The home-brewing community grew, and Papazian started organizing parties in the mountains west of Boulder. The highlight of the year was "The Beer and Steer," a bacchanal with music, beer, and good food that was inspired by the historic 1969 Woodstock music festival.

"In the third year we were, like, 800 people, and it was way, way too many," he said. "We wanted to keep it down to about 300 or 400 people, so we just limited tickets to two tickets per person or maybe four at the most. It was a group of us homebrewers who just thought it would be fun to have a great party up in the mountains, all homebrew and staged music; it was like building on the Woodstock community. People would arrive and camp out. If they drove home, they would have to walk a mile to their cars because we were that far away from the road. We had medics there. We had generators. Lots of food. We built a beer house with snow or ice in there to keep the beer cold depending on what season."[12]

About a decade later Papazian and a member of his home-brewing cohort, Charlie Matzen, started a homebrewing magazine that they called

Zymurgy—after the science of fermentation. The beer festivals continued to grow and so did Papazian's empire. He soon founded the American Home-brewer's Association (AHA), which in 2013 would have a membership of more than 30,000, and the Institute for Brewing and Fermentation Studies. Out of these organizations grew many brewers publications—soon to fall under the name Brewers Publications—and the Great American Beer Festival and the Craft Brewer's Conference. Later, Papazian would form the Association of Brewers as an umbrella organization over all of his empire's different pursuits.

The first issue of *Zymurgy* appeared in December 1978, and the first home-brewing competition and conference was held a year later. About a hundred people attended. "I remember there were twenty-nine entries in the first competition and it was kind of like a . . . it wasn't a show, it was a trade show where homebrewers had their stuff on display and [were] offering samples of homebrew to the public," Papazian said. The next event, in 1980, attracted a few hundred people, and then in 1981 beer writers Michael Jackson and Fred Eckhardt and some professional small brewers, Boulder Beer Company and Cartwright Brewing Company showed up.

"Cartwright—that was a religious guy," Papazian said. "His beer was going bad, but he said, 'Oh, God will take care of it.' [Brewmaster] Tom Burns was working for him then. Burns bailed and came to Boulder, and shortly thereafter the Cartwright brewery closed, and Tom ended up brewmaster at Boulder Beer after the founders hired him to help. They were doing it themselves up to then."

The word *microbrewery* was not yet in use. According to Papazian, Stuart Harris, a volunteer staff writer for *Zymurgy*, coined the term in the early 1980s. "He was working for the microcomputer industry . . . and he said, 'You know, these small breweries are kind of like microcomputers, micro-breweries,' so that's how that name was coined. Harris was just a homebrewer and a volunteer doing beer news for us, for *Zymurgy* magazine."[13]

Papazian and his publications invented much of the terminology for the craft brewing industry. He first defined a microbrewery as a brewery producing fewer than 5,000 barrels annually. When the small brewers grew, he raised the bar to 10,000 and then settled on 15,000 barrels annually, the standard to this day.

Fritz Maytag said he was irritated by Papazian's definitions because it seemed that the AOB was trying to keep Anchor Brewing out of the micro-brewery category. The threshold was always just below Anchor's production volume. Fritz Maytag always had it in for me," Papazian said. "He thought I was doing it to him on purpose." It would not be the last time a trade association's efforts to define the category would court controversy.

Papazian wrote a column titled "What's in a Name" for the March–April 1987 issue of *New Brewer*, in which he first attempted to define or classify the various kinds of breweries in existence. This was the earliest attempt to differentiate "craft breweries" from others. "The names we use to help communicate our position in the industry serve as an introduction and we need that," he wrote. Here is a list of the terms:

Craft brewery—Any brewery using the manual arts and skills of a
   brewer to create its products.
Brewpub (also pub brewery)—A retail establishment, restaurant, bar,
   lounge, taproom, nightclub, or eatery that sells beer brewed on
   the same premises as the retail establishment. A brewpub is a
   type of microbrewery.
Microbrewery—Generally any brewery producing, or able to
   produce, no more than 15,000 barrels of beer per year.
Small brewery—Generally any brewery producing, or able to
   produce, 15,000 to 100,000 barrels of beer per year.
Large brewery—Generally any brewery producing, or able to
   produce, 100,000 to 1 million barrels of beer per year.
Mega or giant brewery—Generally any brewery producing, or able
   to produce, more than 1 million barrels of beer per year.

Some of these definitions, like *microbrewery*, would endure. *Craft brewery* eventually was defined as all independent microbreweries and breweries producing less than 6 million barrels a year and whose main beers are defined as traditional. *Craft brewery* would become an important way for small brewers to differentiate themselves from the giant brewers. Many regional breweries would be deeply disappointed when the Brewers Association in the twenty-first century issued a definition of *craft brewer* that excluded them because their main beers were made with corn and rice adjuncts.

Many of the pioneers attended the first Great American Beer Festival (GABF) in 1982 organized by the AHA as part of the Homebrewers and Microbrewers Conference (later called the Craft Brewers Conference) held at the Hilton Harvest House Hotel in Boulder. Grossman gave a presentation about his brewery, which opened that year.

Papazian was proud, and a bit surprised, by the number of brewing-world luminaries who attended his fledgling beer festival. Among them was

David Bruce, the Monty Python of the British microbrewing movement and founder of the Firkin chain of brewpubs. A former brewer of Old Peculier ale at T&R Theakston Ltd. in Yorkshire, England, Bruce made a fortune when he sold Firkin, and he then led a British group that was investing in US microbreweries, including my company. Bruce was a regular speaker at the early microbrewer conferences, walking onto the stage in a Kermit the Frog suit to demonstrate his zany style of marketing. Bruce would go on to start several pub chains in Great Britain and build on the fortune he made with Firkin.

Roger Briess was there, too. Roger was the CEO of Briess Malt and Ingredients Co. in Chilton, Wisconsin, and a staunch supporter of the microbrewing movement. A short plump man with a reedy voice, Briess carried a pistol at all times, his response to having been mugged in his hometown of New York City. Ron Siebel, the CEO of the Siebel Institute of Technology, the brewing school that would train several generations of craft brewers, was there too.

"To me, Roger Briess and Ron Seibel were two people in the professional brewing business that really recognized the potential of what the homebrewers [and] their enthusiasm and passion [could do]. It was Ron Siebel who introduced me to AB and Miller when I gave talks at the MBAA [Master Brewers Association of America] meeting in 1983 and '84," Papazian said. "When people were pooh-poohing the whole home-brewing [movement] and what we were doing here in Boulder, they would say, 'No, no, you got to listen to these guys. They are on to something! They are very excited about beer, and we have never seen that sort of excitement.'"

Papazian said Tom Burns and Ron Siebel introduced him to the BAA, and Papazian attended BAA conferences for a decade. "If it wasn't for Tom, we would not have been able to convince the BAA folks to donate ten cases of beer to the very first beer festival," Papazian said. "He was our go-between. He was the one that made it happen."

Through his friends at the BAA, Papazian got beer from the regional Wisconsin brewers Joseph Huber Brewing Company, Jacob Leinenkugel Brewing Company, and Stevens Point Brewery. These brewers may have been skeptical of the home-brewing movement, but they didn't want to miss anything. Papazian also recalls that the Coors Brewing Company, then selling only in the West, was helpful. "Before we started the AHA, they let us come down there and ask questions, see what they were doing, taste their pilot beers, explain the brewing process. Boulder Beer couldn't have opened up without Coors because they couldn't get malt." (At the time malted barley was sold only to large breweries in large quantities. Few home-brew stores existed.)

Gordon Bowker attended an early BAA conference and talked about starting Independent Ale Brewery (Redhook). Another early speaker was Dr. Michael Lewis, a PhD in microbiology and biochemistry from England's University of Birmingham. Lewis developed the brewing science undergraduate program at the University of California, Davis, with wine chemistry expert Vernon Singleton.[14]

In the early 1980s Lewis visited Jack McAuliffe's New Albion Brewing Company and said it "certainly changed my view of what the industry could be. I saw a new direction for the industry and a new direction for my program."[15]

In his book Grossman credits Lewis and his successor at Davis, Dr. Charles Bamforth, with directing a technical and practical brewing program that "produced dozens of talented brewmasters" who are the foundation of today's craft brewing movement.[16]

The presence of these brewing industry luminaries was encouraging for Papazian, who just a few years earlier was tapping kegs for a bunch of hippie homebrewers at a beer blast in the Rockies.

JACKSON, THE BRITISH BEER WRITER, ALSO HAD A TREMENDOUS INFLUENCE ON THE craft beer revolution. He was tracking down the history of beer long before microbrewing began to gain popularity in the United States. An early proponent of the Campaign for Real Ale, Jackson published his *World Guide to Beer* in 1977, which was an inspiration to many of us who became intrigued by the mysteries of beer.

Jackson's book plumbed the complexities of this wonderful inexpensive beverage that has beguiled young and old for thousands of years. He explained the evolution of ale yeast—which ferments beer at warm temperatures at the top of the fermenting vessel—into lager yeast—which ferments at cooler temperatures at the bottom of the fermenting vessel.

Lagering was "possible where there were caves, and especially if natural ice was plentiful. It was also noticed that, if the casks of beer were stored in caves packed with ice, the yeast gradually settled to the bottom of the brew. The beer was therefore much clearer, and did not have to be 'skimmed' before sale. This technique of bottom fermentation seems to have first been mentioned in 1420, in the minutes of the Munich town council . . .

"Only with the development of artificial refrigeration during the 1800s did bottom-fermentation become a universal technique. In the same period, the behavior of yeast was being explained, notably by Pasteur."

I thought this was exciting stuff. Louis Pasteur? Jackson was ennobling my favorite beverage. I knew there was more to it than "More taste; less filling," and here it was. The 255-page book was filled with fascinating labels and classic posters from the legendary breweries of the great brewing nations of the world and beguiling photos of the grand breweries of Europe. It was a coffee table book with substance. I read it and became an expert on beer.

Jackson later starred in the six-half-hour episode series *The Beer Hunter* on the Discovery Channel, a wonderful account of his visits to the world's most interesting breweries. I spent many wonderful days with Jackson in the 1990s. We had much in common. I had worked for small newspapers in upstate New York when I graduated from college in 1971. Jackson had quit school at sixteen to work as a cub reporter for a small newspaper, the *Huddersfield Examiner* in England. Former BBC editor Geoff Griggs, now a beer writer in New Zealand, recalled that Jackson started writing a column titled "This is Your Pub," profiling all the pubs in the paper's distribution area. Griggs said when Jackson ran out of pubs, his editor suggested he profile local churches. Jackson promptly resigned. He worked his way up to the *Daily Herald* and the *World Press News,* and eventually wrote for the *Guardian,* one of Britain's great newspapers. On a similar career track, I moved from the upstate paper to New York City, got a job with Associated Press, and later went to the Middle East to have my unlikely introduction to homebrewing.

Jackson was proud of his working class roots in Wetherby, Yorkshire. His father was born Isaac Jakowitz, the son of Chaim Jakovitz, who immigrated to Britain from Lithuania. His father worked as a truck driver, married a gentile, and changed his name to Jackson. Michael Jackson of course shared the name of one of the world's most famous people. He often began his lectures by saying, "If there is any doubt as to who I am, I am the real Michael Jackson," and then dramatically raised a sequined white-gloved hand.

Jackson's writing raised beer to a level of prestige that it had never before achieved in the world of alcoholic beverages. In the *World Guide to Beer* Jackson classified the world's beers by style and thus became the inventor of beer styles such as pale ale, amber lager, stout, and porter. He wrote about beer in the high-minded style of a wine writer, using terms like *bananas, cloves, black currant, smoke, coffee,* and *chocolate* to describe the hints of flavors he detected in the beers he reviewed.

For instance, he wrote of Belgium's Chimay Red in his *Simon & Schuster Pocket Guide to Beer*: "It has a full, copper colour, a notably soft palate and a hint of blackcurrant." Of one of his favorites, Orval, he said, "This brew gains its unusual orangey colour from the use of three malts produced to its own specification, plus white candy sugar in the kettle; its aromatic, aperitif bitterness derives from the use of Hallertau and [more especially] Styrian Goldings [hop varieties], not only in the kettle but also in dry-hopping, its characterful acidity comes from its own single-cell yeast in its primary and bottle fermentations and a blend of several bottom cultures in its secondary."[17]

Not everyone appreciated Jackson's elegant descriptions of beer. And he could be defensive about his tendency to be flowery. In his "Jackson on Brew" column for November–December 1987 issue of *New Brewer* magazine, he wrote a column headlined "Harmonic Convergence" that addressed brewers who questioned his style:

> The truth is that a brewery is a minefield: things ready to go off all over the place. Brewing science tries to stop them going off. That is why scientifically-trained brewers are habituated to look for trouble spots rather than G-spots. They know more about agony than ecstacy.
>
> More than one brewer has attacked me with his flavor wheel: "This is how you analyze beer flavors. You use the proper professional language . . . sulfury, rancid, solventlike, papery, cabbage, phenolic. None of your nonsense about beers being flowery, peachy, spicy, seductive. Obviously, you know nothing about beer. What are you anyway . . . a wine writer?"
>
> I have to answer this: "I understand," I murmur, chastened. "I will try to get it right in the future. How would you like me to describe your beer next time I write about it? Sulfury, rancid, or solventlike?"
>
> There are two areas of misunderstanding here. One is perspective. Should beer be judged on its defects (which can be identified objectively, even if they are matters of degree), or on its merits (also a matter of degree, and not wholly subjective)?
>
> The other . . . concerns language. In the privacy of his lab, a brewer will ostracize even his own beer. Perhaps, indeed, he will be hardest on his own product, since his personal standards are at stake. In the public prints, I am hesitant to damn any beer.

Jackson never panned a brewery. If he didn't like a brewery, he didn't write about it.

Jackson peppered his talks and television appearances with such witty aphorisms as "Some people say you live longer if you don't drink, but that is not true. It only seems longer," and "Moderation is all right, as long as it's in moderation."

The first time I went drinking with Jackson was in the early 1990s. My company was distributing its own beers and about fifteen other micro-brewed beers, including Sierra Nevada and all the great beers of Belgium, Britain, and Germany. Jackson's *World Guide* was my roadmap to the world of beer. I sought out beers that he wrote about. I invited Jackson to New York for several nights of beer tastings, one at the blues club Tramps in Manhattan's Chelsea neighborhood, one on Long Island, one upstate in Peekskill, and one in New Jersey. We promised to promote and sell his books at each event. Selling books was as important to Jackson as selling beer was to us.

The owner of Tramps, the Irishman Tony Dunn, could not believe we sold out the house for this rumpled Brit with the professorial manner and inclination to long-winded digressions. After the tasting we toured some of New York City's beer bars. I recall that Jerry Kuziw, the owner of Brews-ky's and Burp Castle, two pioneering microbrew bars, brought out special vintages of Chimay Grand Reserve and Thomas Hardy's Ale for the Beer Hunter to sample at 3 a.m. Jackson scribbled his impressions in a little note-book throughout the evening. I would be willing to bet the notes were not legible.

The next morning we met for lunch at Café Bruxelles, the Belgian-owned restaurant in Greenwich Village that specialized in the Belgian beers that Jackson wrote about. I was badly hung over, and Jackson looked like he was, too. He perused the beer list and ordered an Orval, the highly car-bonated Belgian ale made by monks at the Abbaye Notre-Dame d'Orval in southern Belgium.

"Orval is my favorite hangover beer," Jackson said in his deliberate York-shire accent. I ordered the same. He was right. Try it sometime.

In books and articles Jackson championed US microbrewers and their beers, just as he had championed the great beers of Europe in his *World Guide*. He eventually published *Michael Jackson's Beer Companion* and gave US microbreweries an exalted place among the great beers and breweries of the world. He often declared that the most interesting beers in the world were being brewed in the United States, a declaration derided by many European brewers who had not sampled the new American beers.

The Beer Hunter tirelessly visited breweries all over the world, including Maytag's Anchor Brewing Company. "The smallest brewery in the United States has added a whole new dimension to American brewing," he wrote.[18]

The Brooklyn brewmaster Garrett Oliver and I toured many of the great breweries of Europe in the 1990s. I recall that Rene Lindeman, of the famous lambic brewery near Brussels (lambic beers are fermented with wild yeasts), said that Jackson had saved his company from oblivion. It really did seem that Jackson educated the British, the Belgians, and the Germans about their own wonderful breweries and brewing cultures.

Jackson's *World Guide* also inspired Charlie Finkel, a graphic designer in Seattle, to begin importing some classic European beers and to develop some classic American brews. Finkel's company, Merchant du Vin, brought to the United States the rich lager and wheat beers of the Ayinger Brewery in Bavaria, the English ales of the Samuel Smith Old Brewery, and the lambic beers of Brewery Lindemans in Belgium. Finkel also commissioned beers from the August Schell Brewing Company in New Ulm, Minnesota, one of the country's oldest breweries, and the Cold Spring Brewing Co. in Cold Spring, Minnesota.[19]

Jackson developed Parkinson's disease in his early sixties and died in 2007. "I think it is safe to say, without fear of successful contradiction, that Michael was the most influential voice in food and drink in the twentieth century," Oliver said in his eulogy at Jackson's London funeral. "His was the voice that launched a thousand breweries, especially in America. . . . And what did he tell us? That great brewing was work worthy of honor, practiced by honorable people. That many of the best times of your life will be spent around a table, with your people—you should drink wonderful drinks. That it was possible to brew a form of absolute truth, a perfect thing that could evoke, or maybe even bring about, all the best things in the world. We heard him, and we could not have hoped for more."[20]

In the United States microbrewed beer has had its greatest success in the Pacific Northwest, partly because of the early influence of an American beer writer, Fred Eckhardt. He was one of the earliest evangelists of homebrewing, publishing his *A Treatise on Lager Beers* in 1969, a decade before homebrewing was legalized. Eckhardt developed a taste for the Danish beer Tuborg while serving in the Marines in Japan during the Korean War. Back in Portland, Oregon, he began home brewing and teaching home-brewing classes. In 1989 he published *The Essentials of Beer Style*, which became a bible for the first generations of microbrewers.

FRITZ MAYTAG HAS TALKED ABOUT THE IMPORTANCE OF HIS FIRST AND BEST CUS-tomer, Fred Kuh, at the Old Spaghetti Factory, the man who encouraged Maytag to get involved in the Anchor Brewing Company.

It would be wrong to overlook the importance of early believers like Kuh, the people who saw the value and dynamism of the microbrewing movement long before most others. I know I had some retailers whose support was essential to my success. One was Joe Marino Sr., owner of American Beer Distributing Company, a strange retailer-wholesaler hybrid that is unique to New York due to a loophole in New York's three tier laws. Joe's father started the company in 1945. When I started peddling Brooklyn Lager, Joe ordered a pallet of my beer on day one. He stacked it in the front of his supermarket-style store and he pushed it. He believed in what we were doing. He told me the Budweiser distributor in Brooklyn, Joe Lomuscio, once came into his store and sniffed, "Why do you have that shit displayed in the front?" Marino replied, "I'm selling a pallet a week of that shit, Joe!"

Another early adopter of the microbrewing movement was Tommy Chou, who emigrated from Taiwan when he was twenty-three and got an undergraduate degree in biochemistry from Tennessee Tech. Chou was a doctoral candidate at New York Technical College and doing research on organic synthesis for a chemical company when the recession of the mid 1970s hit.

"I drove a taxi for a while, and then I got the idea to buy a deli," Chou recounted during an interview at his famous Greenwich Village bar, Peculier Pub. "I thought maybe beer is close to my field, organic chemistry." He took in twenty-four German imports from Dieter Steinmann, a Bavarian immigrant who established the Dinkelacker brand in New York.

"They did well," Chou recalled. So he began to learn about German, Belgian, British, and Czech beers by reading Michael Jackson's *World Guide to Beer.* "And then one day Michael Jackson himself popped into my deli. I said, 'I know you. That's your picture in my book. Will you sign it?'" He said Jackson complained that no bar in New York was carrying these special beers.

Chou and his wife did their homework. They visited an English pub on West Fourth Street. He said the two women who ran the pub were paying about 10 cents a serving for draft beer and selling it for $1.25. In the early 1980s, he was buying beer for 35 cents a bottle and selling it for 50 cents. Owning a bar was clearly a better business, so in 1984 he and his wife leased a pub with a capacity of forty-five at 182 West Fourth Street, the site now occupied by the Slaughtered Lamb. They called the bar Peculier Pub, after Old Peculier, the dark ale brewed by Theakston. Chou left out "Old," because he was afraid of being accused of trademark infringement. The pub did well, and the Chous moved to a larger location with church pew seating and stained-glass windows at 145 Bleecker Street, where it continues to operate today. Chou is now training his daughter Ginger, a biology major and recent graduate of Wellesley College, to take over.

When I started selling Brooklyn Lager in March 1988, Chou was among the first to stock my bottles and then my draft beer. "I knew you were a local brewery," he said. "I had to support you."[21]

If only more bar owners felt that way.

I think every craft brewer can tell similar stories about the importance of those early believers—the writers and educators, distributors and retailers, bar and restaurant owners, storeowners, and homebrewers who promoted and sold craft beer before it was fashionable. Their contributions to the success of the craft beer movement were at least as important as that of the artisanal brewers themselves. These people believed in microbrewed beer, and they believed in microbrewers, and many bet their businesses, and in many ways their reputations, on the viability of these entrepreneurs and their quirky beers.

CHAPTER THREE

THE FIRST GENERATION

A BOOM AND THE FIRST BEER WAR
1984-1994

1984: 18 microbreweries
76 noncraft national and regional breweries
1994: 537 microbreweries
22 noncraft national and regional breweries
Anheuser-Busch, Miller, and Coors: 81 percent market share

IN 1984 THE MICROBREWING WORLD WAS POISED FOR A DECADE-LONG BOOM THAT would see the establishment of hundreds of new breweries, contract operations, and brewpubs. And yet everyone already in the business was painfully, quietly aware that no one was making any money with craft beer. All the pioneers—from Maytag to Newman—spoke incessantly of the importance of understanding the business, but none had found the formula for success.

Alan S. Dikty, the acerbic editor of the *New Brewer,* wrote an editorial for the May–June 1984 issue that noted, "One common denominator shared by most failed, failing and still born microbreweries is that the primary motivation of the founder(s) is to brew good beer."

His point was that no one was motivated to make money. So how long could any of these ventures last?

Dikty noted that twenty-five microbreweries had opened for business in the United States and Canada since 1976. Eight years later six were out of business, one had suspended production, and all were, from a profitability standpoint, marginal. From a business point of view microbrewing probably didn't make sense. But that did not stop the rush. People who wanted to brew good beer were not in short supply.

Later in 1984 Dikty marveled at how attendance at the microbrewers convention in Denver was burgeoning. He wrote: "Item: Investment-hunting businessmen were present to 'check out' this new business. Participants at previous conferences have generally tended to run the gamut from over-educated and underemployed liberal arts majors to slightly dog-eared counter-culture types. This year saw an influx of people suffering from midlife crises who were looking for new fields to conquer and a leavening of businessmen contemplating microbreweries as the next logical step beyond franchised salad bars. Both groups shared an obsession with secret beer formulations and a realization that perhaps this business is a little more complicated than they thought."[1]

Matthew Reich was the volume leader; his Old New York Brewing Co. produced 15,000 barrels annually under contract at the Matt Brewing Company in Utica. Reich, however, was not satisfied with contract brewing. He was determined to open a brewery in New York City. He had the capital, and he was building.

Yet dozens of other wannabe brewers saw Reich's contract-brewing arrangement as the smarter course. Why not contract with an existing brewery? Leave all the messy brewing to someone else and focus on marketing and selling the beer. Making good beer was step one; selling it at a profit was the hard part.

In the four years after the pioneering period, 1984–88, fifty-four microbreweries, sixty-five brewpubs, and twenty-seven contract breweries popped up across the country. Somehow it did not matter that no one was making money. The lure was so strong and the new brewers so idealistic and dedicated that most of them figured if they did what they loved, the money would magically follow.

One of those contract brewers was the business-suited Harvard MBA Jim Koch. He was a brilliant student, one of only a dozen students to qualify for a three-year program that awards not only an MBA but also a law degree. Among his classmates was Mitt Romney.[2]

Jim Koch was born in Cincinnati in 1949 and grew up in the city and on the family farm in Georgetown, Ohio. He was the second of four children and attended Cincinnati public schools. His grandfather was a graduate of Siebel Institute and worked for Anheuser-Busch (AB) for a few years after Prohibition. Koch's father was an apprentice brewer in the 1940s and graduated from Siebel in 1948. He worked for several Cincinnati lager breweries—

Hudepohl, Schoenling, Weidemann's, Burger, and Bavarian—but was out of work when these breweries closed. He said his Dad made only $500 during his last six months as a brewer. He later sold brewing chemicals and supplies to the brewing industry. His mother, an elementary school teacher, worked to put all her children through college.

At the Boston Consulting Group (BCG), where he worked after graduating from Harvard, Jim Koch was an expert on industrial enterprises. He was tall, thin, and boyish, with a reedy, nasal voice eventually made famous by his brewery's ubiquitous radio advertising. You couldn't help but think he probably got slapped around by the guys on the football team in high school. In fact, a prankster at the Institute for Brewing and Fermentation Studies once changed the address label on Koch's copy of the *New Brewer* to read: Jim "Dweeb" Koch. Koch was a guy with something to prove. He had been an Outward Bound leader and had climbed a few serious mountains, including Argentina's Aconcagua, the highest peak in the western hemisphere at 22,831 feet and a notoriously difficult slog.

So it was fitting that he chose as his brand name Samuel Adams, a Bostonian who was one of the fieriest early patriots. Adams was a rabble-rouser or, as Koch put it when I interviewed him, "Sam Adams saw how you could radicalize people."

Adams was a cousin of John Adams, the second president of the United States. He was a signer of the Declaration of Independence. A graduate of Harvard, like Koch. Sam Adams failed in business, including a stint with the family's malt house, which produced malted barley for brewing. He then got into politics, opposing British efforts to tax the American colonists. He led the opposition to Britain's Tea Act, which exempted the British East India Company from an aggressive export tea tax in an attempt to give them a monopoly in the colonies and reinforce the British government's right to level taxes on the colonies. The resistance peaked when a group of Bostonians boarded a British East India Company ship and dumped the tea shipment into Boston Harbor in protest. Koch embraced the revolutionary spirit of Samuel Adams, and it did not take long for his ambition to make good.

When Koch started selling Samuel Adams beer in 1985, he released a series of memorable radio ads attacking the leading European beer imports, Heineken and Beck's, for using corn and sugar as preservatives in the beers they sent to the United States. He claimed their beer was stale by the time it arrived here. In his whiny, insistent, and memorable voice, Koch intoned:

When America asked for Europe's tired and poor, we didn't mean their beer.
But instead of their best, Europe sends us mass-produced beer. They send us
Heineken, which contains adjuncts forbidden by Germany's strict beer purity
law, and Beck's, which is brewed lighter and less flavorful for Americans. The
St. Pauli Girl brand was invented to sell to Americans. So how can we get a true
handcrafted beer over here? Drink my Samuel Adams Lager. I'm Jim Koch. I
brew in a year what the largest-selling import makes in just three hours because
I take the time to brew Samuel Adams right. I use my great-great-grandfather's
recipe, all malt brewing, and rare hops that cost ten times what they use in the
mass-produced imports.[3]

Heineken and Beck's leaped to the bait, and the controversy garnered
much attention in the media, including a long piece in *Newsweek*. I've never
met a headline writer who could resist "Beer War!"[4]

Philip Van Munching, the son of Leo Van Munching, importer of
Heineken, dedicated a chapter in *Beer Blast,* his fine chronicle of Heineken in
America, to the battle with Koch—"Samuel Adams: Brewer, Patriot, Pain in
the Ass." Van Munching writes that his father viewed Koch as the Antichrist,
and the author himself refers to Koch as a scoundrel, but he also clearly recog-
nizes that Koch and the other microbrewers were a force to be reckoned with.

"Because of the tremendous growth of imports, a number of entrepreneurs began asking themselves if the traits that made foreign beers sell
couldn't be replicated here in the States," Van Munching writes. "In asking
that question, they—overnight, it seemed—redefined the beer business. No
longer was the equation domestic/imported; now it would be mainstream/
sophisticated."[5]

And what of Koch's allegation that the American version of Heineken
could not be sold in Germany because it violated the Reinheitsgebot, the
sixteenth-century German purity law, which stipulates beer can have only
four ingredients: water, barley or wheat malt, hops, and yeast? The Samuel
Adams ads declared that Heineken also contained adjuncts. Van Munching
grudgingly acknowledges the charge was mostly true: "In addition to the classic ingredients . . . Heineken used corn in its brewing. Corn acts as a stabilizer
and is often used by larger breweries to add crispness to a beer that may take
a while to reach its destination."[6]

The ads were close enough to the truth that Heineken did not dare sue
Koch. "If I had been wrong, do you think they would have let me get away

with saying there's something fishy in their beer? They would have crushed me like a bug."[7] That arresting image of an international mega-brewer crushing a tiny American microbrewer is one that served Koch well in the 1980s and continues to serve the US craft beer movement to this day.

The David and Goliath metaphor had once been a staple of Van Munching's repertoire. He wrote that he never missed an opportunity to tell a reporter that Budweiser spills in a week what Heineken sells in a year. He adds: "Imagine my horror, then, when this eventually showed up in a Sam Adams ad: 'I brew in a year what the largest-selling import makes in just three hours, because I take the time to brew Samuel Adams right.'"[8] Heineken had a little more than 1 percent of the US beer market in the 1980s.

The Van Munchings later learned that Koch did not even own his own brewery; he contracted with the Pittsburgh Brewing Company to produce Samuel Adams. But by then Leo Van Munching did not have the stomach for a public battle with Koch. Calling the *Newsweek* article unfair, he pulled his advertising from the magazine.

The younger Van Munching paid Koch a compliment, comparing him to his grandfather, Leo Van Munching Sr., the man who introduced Heineken to America after Prohibition and made it the best-selling imported beer by doggedly peddling it to bars and restaurants in New York City.

"Both Koch and Leo Sr. owed a debt of gratitude to P. T. Barnum, and both harbored egos the size of a small town," Philip Van Munching writes. "Both proved tireless promoters, and both understood old-fashioned barstool-to-barstool salesmanship. The major difference between the two is that my grandfather managed to accomplish what he did without pissing off everyone else in his industry."[9]

Koch's assault on Heineken and Beck's was the opening salvo in a career that would always court controversy. Koch was not afraid to mix it up with companies far larger than the Boston Beer Company. "I made my way through the world by pushing the envelope," Koch said. "We were small. We were scrappy. We had to shake things up. I had a better quality product, and they [Heineken and Beck's] were selling skunky beer. It was the strength of the weak."

Koch said that Matthew Reich had suggested he hire a public relations firm to tell his story. He hired Sally Jackson, and she parlayed the controversy with Heineken and Beck's into the *Newsweek* article. Jackson remains Boston Beer's representative to this day.

In the beginning the Boston Beer Company consisted of two people, Koch and Rhonda Kalman, a smart executive secretary from BCG. She left the security of BCG to join Koch in a humble office in Boston. To entice Kalman to join him, Koch told her, "I've never failed at anything that was really important to me, and this is really important to me."[10]

They launched Samuel Adams Boston Lager in the summer of 1985. They missed the truck that shipped beers from eastern microbreweries to Denver for the GABF, so Koch air-freighted several cases to get them there before the deadline. On its first try Samuel Adams won the Consumer Preference Poll, in which festival goers voted for their favorite beer.

The citation for the Consumer Preference Medal called the winner the Best Beer in America, and it didn't take long for the losers to start crying foul. Who would deny there might be better beers in America than Samuel Adams Boston Lager, not to mention the second and third place winners, Hibernia Brewing Company and Snake River Brewing? As such, the Consumer Preference Poll was a lightning rod for controversy. Some brewers accused Koch of using sexy models to pour his beer and gain votes. He protested that his pourers were his partner, Rhonda Kalman, and his publicist, Sally Jackson, and both had dressed modestly.

Of course he ran with the citation. He trademarked "Best Beer in America" and printed the claim on his packaging and his marketing materials. He used it as a tagline in his radio advertising.

The next year he was back, this time handing out Samuel Adams painter's caps to festival goers and winning the Consumer Preference Poll once again. This time the accusation was that Koch had bought votes by giving away tickets to people sure to vote for his beer.

In an interview, Koch denied he ever bought votes. But he did say it was common for Boston Beer salesmen to give out festival tickets to distributor sales representatives and customers in Colorado. "We didn't give away baseball or football tickets, but we did use GABF tickets as an incentive to waitstaff at restaurants," he said.

"Last year, it was the use of sex appeal that stirred complaints, and this year it was hats and too many brewery staff people," said Daniel Bradford, director of the festival, in an interview at the time. "There's always a bad boy of the GABF. Someone always spends the time and effort to think up ways of legally getting around the rules."[11] Craft brewers were upset enough that they forced the festival to adjust the rules, limiting samples to two ounces, the number of servers per brewery to three, and the value of giveaways to a dollar. But controversy flared anew when in 1987 Boston Beer Company won the Consumer Preference Poll for the third straight year, this time with Samuel Adams Festival Lager, a beer brewed specially for the event. Second went to Boulder Beer Company's Festival Brew and third to Chinook Alaskan Amber Beer. The crowd of 4,500 at the festival booed loudly when Boston Beer and Boulder's first and second place finishes were announced. It was pretty clear who the perennial "bad boy" of the GABF was—Koch.

Koch's victories were particularly galling to many who operated their own microbreweries and felt that contract-brewing operations like Boston Beer's were deceitful and an unfair advantage. Koch was also on track to sell his beer in every state, putting him into direct competition with virtually every brewery in the country. Within a decade after starting his business, Boston Beer was the only microbrewer with nationwide distribution, making Samuel Adams the face of the industry.

Some brewers boycotted the GABF for several years in a silent protest against the Consumer Preference Poll and Boston Beer's domination. Kurt and Rob Widmer, who started their draft-only brewery in Portland, Oregon, in 1984, were two high-profile boycotters. Kurt Widmer said that Koch had pretty girls serving his beer and was using giveaways to entice festival goers to vote for his beer. It was not an impartial poll, he said. "We decided at that point that we didn't want to participate in this sort of thing. We didn't have the money to compete like this and we didn't have any interest in this kind of competition. So we stopped going to the festival."[12]

Daniel Bradford was marketing director of the Association of Brewers (AOB). As director of the festival, Daniel Bradford was at the center of the storm. He recalled it as a very trying time and said he and his staff investigated every accusation of abuse of the voting system.

"During that time, every story that I heard, I chased down, and they were not true," he said. "I mean, Vince Cottone [a writer for the *New Brewer*] would say, so-and-so said such-and-such, and I would find them, sit down, and the stories never were true. Secondly, I maintained steady vigilance on all the ticket outlets. And I think they couldn't sell more than six at a time and there never was any bulk buying, so he may have given out tickets that we gave him. Third thing, the difference between the winner and second [place] was way up there. No way Koch bought that many tickets. We never released the numbers, but it was huge."

Bradford said that when people complained about Boston Beer giving away painter's caps, he spoke to Koch and he stopped distributing caps after one public session. He said the accusation that Koch hired models to pass out beer was simply not true, confirming that the servers were Rhonda Kalman and Sally Jackson.

Some breweries did hire pretty women to hand out beer samples, but it was Boulder Beer, Chesbay, and a few others, not Boston Beer, Bradford said. "There were a couple of others that had come straight from the NBWA [National Beer Wholesalers Association] convention in Vegas, so they didn't know any better," he said.

Bradford said many breweries blamed him for the alleged abuses, and he took the criticism personally at the time. He recalls being berated by a German journalist from the trade magazine *Brauvelt*.

"You know nothing until you have been chewed out by a German magazine writer, in German," he said. "I was probably oversensitive to it. I got accosted in the halls by brewers ready to punch me out . . . because they thought I was a crook. One brewer sent a letter to every brewer saying I was in bed with Jim Koch. Actually in bed, not figuratively."[13]

Jeff Mendel, who worked with Bradford on the festival, said none of the alleged abuses were ever proven. "I never knew Jim [Koch] to be a rule breaker, but he certainly was a boundary tester. If something was not expressly forbidden, then it might be OK. It was: ask for forgiveness, rather than permission."[14]

To address the criticism Papazian and Bradford established a professional blind tasting of beers in thirty-six style categories. Michael Jackson helped set up the system, an important improvement in the development of the GABF. The judges, many of them certified beer judges and professional brewers, could award gold, silver, and bronze medals in each category. The judging was supervised by Jim Homer, codirector of the National Beer Judge Certification program.

Today the Professional Blind Tasting Panel judges eighty-five style categories—a testament to the innovation of the craft brewing industry. The judging system is widely copied and recognized internationally as the standard for brewing industry competitions. The Consumer Preference Poll battle is a prime example of how microbrewers were struggling in the early years to define their craft and to develop something valuable and lasting.

"I thought it ended up good for the industry," Bradford said. "It was a kind of values clarification. A lot of brewers took a hard look and said, 'Who are we? Let's do this the right way.'" Mendel added, "The blind tasting protected the integrity of the festival and the awards."[15]

Many other critics focused on the practice of contract brewing made famous by Koch. "I think a contract brewer should stay with the truth and make it real clear," Mark Carpenter of Anchor Brewing said in 1986. "If he leads people on that he has a brewery and doesn't, he'll be in a lot of trouble when that fact comes out."[16]

Though Matthew Reich ushered in the modern era of contract brewing with his New Amsterdam Amber Beer, brewed at Matt, after he built his packaging brewery in New York City in the mid-1980s, he became an outspoken critic. "Until you run a brewery, you don't know what it takes to brew beer," Reich declared. "If a contract brewer wants to sell beer, he has to lie. Basically, he has to perpetrate fraud."[17]

"I was the contract-brewing pariah," Koch said recently. That may have been true, but he was selling a lot of beer. In 1987 Boston Beer Company sold 35,000 barrels of beer, more than double the sales of its closest rival, Reich's Old New York Brewing Co., which sold 15,000 barrels. The bad boy was on a roll that would push him to 113,000 barrels in 1990, way beyond his nearest competitor, a supreme market position he holds to this day.

Koch had made his mark in the beer industry with his attacks on the leading importers and his soaring sales. He also got the attention of Hambrecht & Quist, one of the most successful venture capital firms in America, best known for investing in tech companies in California. Koch said he was surprised and pleased when Bill Hambrecht told him his favorite investments were consumer goods, like Neutrogena and Chalone Vineyard.

Hambrecht invested $7 million in Boston Beer Company, buying a 20 percent stake in the company. That gave Koch a $35 million valuation, not bad for a company that had opened two years earlier with $300,000 in startup capital. Koch's idea was to build a brewery in the old Haffenreffer Brewery in Jamaica Plain, a rundown industrial section of Boston. But Koch knew that Bill Newman was closing his brewery in Albany and that Reich was struggling in New York City. Koch also calculated that a large brewery in Boston could not be built for $7 million. It would more likely cost twice that. So he bought Newman's equipment and scaled back his plans for Jamaica Plain. By the time Koch opened in Boston, Reich had shut his brewery. Koch hired Reich's brewmaster, Andy Bernadette, to run Boston Beer. Andy tracked down and brought in Dave Grinnell, a former brewer at Old New York, by placing an ad in the *Village Voice*. Koch had spent only $200,000.

He would spend the rest of the $7 million in venture money brilliantly, but not without attracting new controversies.

Koch's Samuel Adams Boston Lager was outpacing all rivals. By 1988, the year I started selling Brooklyn Lager, Koch was selling 40,000 barrels annually. Here at last was a small brewer who knew how to make both good beer and real money. He was the only small brewer using mass advertising, and it was amazingly effective. Many of my colleagues dismissed him as a huckster, but few denied that Samuel Adams Boston Lager was good beer, and all underestimated the dogged determination of the brilliant guy from Cincinnati to reestablish his family's place in the American beer business.

Somehow my own fledgling craft brewery got caught up in the beer war, although we were so small, we probably weren't even on his marketing radar. In our first year in business in Brooklyn, we sold 3,000 barrels of beer. The next year, 5,000, and then in 1990, 7,000. It was tough going, but we were proud of our progress. In 1989 we won a beer-tasting event sponsored by a bar in Manhattan called riverrun, after a passage in James Joyce's *Finnegan's Wake*. The bar owner, Don Berger, promoted the event and included both New Amsterdam and Samuel Adams beer. Berger called it the Great American Beer Tasting. It was a thrill and an encouraging accomplishment for our struggling company to win the competition. We had table tents (those small cardboard A-frames that adorn most chain-restaurant tables) and cooler stickers printed announcing that Brooklyn Lager was the winner of the Great American Beer Tasting. It was no match for Koch's radio advertising, but it was the best we could manage. When we told beer drinkers about our accomplishment, they often replied: "I thought Sam Adams won that thing."

In 1992 Brooklyn Lager won a gold medal at the Great American Beer Festival in Denver. Our Brooklyn Brown Ale won a bronze. Our designer, Milton Glaser, did a wonderful poster showing our two bottled beers with ribbons and medals hanging on their necks. The poster announced "Brooklyn's First National Champions Since 1955," a reference to the Brooklyn Dodgers' celebrated, one-time World Series victory against the New York Yankees. Again, many of our customers were puzzled by our victory at the GABF. Didn't Samuel Adams win that thing?

In December 1992, a few months after we garnered our medals in Denver, I attended a holiday party for the teachers at my wife's public school in Manhattan. I supplied beer for the party. As was customary at these sorts of events, the husbands congregated by the bar. There I met a tall attorney in a dark suit and tie named Robert Martin. His wife was a teacher. He asked about Brooklyn Brewery and I told him the story of the company and our recent victories at the GABF.

He asked if I had heard the radio ads that claimed Samuel Adams was the Best Beer in America and that it had won the Denver festival four years running. I explained the controversy about the Consumer Preference Poll and that Koch had won the poll in 1985, 1986, 1987, and 1989, not four years running. Martin said one ad claimed you could balance a quarter on the head of a Samuel Adams Lager. He said he had tried this, and it didn't work. When I asked Martin what he did for a living, he said he was deputy counsel for New York City's Department of Consumer Affairs. Within a few months the agency announced it was investigating Boston Beer for violations of New York City's consumer protection law.

On May 6, 1993, the *Boston Globe*'s business section carried a story whose headline announced: "Barroom Brawl: Tiny Brooklyn Brewery Takes on Boston's Sam Adams. 'It's smarmy,' says Jim Koch." Once again, headline writers were unable to resist a beer war. The article went on to explain that Consumer Affairs had sent an April 19 letter to Koch stating: "Your current ads claim that Samuel Adams Lager 'won the Great American Beer Festival four years running.' However, our preliminary investigation indicates that while you received awards in 1985, 1986, 1987 and 1990, awards were never received for more than three consecutive years."

The article quoted Charlie Papazian's explanation that the Consumer Preference Poll had been replaced by the more objective Professional Blind Tasting Panel because of complaints from rival brewers. "It was becoming a popularity contest, and it didn't really reflect our mission," Papazian told the reporter. New York City's consumer affairs department wrote that "there is a clear potential for consumers being misled when you refer in the aggregate to 'winning' the Great American Beer Festival without being specific as to the nature of what you won."

Ever the wordsmith, Koch countered: "I used to say we won four years in a row. If you go to bat three times, get three hits and a walk, and then a fourth hit, didn't you get four hits in a row?"

The *Wall Street Journal* followed up with a story headlined: "Brewers Go Head to Head over Beer Ads." *Newsday*'s story said, "A Brewsky Brouhaha." The beer industry newspapers and newsletters also wrote stories.

But the controversy was just beginning. Papazian announced that starting July 1, 1993, brewers who used the festival's awards in advertising would have to name the prize, the year it was won, and the category in which it was won. The cumbersome requirements made it difficult to advertise "Winner of the Great American Beer Festival."

Koch defied the new rules, insisting on his right to use the slogan "Best Beer in America," based on the appearance of that wording on the certificates awarded for topping the Consumer Preference Poll.

I do not agree with the maxim that any publicity is good publicity, but this little dustup undoubtedly helped increase awareness of both Brooklyn Brewery and Boston Beer. I was learning something about the way the beer business is perceived by the media. Win or lose, beer wars are usually good for your company.

I was determined to get Koch to play by the new rules. So when I went to the Denver festival in 1993, I was armed with a petition that declared the signatories would boycott the GABF if all members of the Association of Brewers (AOB) did not abide by the rules of the organization. I circulated the petition at the opening reception of the festival, a brewers-only affair fueled by beer contributed by small brewers from across the country. All were members of the AOB and participants in the GABF. While circulating the petition, I got to know brewers like Larry Bell from Bell's Brewery, Bert Grant from Yakima Brewing and Malting Co., Gary Fish of Deschutes Brewery, and Jerome Chicvara of Full Sail Brewing Company. All were up in arms about what they saw as abuse of the GABF. More than a hundred brewers from sixty companies signed the petition. The *Wall Street Journal* quoted Grant as saying Boston Beer's advertising was "so horrible; it's packed with lies." Koch called the complainers sore losers.[18]

Many people I met at that festival would become lasting friends. Perhaps the greatest opportunity that the AOB created was the collegiality of its members. I learned so much over the years from my fellow brewers. In our beer-drinking sessions at the festival, we exchanged stories about our triumphs and our blunders. The presentations at the annual conferences were important and informative, but the informal drinking sessions were invaluable to me, and I think my fellow brewers would agree. Those relationships were key to the Brooklyn Brewery's success. In a perverse way I owe a debt to Jim Koch for pulling me into the controversy.

At that time, however, brewers were expressing increasing amounts of discontent with Papazian and the AOB. What was the AOB anyway? Was it really an association of brewers? Was it a trade association? Was it a publisher? Was it an organization that ran events, like the GABF and the Craft Brewers Conference? Was it for homebrewers, or brewers? Or was it all the above?

After quizzing Papazian, I learned that it was a private nonprofit corporation run by a board of directors made up of businesspeople from Colorado—lawyers and realtors—so it was more like a chamber of commerce than an association of brewers. Perhaps to address the concerns, Papazian had appointed an advisory board made up of small brewers. Eventually he would appoint John Hickenlooper, founder of Wynkoop Brewing Company to the board of directors.

Papazian was not happy about the petition. When I told him about it at the opening reception, he looked like someone had just punched him in the stomach. I was not a member of the board of advisors, and now it was unlikely I ever would be. But Bert Grant, the delightfully arrogant and iconoclastic brewer was a member, and I think it is no exaggeration to say he hated Jim Koch. Grant's Russian Imperial Stout won the first-ever Consumer Preference Poll in 1984. He was livid that Koch had dominated the poll in subsequent years.

Grant was aware that I had spearheaded the petition against Boston Beer, and he wrote a note saying he could not attend the advisory board meeting scheduled during the festival and appointed me as his proxy.

I appeared at the board meeting, to the consternation of Papazian and some of the other board members, and presented the protest petition. Koch was also a member of the board of advisors. As always, he was ready to do battle. As I presented my case, Koch interrupted by brandishing a copy of my 1989 cooler sticker proclaiming Brooklyn Lager the winner of the Great American Beer Tasting. He demanded that the AOB stop me from using this bogus award. I protested that the cooler sticker and table tents had been in use during 1989 and 1990 but were long gone. After making my case for the petition, I left the meeting and promptly got into a shouting match with Koch in the foyer outside the meeting room. I was surprised at his emotional response to me and the petition. I recall his shouting, "You are trying to fuck my company!" over and over. I replied that I had nothing against his company. I simply wanted him to play by the same rules as the rest of us. I was impressed by his earnestness, although he did seem a bit overwrought. I was also impressed by the way he countered my attacks. Koch would sell 450,000 barrels of beer that year, far more than the 10,200 barrels Brooklyn Brewery would sell. The idea that my little petition could in any way thwart Samuel Adams' surging popularity was laughable. But I guess he knew better than any of us the danger implicit in the *Boston Globe* headline that suddenly cast the tiny Brooklyn Brewery as David and Boston Beer as Goliath.

In a private meeting involving Koch and the lawyers on the AOB's board of directors, Papazian agreed to give Koch time to use up the marketing materials he had already printed touting his Consumer Preference Poll victories. Koch agreed to abide by the AOB's rules as of May 1994.

Papazian says he doesn't recall the petition, but he does recall that the "four years running" verbiage was a violation of the rules. He knew he had to address the discontent of the other brewers. "There were other violations happening too, and we knew we had to get a handle on it," he said. "And at that point, we had a million dollars in reserve, and we weren't afraid to spend it on any litigation if we had to. So we had a foot to stand on—[in fact,] two feet to stand on. We weren't afraid of confronting brewers with the rules we had established, because we knew [if we didn't,] if we let it get out of hand, the credibility of the beer festival would have just dissipated."[19]

Papazian will not reveal the details of the closed-door meeting that led to the agreement with Koch, but his reference to litigation could be a hint that Koch threatened to sue to enforce his right to promote the Consumer Preference Poll wins. In a 1994 article in the *New Brewer,* publisher Virginia Thomas wrote, "The flap engendered backbiting and criticism that brewers considered negative to the microbrewing industry as a whole. Koch's supporters pointed out that he was originally authorized to use the phrase 'four years running' by festival management: they say that envy of his success with Samuel Adams beers has motivated his detractors."[20]

Carol Stoudt, president of Stoudt Brewery, helped circulate the boycott petition. Part of the problem, Stoudt said, was that "we wanted compliance with the GABF rules, with no exception. Jim Koch was caught in the middle of it. It was the festival's problem that it didn't enforce the rules, but it turned out to be everyone's problem. Hopefully, this will resolve everything."[21]

John Hall, founder and president of Goose Island, was vice chair of the board of advisors of the Institute for Brewing and Fermentation Studies. He said unity was important for an industry that prided itself on its close connection to consumers. "It's been confusing, and the last thing we want is to confuse customers. We have much bigger issues to fight than to squabble among ourselves."[22]

Amen. But it wasn't the last challenge to that unity.

CHAPTER FOUR

THE CLASS OF '88

THE DECADE BETWEEN 1984 AND 1994 SAW A DIZZYING PROLIFERATION OF BREW-pubs and microbreweries across the country. I have chosen 1988, the year Tom Potter and I started Brooklyn Brewery, to profile many of the breweries that started that year and still are operating in 2013. I could just as easily have chosen 1987 or 1989. This critical decade was a period of incredible expansion for the craft beer revolution. The companies started in this period were not pioneers in the sense that Fritz Maytag and Jack McAuliffe, Suzy Denison, and Jane Zimmerman were pioneers, but they were the brewers who laid the foundations of the craft beer movement. They created the craft beer segment of the US market. Brewers coming after them would not have to explain that they were selling an American-brewed beer that was as interesting and as good as the imports. "Microbrewed beer" or "craft beer" became a respected segment of the beer industry as a result of their efforts.

Craft breweries now employ 100,000 people across the country and are responsible for more than $10 billion in annual sales. They have had an outsized impact on the health and growth of the communities where they began. And they represent a pretty good geographic distribution. The Brewers Association (BA) says virtually every American lives within ten miles of a brewery today.

Nine of the eleven breweries profiled in this chapter started out as brewpubs. Brewpubs, like homebrewing before them, are an important part of the early history of craft brewing. Bert Grant established the first brewpub in Yakima, Washington. After that came the Mendocino Brewing Company in Hopland, California; Bill Owen's Buffalo Bill's Brewery in Hayward, California, and the Manhattan Brewing Company in New York City's then-rising

SoHo neighborhood. The last was started by Richard Wrigley, a Brit who would also start the Commonwealth Brewing Company in Boston.

Many of the '88-ers expanded to become production breweries, as you will see, and all now distribute their beers well outside their neighborhoods.

I am including Matt Brewing Company in Utica, New York. Matt is an '88-er, too. The Matt family started brewing beer in 1888, and they have played an important role in the craft beer revolution. Like some other regional breweries, most notably D.G. Yuengling & Son of Pottsville, Pennsylvania, Matt Brewing has transformed itself into a player in the craft segment.

Here is the Class of '88 in reverse alphabetical order. (It wouldn't feel right to put Brooklyn first.) I think each one, in its unique way, illustrates the outsized positive impact that craft breweries have had on communities across the nation.

WYNKOOP BREWING COMPANY, DENVER

130 employees
Estimated 2013 sales: 4,500 barrels

Craft brewers pride themselves on involvement in their home cities. No craft brewery epitomizes that commitment like Denver's Wynkoop. One of its founders, John Hickenlooper, a Pennsylvania native who moved to Denver to work as a geologist, ran for and became mayor of the city in 2003. He was elected governor of Colorado in 2010 and has been mentioned as a potential presidential or vice presidential candidate for 2016.

Hickenlooper, a homebrewer since 1971, was laid off from his job as a geologist in 1986 and soon after visited the Roaring Rock Ale House (later renamed the Triple Rock Ale House), a brewpub in Berkeley, California. He was impressed by how busy the restaurant was on a weekday night. Back in Denver he borrowed a library book on writing business plans and developed a plan for a brewpub. He connected with Russell Schehrer, the 1985 American Homebrewers Association's Homebrewer of the Year, and opened Wynkoop two years later.

Hickenlooper's amazing political career began with his decision to locate his brewpub in a crime-ridden neighborhood of Denver known as LoDo (lower downtown). The rundown warehouse district was located on the site of the original settlement of Denver, not far from the South Platte River. Hickenlooper first had to lobby the Colorado Legislature to allow brewpubs—a change that clearly paid dividends, as the state has since become

John Hickenlooper at Wynkoop's Running of the Pigs. Photograph courtesy of Wynkoop Brewing Company.

one of America's most important craft brewing centers. Hickenlooper and his partners then bought and restored the former J.S. Brown Mercantile Building, built in 1899. The restoration included the building's hardwood floors, thick timber columns, and pressed tin ceilings. You can imagine how the building must have once bustled with miners, ranchers, and cowboys. The ground floor is now home to the main bar and restaurant. The expansive second floor has twenty-two pool tables, dart boards, and a second bar. The year the brewery opened, the city designated the area the Lower Downtown Historic District, protecting 127 buildings. Hickenlooper soon moved into a loft apartment on one of the upper floors of his building. A few years later Leo Keily, CEO of Coors, would become Hickenlooper's neighbor in the nearby Platinum Building.[1]

Wynkoop sparked the redevelopment of LoDo. Today the area hosts the most vibrant nightlife in Denver. In 1996 the gentrification of LoDo was capped by the building of Coors Field, the home stadium of the Rockies, right around the corner.

I have known Hickenlooper for many years. He has always had a buoyant personality and is a fast talker with an impatient can-do attitude. At one point in the late 1990s both of us were courting the investor David Bruce, the legendary British pub chain developer. We shared lunches with Bruce and his entourage in both Brooklyn and Denver. Bruce, a former brewer at Theakston, was an early presence at the Great American Beer Festival (GABF) and microbrewing conferences.

"In my 47 years of brewing around the world, John Hickenlooper stands out as a true pioneer of the global micro-brewing and brewpub revolution," Bruce writes. "Not only did John back in 1988 create Wynkoop and its subsequent chain of brewpubs and microbreweries, he is also one of the best, kindest and [most] dynamic men one could ever hope to meet. No wonder he has carved out his new career in politics so successfully."[2]

Wynkoop's original business plan projected sales of $1.6 million in five years. Wynkoop did $4 million in its fifth year alone. But Hickenlooper was honest about Wynkoop's rough start in an award-winning article that appeared in *All About Beer* magazine in 1998, when Wynkoop was celebrating its tenth anniversary. "We had no financial controls," he said. After six months in business, an accountant told Hickenlooper that Wynkoop was $45,000 in the red and the company had no cash. "I'd lay awake at night . . . we went back to working sixty to seventy hours a week."

Hickenlooper had to walk through the brewpub to get to the elevator to his apartment. Many entrepreneurs would have loathed this proximity, preferring to live further away from their work. Hickenlooper reveled in the close connection to his customers. "My favorite task is busing tables," he said, referring to the lowliest position in a restaurant save dishwasher. "You get to talk to the customers and see what they really think. They have no idea who you are."[3]

Like many craft brewers, he was a master of inventive, inexpensive promotions. In 1990 he borrowed a dozen sixty- to seventy-pound piglets from the East Lake County farmers who picked up Wynkoop's spent grain for feed. He organized the Running of the Pigs, a race around the block modeled on the Running of the Bulls in Pamplona, Spain, made famous by Ernest Hemingway. Hickenlooper employed local television celebrities to back each squealing entry. A Denver columnist dubbed it "Pamplona on the Platte." It was all great fun until PETA, People for the Ethical Treatment of Animals, protested in 1993. Not one to shy away from controversy, Hickenlooper eventually bought the pigs from the farmers and staged a new promotion, the Liberation of the Pigs. The pigs were retired to PETA's Loving Nature Ranch.[4]

Hickenlooper led an ambitious effort in 1998 to take the Wynkoop concept to several other cities. Bruce and his British investors funded the plan to establish brewpubs in Green Bay, Wisconsin, Buffalo, New York, Lincoln,

Nebraska, Rock Island, Illinois, and other cities. The goal was to develop thirty-four brewpubs and eleven satellite pubs by 2000. That project failed, and the pubs were sold off, but Hickenlooper still had the successful Denver pub.[5] Two years later he decided to run for mayor after discussing the idea with Papazian in Papazian's backyard tipi in Boulder.

"Anyone who entered the plains-style tipi, located in a secluded area of our property, enjoyed its spiritual ambience," Papazian explained. "As the American Indians did, we would only walk clockwise around the fire center-piece. [During] one of the original late-night beer-and-mead-drinking gath-erings, David Bruce, John Hickenlooper, and I agreed to the rule that only the truth could be spoken within the tipi. Furthermore intimate parts of any conversation we had must stay within the tipi. We talked in the tipi until early dawn. What we discussed immensely influenced all three of us in some very personal ways which I cannot reveal.

"That gathering set the stage for when John, his soon-to-be wife, Helen, and I gathered at the tipi one evening several years later. Even today, when-ever we meet, John and I knowingly reminisce about the conversations we had. This night John and Helen were still struggling with the decision on whether he would run for mayor of Denver. He has said in public that the tipi experience helped him make his decision. In the tipi we spoke only the truth then, as we would now."[6]

Hickenlooper said his background as a brewer has been an asset in his political career. He said a key part of his stump speech points out that craft beer is less than 10 percent of the Colorado beer market, but craft breweries provide 64 percent of the brewing industry jobs in Colorado, a state that is home to AB InBev and MillerCoors breweries. "When I ran for governor, I visited all sixty-four counties in Colorado, and we held events at brewpubs and microbreweries around the state. We got a lot of benefit from that be-cause the breweries are often an important part of the community."[7]

For his adventurous development of the Wynkoop Brewing Company, Hickenlooper and his partners received a prestigious award for inner city development of historic buildings from the National Historic Trust Founda-tion in 1997.[8]

VERMONT PUB & BREWERY, BURLINGTON
60 employees
Estimated 2013 sales: 1,000 barrels
Greg Noonan was writing about beer styles for the *New Brewer* magazine long before he started Vermont's first brewpub in 1988. He was also the author of

Greg Noonan and Steve Polewacyk of Vermont Pub & Brewery.

Brewing Lager Beer (1986), a favorite reference for homebrewers and the first book ever published by Charlie Papazian's Brewers Publications.

Noonan was an avid homebrewer working for a wood and paper products company in Massachusetts when he decided to start the brewpub in Vermont. He had sampled beers from America's besieged regional breweries while hitchhiking across the country in the 1970s. He said his interest in homebrewing started with the discovery of a Prohibition-era homebrew stored in a rural New England root cellar.

"I was at a party once in the middle of nowhere in New Hampshire, and during the party we ran out of beer," he told *Yankee Brew News* in 1996. "As we're collecting money to go buy more beer, the guy who owned the cabin said there are two cases downstairs in the root cellar that look like they might be beer. So we go down to this root cellar and sticking out of the dirt floor are the necks of some bottles. We dig it all out, and it's two cases of homebrew, been there forever, with wax corks in the tops. Cracked those, and had a great time drinking this homebrew, and I think that's what did it for me. I was thinking, 'Man, this stuff's 50 years old.' It was pretty neat drinking it. It had a very interesting flavor, sherry-like as you might expect, almost whiskey-like in flavor. It probably had no alcohol in it, after that many years, it had probably evaporated away."[9]

"I specifically sited my brewery in Vermont because that is where I wanted to live," Noonan told a reporter in 2007. (He died in 2009, at fifty-eight.) "I admired the politics in Vermont. I had $175,000, which is a shoestring budget in the brewing industry. Brewing equipment is very expensive."[10]

The cash came from savings and an early retirement package he negotiated with his employer, who was about the sell the company. Vermont is known for its liberal politics and today for one of the most vibrant craft brewing cultures in the nation. But back in the 1980s, Vermont banks spurned Noonan. He pressed ahead, a determined blond-haired Yankee with an infectious smile and an energetic personality. "The banks all said, 'What is a brewpub?' but I plunged ahead anyway with the money I had."[11] He lobbied the state legislature for three years before gaining approval for the microbrewery.

A friend from his college days at St. Anselm College in New Hampshire, Steve Polewacyk, helped Noonan. A former database consultant in New York, Polewacyk now runs the Vermont Pub & Brewery, a New England institution. Like all other members of the Class of '88, the Vermont Pub & Brewery struggled through its first few years. Craft beer was not well known in those days.

"It was an inauspicious beginning," Noonan recalled. "We eked our way through the winter of '88 to '89, barely by our teeth, with no cash reserves. . . . We ran it mom and pop for the first five years or so, which means we were here all the time. We put in 80-plus-hour weeks."

Polewacyk recalls nights sleeping in the booths and then waking at 6 a.m. to mop the floors and get ready for a new day. Noonan and Polewacyk didn't cash a paycheck until 1990.[12]

The pub's Church Street location in Burlington was in an abandoned warehouse. Like many craft breweries across the county, Vermont Pub & Brewery planted the seeds of revitalization in a foundering urban center. Ann Heath, property manager for the pub's landlord, said she had never heard of a microbrewery but took a chance on Noonan's plan anyway.

"It was different and innovative," she said. "They enticed people with the product. It expanded the scope and vitality of the city."[13] Noonan won medals with the lagers, wheat beers, and ales brewed in the cellar of a fourteen-barrel brewhouse. The restaurant served English pub-style fare with Vermont cheeses, seasonal produce, and Vermont roasted coffees. "We wanted a populist menu," Noonan said. "Every brewpub back then was doing new American cuisine. We wanted to prepare good, basic food at reasonable prices."[14]

Noonan continued to write for craft brewing trade publications and to speak at conferences. He published *Scotch Ale* in 1990, *Seven Barrel Brewers' Handbook: A Pragmatic Guide to Homebrewing* in 1996, and *The New Brewing Lager Beer* in 2003. He opened the Seven Barrel Brewery in West Lebanon, New Hampshire, in 1994 and the Amherst Brewing Company in Massachusetts in 1997, but stepped away from those ventures when he found himself stretched thin.

"I liked the excitement and challenge of opening," he said. "However, I decided I was working myself out of the hands-on work and into a job I didn't really want. Both [pubs] are doing quite well without me."[15]

John Kimmich, a former head brewer at Noonan's Burlington brewery, opened the Alchemist Pub and Brewery in Waterbury, Vermont, in 2001 with Noonan's assistance. "Greg is a major reason that the Alchemist is a success," said Kimmich. "He's been a wonderful mentor. He's got the blending of the chemistry knowledge with the esoteric side of things."[16]

After Noonan died, Alan Newman, cofounder of Vermont's Magic Hat Brewing Company, told the *Burlington Free Press* obituary writer: "He was here at the beginning. You could easily argue he is one of the two grandparents of Vermont brewing. If you are talking about brewing in Vermont, here is Greg; he was there at the beginning of it all."

Noonan was a brewer's brewer, a man who embodied the collegiality that has been a hallmark of the craft beer revolution and an important factor in the spread of craft beer culture in America.

He was respected throughout New England and beyond. There is no better mark of the esteem his fellow brewers felt for him than a commemorative beer recently developed by Peter Egelston and his team at Smuttynose Brewing Company. They brewed a black India pale ale, and called it Noonan IPA. They call it a tribute to the man who invented the black IPA style. I will not debate who invented this now-popular style, but I will be happy to buy one of these tribute beers and raise my mug to the memory of a brewer who gave much to the craft beer revolution.

ROGUE ALES, NEWPORT, OREGON

305 employees
Estimated 2013 sales: 114,000 barrels
Jack Joyce, the founder of Rogue Ales, is a rogue. I don't mean the first definition—"a dishonest, knavish person; scoundrel"—I mean the second definition—"a playfully mischievous person; scamp."[17]

Brett and Jack Joyce of Rogue Ales.

Joyce is sometimes maddening to work with. He is ornery and contrary. Sometimes you think, *If I go this way, Jack will surely go that way.* But there is usually a point to his position. He does not play devil's advocate. He is a serious man. He is also a lot of fun.

If you order a craft beer at a bar, Joyce will order a Budweiser longneck.

If you ask him, he will tell you he is just a country lawyer. He is indeed a lawyer, and a smart one. He advised Phil Knight, the founder of Nike, for many years. Joyce also negotiated Michael Jordan's precedent-setting sponsorship deal with Nike. Joyce recalls telling Phil Knight to "just do it" at one point, but the ad firm Weiden & Kennedy got the credit for that famous slogan.

Joyce and his University of Oregon classmates Bob Woodell and Rob Strasser were approached by Bob's accountant, Jeff Schultz, an avid home-brewer, about starting a brewpub. They liked the idea and built one on Lithia Creek in Ashland, Oregon. They made an amber and a gold brew, opened in October 1988, and promptly started losing their shirts.

Undeterred, Joyce wandered to Newport, Oregon, looking for a spot to build another Rogue brewpub. The story goes that, caught in a snowstorm, he found himself stranded on the waterfront. "He was forced to walk the streets, until he met up with Mohave Niemi, founder of the famous Mo's Clam Chowder. She took him to the original Mo's restaurant, gave him a bowl of clam chowder, and told him about her dream of living above a bar, and how she might just have the perfect spot for the next Rogue brewpub."

She showed him an empty storefront and a garage that was being used to store antique cars. "Mo offered the vacant space and garage to Jack at a very generous price, under two stipulations: that a picture of Mo herself, naked in a bath tub, be forever displayed at the Pub, and that Rogue 'feed the fishermen,' meaning that we give back to the local community."[18]

That's an offer no true craft brewer could refuse.

Brewmaster John Maier, formerly of Alaskan Brewing Company, joined Rogue and began brewing more than sixty fine ales that were packaged in twenty-two-ounce painted bottles and are now sold in every state and thirty-two countries. Rogue now has brewpubs in Oregon, Washington, and California. It operates distilleries in Portland and Newport. Maier did a special beer with Iron Man Chef Masaharu Morimoto, and one with the journalist Fred Eckhardt. One of their best-selling beers is Rogue Dead Guy Ale; another is Rogue Yellow Snow Ale.

They spin out brands the way Nike spins out shoes.

"We try to do four things: keep making great product, keep trying to make our packaging great, keep trying to integrate ourselves in our communities, and keep creating unique thunder," Joyce said.[19]

Rogue is growing its own hops and barley and continues playing a large role in its communities: It helped the city of Newport celebrate its 125th anniversary with a special ale, Rogue donates to the Oregon Coast Aquarium, and it sponsors the Gathering Longboard Classic, a surfing event on the Oregon coast.[20]

These days when I call Joyce, he is often in Hawaii. He still keeps up with the world of craft brewing. But he has turned day-to-day management of the company over to his son, Brett. I met Brett years ago when he was doing marketing for TaylorMade, the most dynamic manufacturer of golf clubs in the world. Brett does not have the swagger of his father, but he is a serious young man.

I think the Rogue legacy is in good hands. Witness the latest Rogue Ale, unveiled in April 2013 by Brett Joyce: The Beard Beer, an ale made with a yeast harvested from the beard of the brewmaster, John Maier.

Nick R. Matt, fourth generation and Brand Manager, Fred Matt,
fourth generation and President, Nick Matt, third generation
and Chairman, standing in the F.X. Matt Brewing Company
Brewhouse as they celebrate their 125th anniversary in 2013.
Photograph courtesy of F.X. Matt Brewing Company.

MATT BREWING COMPANY, UTICA, NEW YORK

130 employees
Estimated 2013 sales: 220,000 barrels

The most venerable member of the Class of '88 is the Matt Brewing Company, which celebrated its 125th anniversary in 2013. Over the years I have heard many brewing industry veterans marvel at how Matt endured the difficult years of consolidation, reinvented itself, and emerged as a leader of the craft brewing revolution.

As F.X. Matt Jr., who died in 2001, would tell you—and I'm sure Nick Matt, his brother and the CEO, and F.X.'s son Fred, the president, would concur—it wasn't easy. The Matt Brewing Company opened for business in 1888, one of hundreds of breweries started by German immigrants in the nineteenth century. Matt, D.G. Yuengling & Son of Pottsville, and August Schell Brewing Company, all survived Prohibition and the consolidations of the twentieth century, and all have transformed themselves to become part of the craft beer revolution.[24]

The Matt brewery, originally called the West End Brewery, survived Prohibition by producing a line of soft drinks under the Utica Club trademark, along with malt syrups, extracts, distilled water, and malt tonic. The sons of F.X. Sr., Walter and Frank, joined the company after Prohibition. They expanded the brewery and bought new equipment. Nick Matt said one of F.X. Sr.'s favorite sayings was, "A business is like a man: you have to feed it to keep it alive." That saying has become a motto for the company's policy of continual modernization. In 1951, when F.X. was ninety-two, he made his son Walter president and F.X. became chair of the board, a post he held until his death seven years later.

In the 1960s Utica Club Beer sales soared, and production reached record levels, thanks to an animated television advertising campaign that featured talking beer mugs, Schultz and Dooley.

Sales of Matt's main beers, Utica Club Pilsener and Matt's Premium, were declining in the 1970s under relentless competition from the industry giants. In 1982, Matthew Reich, on the advices of Joseph Owades, came to Utica to ask F.X. Jr. to brew his New Amsterdam Amber. New Amsterdam added volume at a time when the Matt brewery sorely needed it.

"We were in a very difficult competitive situation," Nick Matt said. "On the one hand you had Budweiser and Miller, which were recognized as premium, superior national products, higher priced, advertised; on the other hand you had, from those same companies, Milwaukee's Best, Busch, the lowest end, and in some cases those beers were being sold at less than the price at which we could even make beer."[21]

In 1985 Matt began to change the way it made its own beer. F.X. Jr. had had an epiphany during a visit to the Duke of Baden Brewery in the Black Forest region of Germany, where his grandfather worked before immigrating to the United States.

"The story goes that F.X. was driving a Mercedes-Benz down the autobahn at 140 miles an hour, and it all of a sudden occurred to him, 'Why can't we make a beer as good as this car?'" Nick Matt said. F.X. returned to Utica, conferred with Owades, and created Saranac Adirondack Lager, a "beer that was what American beer used to be like, imported from the past."[22] In practice, that meant all malt, carbonated naturally by adding wort—a concoction of water, barley, and hops before it's fermented to become beer—to the conditioning tanks.

Saranac did well, but its sales were not great. In the late 1980s some Matt family shareholders expressed an interest in selling the brewery. Nick, who was president of the Richardson-Vicks division of Procter & Gamble, and Fred, an account manager at Grey Advertising in New York City, bought out the dissenting family members and returned to work with F.X. at the brewery.

"Saranac was one percent of the brewery's sales when we came back in 1989," Nick said. They entered Saranac in the 1991 GABF and won the gold medal in the American premium lager category. The Matts decided to focus on Saranac instead of Utica Club and Matt's Premium. Fred Matt went on the road to drum up sales.

"Today, the decision to go with Saranac seems obvious, but at the time it was a fairly difficult decision. But it has worked out," Nick said. "Saranac doubled for four or five years in a row, and that really changed what this brewery was all about."[23]

The Matts also expanded their contract-brewing relationships, making beer for Brooklyn Brewery, Dock Street Brewing Co., Olde Heurich Brewing Co., Harpoon Brewery, and Boston Beer Company.

"We were the place where a lot of the East Coast craft beers started," Nick Matt said. "We have an unusual role in the category. It's a piece of our history, and it is a good piece. We care very much about those beers. Their success was our success."

As chair of the Brewers Association of America (BAA), F.X. Matt encouraged the participation of the new breed of craft brewer in the organization, which had long been dominated by the old regional brewers that had fallen on hard times.

Nick's son, Nick Jr., joined the brewery in June 2013. A former Procter & Gamble marketing manager, he now manages the Saranac brand and oversaw the creation of new packaging to highlight the brewery's 125th anniversary in 2013. He and Fred are the third generation of the company. And, according to Nick, Fred's son Telpy is interested in becoming the fourth—a testament to how much this family business means to everyone.

NORTH COAST BREWING COMPANY, FORT BRAGG, CALIFORNIA
110 employees
Estimated 2013 sales: 67,000 barrels

Mark Ruedrich was born in the Bronx, New York, and grew up just up the Hudson River in Poughkeepsie. He recalls visiting his grandparents in the Bronx about twice a month and swimming in the Long Island Sound. He graduated from North Carolina State in 1973 with a degree in zoology and an expertise in extracellular enzymatic reactions.

He dreamed of being a photographer or a writer. As an unencumbered young man, he wandered out to San Francisco, where he worked for Mel Novikoff, an entrepreneur who started the Surf Theatre, a chain of art movie

Mark Ruedrich and Tom Allen of North Coast Brewing Co.
Photograph courtesy of the NCBC archives.

houses showing films by François Truffaut, Jean Luc Goddard, Akira Kuro-
sawa, and the Italian neorealists. Ruedrich also managed the Castro Theatre,
which featured retrospectives on the great directors of the twentieth century.
He fell in love with Merle Hilary, an Englishwoman living in San Francisco,
and they moved to Totnes, Devon, a town of 5,000 in southwest England,
near Dartmouth.

"I was working as a writer, soaking up the ambience and the beer culture,
and our English friends started training me in the art of real ale," he recalled.
"Let's say they addressed my deficiencies in beer appreciation. The guys in the
village where we lived were very serious about this." They were advocates of
the Campaign for Real Ale.

Ruedrich and Hilary returned to California in 1979. He brought with
him a copy of Dave Line's book, *Big Book of Brewing,* and, "I began brewing
my own beer in 1979, pretty much because there was no good beer available
at that time."

They ended up in Fort Bragg, California, a town north of San Francisco
that was about the size of Totnes. Ruedrich was working as a carpenter and
construction foreman for Joe Rosenthal, a contractor who also hailed from
the Bronx. With Rosenthal and one of their clients, Tom Allen, owner of a

bed and breakfast, Ruedrich and Hilary visited the Roaring Rock Brewery & Alehouse in Berkeley. The beer was fresh and tasty; the pub was packed with happy customers. "We had an 'Our Gang' moment," Ruedrich said, echoing the experience of thousands of entrepreneurs since. "We said, 'We can do this.'" After all, Ruedrich was a homebrewer. Suddenly he was putting his knowledge of extracellular enzymatic reactions to work.

The partners visited Buffalo Bill's Brewery in Hayward, just south of Oakland, and soaked up the free advice of Bill Owens, a famous photographer with a distinctive white flat-top haircut and cotton vest who became a brewpub pioneer. They visited Santa Cruz Brewing Co. and marveled at its miniature open fermenters. They visited the Mendocino Brewing Company's pub in Hopland. "Don Barkley was a great guy, very open and sharing but realistic, too," Ruedrich said. After all, Barkley had learned at New Albion that it took more than passion to build a business.

Ruedrich, Allen, and Rosenthal went to the 1986 microbrewers conference in Portland, Oregon, the same year my partner, Tom Potter, attended. There they encountered all the pioneers of the fledgling industry, Fritz Maytag, Ken Grossman, Bill Owens, and some wannabes too, like Dean Biersch, who would go on to found Gordon Biersch Brewing Company with Dan Gordon. The conference was the inspiration Ruedrich, Hilary, and their partners needed to get serious about starting a brewery in Fort Bragg.

They raised $200,000 in a limited partnership offering and began restoring an old mortuary in downtown Fort Bragg. They imported a shipping container of Grundy tanks from England. A local boat builder crafted a kettle and mash tun to Ruedrich's specifications. They opened their brewpub on August 17, 1988, with Red Seal Ale, Scrimshaw Pils, and Old No. 45 Stout on tap. The pub filled up with happy customers enjoying good beer, good food, and good music.

From the outset North Coast Brewing Company supported local jazz musicians. This interest in jazz grew into a major commitment. In 2012 North Coast donated about $60,000 to the Monterey Jazz Festival and the Mendocino Music Festival. It donated $80,000 worth of beer to smaller festivals and concerts. And it donated $120,000 to the Thelonius Monk Institute of Jazz in Washington, DC.

"This is something that is in the fabric of our business," Ruedrich said. "None of us had thoughts of getting rich. But we wanted to support good works in our community. About five years ago we stopped spending on advertising all together. You get a lot more out of donating to good causes than placing ads in marginal publications that don't really get noticed anyway."

They built a production brewery across the street in 1994. Today they sell Red Seal Ale, Old Rasputin, and other beers in forty-seven states. North Coast is the biggest employer in Fort Bragg, a mill town that once turned out lumber from Northern California's redwood forests. Ruedrich said the local government has finally recognized that North Coast is key to the local economy. He is hoping it will support his effort to locate the brewery on ten acres of coastal headland that is owned by Georgia Pacific, so he can expand the brewing operation.

Hilary ran the restaurant for many years, then turned it over to a young manager. She also ran the retail store but now is semiretired. Mark Ruedrich is sixty-one and, like many entrepreneurs in the Class of '88, concerned about the future of North Coast. He wants it to stay in Fort Bragg, even though a more hardheaded businessman might want a more practical location. Fort Bragg is four hours from the nearest interstate, but that is part of its charm. He is thinking of inaugurating an employee stock ownership plan because many of his dedicated employees are in their mid-forties and committed to a future in Fort Bragg.

Like many members of the Class of '88, he is not rich, but he has enjoyed a rich life and he's proud of his achievement.

"I feel lucky to have been a part of changing so fundamental a thing as the beer culture in this country," he said. "It's been great to have had an impact on something like beer, which is really an important part of daily life."[25]

GRITTY MCDUFF'S BREW PUB, PORTLAND, MAINE

180 employees

Estimated 2013 sales: 10,000 barrels

When the stock market crashed on Black Monday, October 1987, Richard Pfeffer, a stockbroker, was sitting at his desk at an investment bank in Portland, Maine, dreaming of starting a brewpub.

"I was already leaning in that direction, so I called David Geary [of D.L. Geary Brewing Company, Maine's first microbrewery], and I said, 'I'm thinking of building a brewpub, can I come talk to you?' He said sure, so I went over and he said, 'First thing you have to do is go get the money.'"

Black Monday shook Pfeffer out of the comfortable life for which he had trained as an economics major at the University of Rochester. He had been in

Richard Pfeffer and Ed Stebbins of Gritty McDuff's Brewpub.

the finance business for eighteen months, but he had never stopped dreaming about an idea planted by an Aussie friend in Hawaii.

"Before I graduated from the U of R, I was going down to New York City, doing all these interviews. And I walked out of one with Salomon Brothers or whatever it was," he recalled. "I just thought to myself, 'I'm not quite ready for this.' So I did a road trip. I got out of school and rode my motorcycle (a Yamaha Seiko 750) up across Canada, down the West Coast. I hopped on a boat and sailed from San Diego to the Marquesas, the Tuamotus, the Societies, up to Samoa. I got thrown off the boat and ended up in Hawaii, where I worked for about six months on a boat. And I decided it was time to go home. I was talking to an Australian fellow who I was working with. I said, 'I'm going to go back to Maine and open a pub,' and he said, 'You should open a brewpub. There's one in Brisbane and it is just killing it.' I didn't know what a brewpub was. That was the spring of '86."

While at the bank Pfeffer had watched Richard Wrigley open the Commonwealth Brewing Company in Boston. Wrigley was the dynamic Brit who had also opened the Manhattan Brewing Company in SoHo. Then Pfeffer watched Geary open a production brewery in an industrial park outside Portland, Maine, with the brewer Alan Pugsley as his partner. The first microbrew

Pfeffer tasted was Geary's Pale Ale. I drank it myself that summer while vacationing in Maine. It had a lobster on the label, and it paired beautifully with fresh lobster.

After talking to Geary, Pfeffer started raising money. He hired Geary and Pugsley as advisers to train his brewing staff and help buy brewing equipment from Peter Austin, the founder of Ringwood Brewery in Britain.

"I was thinking it was going to cost $250,000 to $300,000, and I think, given the mistakes and all the hard lessons learned, it probably cost $400,000 before we were done, which is quite a bit of money for a twenty-four-year-old guy," Pfeffer said of the Gritty McDuff's Brew Pub.

"When I started working on it, I was twenty-three. When you are twenty-three, you can do anything. You don't have anything to lose, and you don't know enough to be scared. You stay there all night and you get it done. You can work 24/7."

As for the name, Gritty McDuff's, "I made it up," Pfeffer said. "Did all kinds of geographical research, British pub names. I wanted a UK flair, and a fun, not too serious, attitude. . . . All in all, it works, and we have a pretty decent brand."

Pfeffer's partner, Ed Stebbins, was a friend of one of Pfeffer's college buddies. Stebbins was working in a bookstore in Portland in 1986. "We kind of hit it off, and he was looking for something to do," Pfeffer said. "[Stebbins] was raised in England, and he was pretty familiar with CAMRA [Campaign for Real Ale] and real ale and pubs and that whole lifestyle. He came in right about the time we opened. He came in financially but also working at the pub at the same time. Ed took to the brewing side, pretty much right away. We trained at Geary's with Alan for a couple of months, Ed more than I, because I was working on the rest of the startup. He's still the brewer. Well, he oversees all the brewers."[26]

Most of the $400,000 came from friends and family. They opened with four partners, Pffefer, Stebbins, their bar manager, and their handyman-accountant. They chose a location in the heart of Portland's Old Port, then a rundown warehouse district and now a thriving commercial and retail center.

They now have four brewpubs in Maine, two in Portland, and one each in Auburn and Freeport, home of L.L. Bean. All are Peter Austin brewing systems. The two in Portland are seven-barrel systems, and the system in Freeport is fourteen barrels. They make fine English-style ales and a silky Irish-style stout. The Freeport location brews all the draft beer and twenty-two-ounce bottles that are wholesaled in New England, upstate New York,

New Jersey, and Pennsylvania. Geary started producing twelve-ounce bottles of Gritty's in 1994.

Does Pfeffer wish he had continued as a stockbroker?

"Oh, God, no," he said without hesitation. "The best decision I ever made in my life was getting into the brewpub business, and I think about what people have done in this career for so long. I look at Alan [Pugsley]'s record. I was instrumental in getting Fred Forsley and Alan [founders of Shipyard Brewing Co. in Portland] together. And I'm very proud of all the great stuff that has grown up around us. I'm pretty comfortable with where we are."

He said he and his partners did get sidetracked with a separate business a few years ago. They decided to get into craft distilling, which was just getting started in a few places. "One thing led to another, and I ended up buying a potato starch factory in northern Maine—go figure," he said. "I've spent the last six years basically working it out. . . . I learned a big lesson—*focus*," he said. "[The distillery] has been a real distraction from running the brewpub company."

He said he and his partners think about building a big brewery and expanding production and distribution of their bottled beer rather than expanding their brewpubs. They really want to do both, but they know they can't. He knows that the distribution channels are already crowded with craft brands, and more than a thousand new brewing companies are in the works.

"The packaging side for us, we've looked at it almost like marketing, because we have such little margin in it," he said. "But it gets our name out. And creates jobs. We've got half a dozen people working at that, and they are working at basically promoting Gritty's, but the only way to actually make any money at it is to triple, quadruple, its size—build our own."

He sees an advantage in the brewpub business.

"I know that the market is going to get more crowded," he said. "The brewpub creates cash flow. In your own pub it is never crowded. You are in control. And you are really in the entertainment business more than anything. And I think that is what we are good at, so my sense is we will focus more on brewpubs."[27]

GREAT LAKES BREWING COMPANY, CLEVELAND

200 employees
Estimated 2013 sales: 160,000 barrels

Of all the members of the Class of '88, Great Lakes Brewing Company, Ohio's first craft brewery, has perhaps distinguished itself the most with its

Pat and Dan Conway of Great Lakes Brewing Company. Photograph courtesy of Great Lakes Brewing Company.

sustainability programs, which have helped usher in a new era for Cleveland, a Rust Belt city once famous for a fire on the polluted Cuyahoga River but now better known as the home of the Rock and Roll Hall of Fame.

The Cleveland brothers Pat and Dan Conway opened their doors on Market Avenue as a brewpub producing 1,000 barrels annually and then quickly, but carefully, expanded their operations to a packaging brewery in six buildings that in the 1870s served as stables and kegging facilities for the old L. Schlather Brewing Company, one of dozens of breweries that once served northern Ohio.

"We bought that building with the goal of gradually growing into it, which we've done over time," Daniel Conway told *Crain's Cleveland Business* in 2010. Pat Conway added, "We've been careful and patient. We don't want to compromise our quality. I'd say that's a good strategy after two decades."[28]

From day one, Great Lakes pursued a mission that included sustainability:

Great Lakes Brewing is a principle-centered, environmentally respectful and socially conscious company committed to crafting fresh, flavorful high quality beer and food for the enjoyment of our customers. We aspire to maintain our status as the premier craft brewery in the Great Lakes region and are dedicated to uncompromising service, continuous improvement and innovative consumer education.

Pat Conway told the blog *Renovating the Rust Belt* in 2009 that the brothers asked themselves at the inception of the brewery, "What can we do with this waste?" They started with simple recycling of paper, plastic, metal, and spent grain.

"It meant a cultural shift because we as a company, along with our city and our culture on a larger level, didn't think in terms of recycling," Pat Conway said. "Simply segregating the waste was cumbersome at first, but now it is part of the DNA of the company." The original mission has evolved into a zero waste and "triple bottom line" philosophy to develop their business environmentally, socially, and financially.[29]

Great Lakes operates Pint Size Farm at Hale Farm and Village in Bath, Ohio, growing organic vegetables, herbs, and flowers for use in the brewpub. What Great Lakes cannot grow, it buys from organic and environmentally sensitive farmers and suppliers. Great Lakes brewery employees also work on the farm.

Since 2002 the company has run the Burning River Fest, a remembrance of the 1969 fire on the Cuyahoga, which was a low point for the city but a rallying point for a change in environmental responsibility. The festival features educational exhibits from local environmental groups, food from local farms and eateries, and live music. Some of the proceeds from the event go into the Burning River Foundation, which makes grants to groups committed to cleaning up Ohio's waterways.[30]

Great Lakes' trucks and other vehicles run on used vegetable oil. Spent grain is sent to local farmers and bakers. Some is fed to worms, which create the fertilizer used at Pint Sized Farm. In winter chilly Cleveland air cools the brewery's fermenters. Skylights and light sensors maximize energy efficiency, and a dozen solar panels create electricity for the brewpub. Edmund Fitzgerald Porter and Christmas Ale in short-filled bottles are used in soups, sausages, soap, and even by a local ice cream maker.[31]

Great Lakes has completed a $7 million expansion of its brewery that was financed with $3 million in tax-free Cuyahoga County industrial development bonds and another $3 million in Recovery Zone bonds, a part of the federal government's American Recovery and Reinvestment Act, created to encourage economic investment in distressed areas.[32]

"We feel we are doing something that helps our community and the planet," Pat Conway told *Renovating the Rust Belt*. "We do it, and we do it successfully, and then you hope—like throwing a pebble in a pond—that the rings continue to grow out further and further, that many more restaurants will adopt these menu ideas, and that people on an individual level will do this in their own lives. It's a game of inches, one step at a time."[33]

GORDON BIERSCH BREWING COMPANY, SAN JOSE, CALIFORNIA

2,400 employees

Estimated 2013 sales: 155,000 barrels

With thirty-six brewpubs in the United States and Taiwan, Gordon Biersch Brewing Company is the largest employer of the Class of '88 and an amazing story of two guys who were determined to grow their brewpub business with private equity capital.

San Jose-born Dan Gordon, a Berkeley graduate in economics, was a homebrewer who took his craft to a new level with an education at Munich's prestigious Technical University. San Francisco native Dean Biersch got his first restaurant job, cleaning the deep fryer, at fifteen and worked in restaurants until he graduated from San Francisco State College. He completed a Hilton Hotels management program before becoming the catering manager for Hornblower Day Yachts.[34]

Biersch visited Mendocino Brewing Company's brewpub in Hopland in the early 1980s and began to dream of a brewpub that served great food and great German-style beers. Mutual friends introduced the two men, and they found their talents and interests were complementary.

"We spent a week around my parents' swimming pool getting to know each other," Gordon told the *Business Journal*.[35]

That initial meeting would launch a roller-coaster ride of fund raising and corporate partnerships, culminating in the brewpub empire we know today. Gordon was director of brewing operations for the Gordon Biersch Brewing Company, and Biersch was director of restaurant operations for the Gordon Biersch Brewery Restaurant Group.

The two partners gave up control of their company early on. By 1995 they were doing $20 million a year with five locations. They partnered with Lorenzo Fertitta, a Las Vegas casino operator. He invested $11.2 million in a plan to develop twenty more brewpubs and a production brewery. Fertitta also bought out a number of small shareholders for $7 million and gained control of the company.

Dan Gordon and Dean Biersch of Gordon Biersch.

Dan Gordon reflected on the decision in a Stanford Business School case study titled, "Gordon Biersch: New Challenges and Opportunities."

"The decision was actually quite easy and was made in the San Francisco restaurant that night," he said. "The Fertittas have a background in food and beverage, so they provided instant expertise and value-add . . . they had a stellar reputation in Las Vegas. Finally, they were a sophisticated, one-stop investor that provided patient capital. I think the biggest difference between venture capital and private equity financing is the level of patience that the investor is going to have. You hiccup once with venture capital, and there is a good chance that they don't forget it."[36]

Fertitta, Gordon, and Biersch opened the brewery in San Jose in 1997, as well as six new brewpubs in California, Washington, and Arizona.

In 1998 a change in California law enabled them to start selling liquor in their pubs. Gordon Biersch obtained liquor licenses for its California brewpubs, but the California beer wholesalers association quickly got the law changed, to restrict hard liquor licenses to companies selling fewer than 60,000 barrels of beer annually. Gordon Biersch's new brewery in San Jose put the company beyond 60,000 barrels.

Fertitta, Gordon, and Biersch decided to sell the restaurants to Big River Breweries of Chattanooga, Tennessee, in 1999. Gordon and Biersch do public relations work for both companies, Big River and the Gordon Biersch Brewing Company. Gordon Biersch also makes beer for the Trader Joe's chain of grocery stores.

In 2010 Centerbridge Partners merged the Gordon Biersch Brewery Restaurants with the Rock Bottom Restaurants and Breweries group to form CraftWorks Restaurants & Breweries, which also owns the Old Chicago Pizza & Taproom chain and other restaurants. The CraftWorks Foundation is dedicated to combating hunger in the markets served by its restaurants.[37]

GOOSE ISLAND BEER COMPANY, CHICAGO

150 employees
Estimated 2013 sales: 320,000 barrels

In an interview with *All About Beer* magazine in 2010, Greg Hall reflected on his father's decision to leave the corporate world and start a brewery when Greg was still at the University of Iowa, majoring in English and creative writing. (It is remarkable how many English majors you'll find in craft brewing.) "My father was in the paper packaging business, which was a good business, but about the least sexy business there is," Greg Hall said. "And he was on the financial side, the least sexy part of the least sexy business. In the mid-1980s, the company he worked for was bought by a competitor and he had the opportunity to move to another city or take the early retirement package. He was about the age I am right now. I was going to college and my sister was in high school. He went out on a limb, for a pretty conservative guy, and decided to start a brewery and a restaurant at the same time, without any experience in either one of them."[38]

Greg worked at the brewery one summer and then decided to go to Siebel Institute to learn brewing. He joined the company in 1991 as head brewer. People in Chicago loved the beers at the pub, so he and his father built a packaging brewery on Fulton Street that opened in 1995. He said he and his dad worked well together.[39]

"Well, we often don't agree on things, but the nice thing is, he's most comfortable sitting behind a desk looking at spreadsheets all day," Greg said. "I would rather poke my eyes out and set them on fire. . . . He's really not a technical brewer, and he's not quite as comfortable in front of an audience, so I do a lot of that."

Having a brewpub allowed the brewers at Goose Island to experiment with many different yeast strains and beer styles. And being in Chicago

*John and Greg Hall of Goose
Island.*

afforded them access to many of the talented brewers attending the courts at Siebel, among them, Matt Brynildson, now at Firestone. Brynildson is famous in the craft brewing world for his knowledge and use of hops.

"Matt was a brainy, skinny kid with a bit more hair than he has now and a lot more on his chin," Greg Hall said. "He was at Kalamazoo Spice Extraction Co. and went through Siebel. Christopher Bird, who had worked for us several years in the brewpub, at the time was registrar for Siebel, and he called me up and said, 'This kid is so sharp. You've got to hire him before somebody else does.' We brought him in and within eight or ten months made him head brewer, because he delved into every single thing we were doing and helped us set up a lot of the stuff we've got now."

The sale of Chicago's Goose Island Beer Company for $38 million to Anheuser-Busch (AB) InBev in 2011 was a shock to the craft brewing industry. Founder John Hall and his son Greg had been prominent figures in the craft brewing world, with John serving on the board of directors of the BAA and Greg a respected brewmaster who helped pioneer the barrel-aging process.

When Greg announced he would be leaving the company shortly after the sale was made public, even his father was surprised because the decision to sell had been a joint decision. John said the sale was the best way to ensure that Goose Island would continue to grow and take advantage of the foundation the Halls had built. Greg has since started a cider company called Virtue.[40]

News reports said Goose Island sold for $38 million, but we will never know how much of that cash ended up in the bank accounts of the Hall family. Business ownership is complicated. It takes a lot of wheeling and dealing to raise the money needed to build a brewery and keep it growing. You never really know how the founders faired unless you know them very intimately.

John said he didn't think Greg wanted to work in the structure of a large company like AB InBev. "He's a very creative guy," John said. "I'm just a businessman who loves beer." The Halls still own two Goose Island brewpubs in Chicago, including their first one. John serves on a craft brewery advisory panel for AB InBev.

I met John Hall for lunch in Chicago a few years ago, just after he sold 40 percent of the brewery to the Craft Brewers Alliance (CBA), a group of craft brewers that now includes Kona, originally from Hawaii, Seattle's Redhook, and Widmer Brothers Brewing Company of Portland, Oregon. AB InBev owns 32.5 percent of the CBA stock and handles distribution for all its products. The CBA falls just outside the definition of craft brewer adopted by the BA.

John said that deal enabled Goose Island to consolidate its distribution in the hands of the AB InBev network.

Distribution had been a headache since Goose Island started. "We couldn't get a good beer distributor in the beginning, so we went with a wine distributor," John said. Later, unwinding the relationship with the wine distributor was arduous and expensive.

John Hall was not happy with the deal with CBA, but he told me he did it to get some cash out for his original investors. I understood. I have had to make similar sacrifices. He was in his late sixties at the time. For many founders a sale is the only way to get any cash out of the business.

John Hall stepped down in 2012. Andy Goeler, one of AB's most successful sales managers, now runs the brewery. AB InBev now makes Goose Island beers in its breweries around the country. It is taking the Goose Island brands into all fifty states. One AB executive vowed to make Goose Island a million-barrel brand within five years. It will be interesting to see if that happens.[41]

Goose Island's flagship beer is Honker's Ale, and the brewery makes a delicious wheat beer called 312 Urban Wheat Ale, after the area code of the brewery. Goose Island has won many awards at the GABF and is famous for its barrel-aged beers, in particular Bourbon County Stout.

DESCHUTES BREWERY, BEND, OREGON

400 employees

Estimated 2013 sales: 285,000 barrels

I know I speak for all craft brewers when I say that one of the greatest benefits of working in this industry is the friends you make along the way. Gary Fish, founder of Deschutes Brewery, is one of my best friends, along with Kim Jordan of New Belgium Brewing Company. The three of us have worked together for years on the boards of both the old and new brewers' associations. We were part of the team that merged the BAA and the AOB to create the BA.

I feel like I know Fish's business almost as well as my own. Over the years we have learned a lot from each other. Fish is the biggest member of the Class of '88 in annual production. He started out in business in 1988 with a brewpub, Deschutes Brewery & Public House, in Bend, a sleepy blue-collar mill town in the center of Oregon. The population was about 15,000. Fish had grown up in the San Francisco Bay area. His father was a grape grower. Fish began working as a dishwasher in a restaurant when he was sixteen, and he worked his way through the University of Utah waiting tables. After earning a degree in economics, he worked in restaurants for about fifteen years and was part owner and manager of a restaurant in Salt Lake City.

Gary Fish of Deschutes Brewery.

"My father and I had talked about what was happening in the brewing industry in the mid-80s, and between his background in the wine business and what I had learned about the brewing business, we decided it would make sense to get into brewing," he told *Oregon Business* magazine in 2008. "I sold my share in the restaurant I was involved in [in] Salt Lake and moved back to California with my parents to help a friend [who was] opening a brewpub in Sacramento, so I would learn about the brewing side of the business."[42]

His parents were from Oregon and suggested he look at Bend, a beautiful little town surrounded by mountains and nestled on the banks of the crystal clear Deschutes River. With support from his family, he opened the brewpub. The brewery sold 310 barrels of beer the first year, and four years later sales were up to 3,954 barrels. "The first few years were a tough slog," he recalled. "There were people in the microbrewing business who knew where they were going. I freely admit I had no idea where I was going." The beers that were brewed by his master brewer, John Harris, pulled the business along. Harris moved on to Full Sail Brewing Company in the early 1990s. Harris now is opening his own brewpub in Portland, Oregon, Ecliptic Brewing.[43]

"We got a call from a distributor friend, Jim Kennedy of Admiralty Beverage Co., saying some tavern owners from Portland had been through the pub in Bend and were interested in pouring our beer," Fish told *Oregon Business*. "We had the beer, and certainly could use the cash flow. We cobbled together some beat-up dented Golden Gate kegs and sent them to Portland on a load of recycled cardboard, and that's how we grew. We had the brewing operation at the pub and we got a little building that we used as a warehouse, and you haven't lived until you've driven a forklift down a sloped parking lot with a full load of kegs, in the middle of winter, with chains on."[44]

Fish recalls with gratitude customers like Don Younger of Portland's Horse Brass Pub, and the McMenamin brothers with their quirky brewery-bar-restaurants. The McMenamins now run sixty-five brewpubs in the Pacific Northwest, many with theaters, performance spaces, and hotels.[45]

In 1993 Fish built a fifty-barrel brewhouse across town on the Deschutes River. The 16,000-square-foot brewery had a capacity of more than 100,000 barrels. He expanded this brewery in 2004, adding another brewhouse to increase production by more than 500,000 barrels. In 2013 Deschutes sells in twenty states. In May 2008 he opened a big beautiful 265-seat brewpub in Portland's trendy Pearl District. The pub's eighteen taps include year-round Deschutes brews, as well as seasonal and experimental beers.

Fish believes there is a market for his beers on the East Coast, but he is reluctant to ship beer across the country because of the high cost of transportation. It costs about $4 per case to get beer from the West Coast to the East. He has explored the possibility of brewing at a partner brewery in the East, if he can find the right brewery.

"The key is we have to make the beer our way," he said. "We're a little eccentric in how we make our beer and have it taste like Black Butte Porter or Mirror Pond Ale. We've only just begun the conversations. There are new business models being developed all the time. And will there be one that no one has thought of yet? Creative intelligent people will find ways to solve problems creatively and intelligently."[46]

Fish is fifty-six. He recently established an employee stock ownership plan with 8 percent of the business to give his employees a way to buy into it and to give his investors, many of them family members, a way to take some cash out. Deschutes Brewery is a pillar of the central Oregon community. For twenty-three years it ran a beer, food, and golf event, the Sagebrush Classic, each summer and raised more than $3 million for local charities, until the recession forced the brewery to end the event.

Fish has hired a solid chief operating officer, Michael Lalonde, and a strong administrative, brewing, and sales and marketing team to give himself some breathing room. But he still is very much a hands-on CEO. Bend and the surrounding area have exploded in recent years and now are home to more than 100,000 people and a downtown with fancy shops and restaurants, not to mention a hotbed of craft brewing. The area now boasts more than 20 breweries. It is no exaggeration to say that Deschutes has played an important role in Bend's transformation from sleepy mill town.

Fish is a past president of the Greater Bend Rotary Club, the Chamber of Commerce, Bend Downtowners, and the Oregon Brewers Guild. He is a past chair of the BAA and current vice chair of the BA. He and his brewery have received numerous awards for excellence in brewing and citizenship.[47]

THE BROOKLYN BREWERY CORP.

82 employees

Estimated 2013 sales: 220,000 barrels

After six years of covering wars and assassinations in the Middle East for the Associated Press, I returned to New York City with my wife and two children in 1984. In my last posting, to Cairo, I got to know Jim Hastings, an employee of the Agency for International Development who had served

Eric Ottaway, Garret Oliver, Steve Hindy, and Robin Ottaway of Brooklyn Brewery.

three years in Saudi Arabia, where alcoholic beverages were prohibited under Islamic law. Hastings had taken up homebrewing during his tour in Riyadh, and he continued to brew in Cairo because his beer was much better than the local beer called Stella, which was reputed to contain a dose of formaldehyde.

My family settled in Brooklyn. I went to work for *Newsday* editing foreign news, and I started homebrewing in my spare time. Being an editor was not nearly as exciting as being a foreign correspondent, and I soon got restless. I started reading about the small breweries that were opening out West, and I watched as Matthew Reich built his brewery in Manhattan. I learned that Brooklyn once was a great brewing center, with forty-eight breweries at the turn of the last century. I was eager to start my own brewery and wanted my downstairs neighbor, Tom Potter, then a junior banker, to join me. Eventually I persuaded him to attend the 1986 Craft Brewers Conference in Portland, Oregon. Potter came back and agreed to start a brewery with me. We raised $500,000 from family and friends. On the advice of a neighbor, Sophia Collier, the founder of a company called SoHo Natural Soda, we decided to put off building a brewery and instead contract with the Matt Brewing Company to make our beer. Collier, who was selling her company to Seagram's for $22 million, told us distribution was the key to the beverage business in New

York City. She said that no established beer distributor was ever going to do the hard work of establishing a new brand. If we wanted success, we had to distribute our own beer.

We took her advice and bought a van, painted our logo on the side, and started peddling Brooklyn Lager on the streets of New York. Within a couple of years we were selling 50,000 cases annually, and the big distributors were starting to notice us. But by then we had learned that many other small brands, American and imported beers, were looking for distribution. So we took on other brands, like Dock Street, Sierra Nevada, the Merchant du Vin line, Chimay, Duvel, and many others. Michael Jackson's *World Guide to Beer* became our road map. If Jackson liked the beer, we took it on.

I will immodestly say that we built the foundation of the craft brewing industry in New York—with the support of the many importers and American craft breweries that we distributed. We did countless beer dinners and promotions, and we courted the local press to explain the world of flavorful beer. Jackson paid tribute to us in 1995, writing in a Craft Brewers Guild advertisement in the monthly *Ale Street News:*

> For lovers of characterful beers, New York was once a disappointment; now it is a delight. Some of the best products from microbreweries across America are here, and so are several of the quirkiest from beer lands like Britain, Belgium and Bavaria. What brought about this metamorphosis? I like to think I encouraged it—but someone had to make the beer available, and it was Brooklyn Brewery who waved the wand. Their notion to distribute their competitors' beers along with their own was a stroke of genius. I thank them for a magical transformation.[48]

In 1996 Mayor Rudy Giuliani cut the ribbon to open our twenty-five-barrel brewery in Williamsburg, Brooklyn. After I introduced him to the assembled reporters, he pulled me up next to him and said: "I want all you reporters to look at this man. He used to be a journalist. Now he is making an honest living." The reporters laughed, and the mayor poured beer for everyone. Garrett Oliver joined our team as brewmaster in 1994 and brewed his first Brooklyn beer, Brooklyn Black Chocolate Stout, the biggest batch of imperial stout ever brewed in the western hemisphere. His next masterpiece was Brooklyn East India Pale Ale, a well-balanced IPA with about 7 percent alcohol by volume. Oliver wrote *The Good Beer Guide* in 1996 and went on to write *The Brewmaster's Table* in 2003 and become editor-in-chief of *The*

Oxford Companion to Beer in 2011. He is widely recognized as one of the world's experts on the history and culture of beer.

Our Brooklyn neighborhood has blossomed along with the brewery. On the first day we delivered beer, Teddy's, a 110-year-old bar that once was owned by the Peter Doelger Brewing Co., was one of our first five customers. For several years Teddy's was our only customer in Williamsburg. Today Williamsburg is home to literally hundreds of great bars, restaurants, hotels, and clubs. The neighborhood has been transformed, and Mayor Michael Bloomberg, in a foreword to the book that Tom Potter and I wrote, *Beer School: Bottling Success at the Brooklyn Brewery*, credited the brewery with an important role in this Brooklyn renaissance.

With our distinctive logo created by Milton Glaser, the man behind the I ♥ NY logo, Brooklyn has become an international brand. We sell beer in twenty-five states and will export 25 percent of our 2013 production. We are building a brewery in Stockholm with Carlsberg, the world's fourth-largest brewery. As I write, we are planning to expand our operations in Brooklyn and Utica.

One of my best friends from my days in the Middle East is David Ottaway, now retired from the *Washington Post*. He invested in our business and eventually bought out Tom Potter. Today I work with his two sons, Eric and Robin, who have been with the company since 1996. Eric, the general manager, and Robin, the sales manager, are the next generation of management at the Brooklyn Brewery.

CHAPTER FIVE

BIG MONEY MEETS CRAFT BREWING

1994–2000

1994: 537 craft breweries

37 noncraft national and regional breweries

2000: 1,509 craft breweries

29 noncraft regional and national breweries;

AB, Miller, and Coors 81 percent share

IN THE SIX DIZZYING YEARS BETWEEN 1994 AND 2000, THE MICROBREWING WORLD was roiled by dramatic successes, spectacular failures, and more bitter public beer wars. Encouraged by a decade of annual double-digit growth from 1984 to 1994, the craft brewing industry saw the construction of hundreds of new breweries, the signing of many contract-brewing ventures, and daring expansions of many existing breweries. The industry grew by 50 percent in 1994 and 1995, then slumped. Some pioneers failed, as did many of the contract operations. But many innovative newcomers appeared.

Brewers would later debate whether a shakeout had occurred. A number of microbrewers took their companies public, raising hundreds of millions of dollars. These were the years of the dot-com boom, when startups burned through billions of dollars in venture capital, hoping to sell everything from music to groceries to wine, beer, hamburgers, hot dogs, and popcorn on the Internet. Some of the first generation of craft brewers allied with the brewing industry giants, Anheuser-Busch (AB) and Miller Brewing Company, which were challenging the cohesiveness of the microbrewing movement. And a brewing and distilling tycoon from India entered the fray, seeking to buy American craft breweries to add to his empire.

After years of ignoring the microbrewing movement, perhaps hoping it was a passing fad, AB, Miller, and Coors invested in some microbreweries and launched their own craft-like, or crafty, beers—with names like Red Wolf, Red Dog, Red River Valley Red Lager, and George Killians Irish Red. But red wasn't the only color on the table. Coors also launched a Belgian white beer called Blue Moon that had been developed by the brewmaster Keith Villa at Sandlot Brewery at Coors Field in Denver. Matt Brewing Company brewed Blue Moon under contract. The large brewers seemed at last to be taking the business seriously, after years of halfhearted attempts to launch microbrew-style brands. (See the chronology in the appendix.)

AB's ferocious leader, August Busch III, unleashed a multipronged war on Boston Beer Company's CEO, Jim Koch, and his contract-brewing operation, which had reached an amazing 700,000 barrels of production in 1994. Busch had clearly had enough of Koch's jabs at big brewers, his oft-repeated comment that the big brewers spilled more beer than Koch made in a year. "We don't spill beer," I once heard an AB executive growl in private.

In 1996 Busch demanded that his wholesalers, the most highly rated beer distribution network in the United States, devote a "100 percent share of mind" to the AB products in their portfolios.[1] Theoretically, and legally, distributors were independent businesses, immune to big brewer control. But in practice many AB distributors were committed to AB brands exclusively. Only some carried imported beers and other non-AB products. As a result of the "100 percent share of mind" crackdown, many dropped imported and craft brands from their houses. Shortly thereafter Busch drove the directive home by presenting so-called equity contracts to his wholesalers, outlining financial incentives for hewing to the "100 percent share of mind" policy.

Four California microbreweries—Anderson Valley Brewing Company, El Toro Brewing Co., Lake Tahoe Brewing Co., and St. Stans Brewing Co.—brought private actions against AB's policy with the Department of Justice Antitrust Division, but the government took no action against AB.[2]

Fred Bowman, cofounder of Portland Brewing Company, said the 100 percent share of mind policy led several AB distributors in Southern California to drop his company. This was a big problem, because he needed statewide distribution to sell in the critically important chain stores in the biggest beer-consuming state in the nation. He had to buy his way out of his contracts with other distributors so he could assign the Portland brands to a wine distributor that covered the entire state. The drain on his cash was one of several reasons why Portland was eventually forced to sell to Pyramid

Breweries.[3] Many other craft brewers were forced out of AB distributors as a result of AB's policy.

In 1996 the board of advisors of Papazian's Institute for Brewing and Fermentation Studies—eleven small brewers and industry suppliers—tiptoed forward with a definition of *craft brewer* that condoned contract brewing and excluded companies with 25 percent ownership by noncraft brewers or whose recipes contained more than 10 percent adjunct, corn or rice. It was a clear shot at the microbrewers like Redhook and Widmer who had sold part of their companies to the large brewers. Redhook and Widmer protested their exclusion from the ranks of craft brewers in a controversy that still rages.

The Association of Brewers (AOB) was shifting toward political advocacy, raising questions among many of its members about its governance. How could an organization fundamentally dedicated to education and run by a professional board of directors—lawyers, business people, and realtors from the Boulder area—set a political agenda for the craft brewing revolution? It wasn't a trade association, was it? Disgruntled, many members turned to the old Brewers' Association of America (BAA) for guidance in government affairs and politics. The BAA was a trade association by definition, run by a board of directors elected by the membership.

The first microbrewer to be publicly traded was the Mendocino Brewing Company of Hopland, California. Mendocino was a cousin of Jack McAuliffe's pioneering New Albion Brewing Company and used the same yeast that had fermented in New Albion's repurposed fifty-five-gallon Pepsi and dairy tanks. When it began selling shares to the public in a limited offering in 1994, Mendocino was producing only 13,600 barrels a year. Running Mendocino were the founders Michael Laybourn and Michael Lovett and the former New Albion brewmaster Don Barkley.

In May 1997 Mendocino was sold to United Craft Breweries, a division of the Indian billionaire Vijay Mallya's United Breweries Group, brewer of Kingfisher, the best-selling beer in India and a favorite of Indian restaurants in the United States. News reports said Mallya gained control of Mendocino by investing $3.5 million in the company. He also announced he was buying Humboldt Brewing for $1.75 million in cash. Then Mallya bought a 45 percent share of Oregon-based Nor'Wester Brewing Co. Nor'Wester's founder, Jim Bernau, became president of United Craft Breweries.[4]

As it happens, Brooklyn Brewery also had a dalliance with the flashy and publicity-loving Mallya in 1998. After inheriting the Kingfisher Brewery from his father, Mallya had expanded the company's holdings significantly.

Mallya had been a Formula One racing driver in his younger days, and he still sponsored a Formula One car. His liquor company in India was second in size only to the international distilling giant Diageo, producer of Guinness, and he owned dozens of chemical companies in Europe. He let it be known that he intended to add other American craft breweries to his portfolio. He sailed into New York Harbor on his yacht, the *Indian Achiever*. The yacht had a crew of twenty-four good-looking men and women, all Brits, a kind of revenge of the colonial. The yacht was about twenty feet longer than the one owned by Malcolm Forbes, the billionaire publisher of *Forbes* magazine, which was docked at Chelsea Piers near Mallya's. Mallya hosted a party on the boat and invited New York's craft brewers. I went to the party and drank Mallya's beer and ate his canapés. This was a novel escape from the daily grind at the Brooklyn Brewery. It turned out that Mallya was interested in Brooklyn Brewery because we were based in the Big Apple, where he had a duplex apartment in one of Donald Trump's skyscrapers. Mallya was also interested in my distribution company, the Craft Brewers Guild.

A few days later I joined Mallya and a coterie of his advisers for a lavish fresh fish lunch on the *Indian Achiever*. He was dressed in a polyester warm-up suit, with gold chains around his neck, his black hair touched his collar. I told him the story of the Brooklyn Brewery, and he told me the story of Kingfisher, as well as his hopes for pulling together a strong group of American craft breweries and gaining a dominant share in the US craft brewing market.

At one point during the long meal the discussion turned to golf. I told Mallya I had been a junior golf champion when I was in high school but had quit my college golf team at Cornell because my 2 handicap was perilously close to my grade point average of 1.9.

"Hindy, have you ever played golf in Scotland?" Mallya asked me.

"No," I said. "One of my dreams is to go to Scotland and play those great courses."

"Why don't you go this summer?" he asked. "I am a member at Gleneagles Country Club. You have heard of it? You can take your family and stay at my castle. It is near the course."

"That would be great," I replied, thinking, yeah, right. Gleneagles is one of Scotland's classic golf clubs, and the site of many championships.

But later in the meal Mallya said, "Hindy, let's get my secretary and pick out some dates for your Scotland trip."

So during the summer of 1998 I took my wife and two children to Scotland, a real vacation from the stress of running the brewery. We stayed at Keillour Castle, which was really a four-story stone mansion built on the site of an old castle at the confluence of two deep gorges. The mansion was decorated with suits of armor, swords, and other medieval artifacts. It was surrounded by acres and acres of finely maintained woods and gardens, a pheasant hunting preserve and farmland. We had a chauffeur, a chef, and a full staff to take care of us. Twenty people must have been working on the grounds every day. We stayed for two weeks, even driving to the ancestral villages of my wife's Scottish ancestors. At the castle we hosted a dinner for the farmer who grew barley on Mallya's land and for the schoolteacher parents of Ewan McGregor, the Scottish film star. They lived in the shepherd's house on Mallya's property. McGregor's father was the grand marshal for the Highland Games in the nearby city of Creiff. We attended the games, sat in the VIP section, and were introduced to the crowd as visiting dignitaries. A day of hammer throws, tossing the caber, and tugs-of-war culminated in the big attraction, a monster truck pull.

Being lord of the manor felt pretty good.

After we returned to New York, Mallya invited me to dinner on the yacht. We met privately on the upper deck, and I told him I had no interest in selling the brewery. Mallya was not offering cash to buy our company. He was proposing we take stock in a US-based subsidiary of his United Breweries group. I knew my partner, Tom Potter, and my investors would never go for this sort of deal, and I had little interest in it myself.

We were contract-brewing Brooklyn Pilsner at Mallya's brewery in Saratoga Springs, New York (one of the former Nor'Wester breweries), and I was not happy that he had yet to install a quality control laboratory there. The brewer at Saratoga was a former AB brewer who knew how to make a great pilsner, but I was concerned that there was no regular reporting on the quality of the beer he was brewing.

I also knew that Ten Springs, the brewery's new name and the brand Mallya was marketing, was not doing well. I told Mallya I knew his New York brewery was struggling and that we would be interested in buying an interest in that brewery if he wanted to sell. Mallya exploded. "Do you think I do not know what I am doing with United Craft Breweries?" he raged. "Are you suggesting my strategy is wrong?"

"No," I said, "This is just between you and me; I am offering to be helpful."

Mallya stormed down to the main deck and told his men that I was trying to steal his brewery. It was time to abandon ship. That was the end of my friendship with the Indian billionaire. One of the Ten Springs executives who was later laid off said to me, "Hey, at least you got a trip to Scotland out of the deal. I got nothing."[5]

Four other brewing companies went public in 1995.

REDHOOK WAS THE FIRST TO GO, AT $17 PER SHARE. BY THE END OF THE YEAR Redhook shares were trading at $25.25, for a market capitalization of $224 million. The company pledged to use part of the money to pay for the $30 million brewery it was building in Portsmouth, New Hampshire, a dramatic commitment to leapfrog across the country and establish a foothold on the East Coast.[6]

Paul Shipman, Redhook's cofounder and CEO, also signed a distribution deal with AB that would allow him access to AB's national network of distributors, widely viewed as the best in the country. Shipman was a key figure in the world of craft brewing from the early 1980s until he gave a fateful speech at the Craft Brewers Conference in Seattle in 1997. After that he virtually disappeared from the public eye.

Shipman dressed in dark suits and ties and looked every bit the president and CEO of a Fortune 500 company. I met him only once, at a Fourth of July picnic in Seattle in 1999. I was there with George Hancock, then CEO of Pyramid Brewery in Seattle. I could not resist complaining to Shipman that his distributor in New York was selling kegs for $65 (our kegs were priced at $100). He batted away my comment, saying that was ridiculous because he was selling the kegs to his distributors at roughly $65 each.

In his early speeches Shipman was fond of grand sweeping statements and prognostications. He once predicted that the imports were going to disappear from the US market and be replaced by American-brewed craft beers. In his keynote speech for the 1997 Craft Brewers Conference in Seattle, he started out by saying his theme was "unity and craftsmanship." In spite of this commitment to comity, it wasn't long before he drew a bead on two segments of the industry: the struggling heritage brewers like Matt Brewing Company and contract brewers. He first said he was going to peer "deep into the future."

He forecast continuing consolidation of the brewing industry and said the future belonged to "great big breweries and then small specialty breweries." In one fell swoop he was consigning to the dustbin of history heritage brewing companies like D.G. Yuengling & Son, the oldest brewery in the country; August Schell, Matt Brewing Company, Rainier Brewing Company, and Genesee Brewing Co., while many of their executives were sitting in the audience.

"And that has, in fact, played out," he said. "There are a few breweries still stuck in the middle, but I think they are doomed. I don't think they fulfill a positive role and in fact, I think, it's just as well for them to quietly go out of business, which would be the natural course."

Shipman said that brewers' attacks on each other undermined consumer confidence in the craft brewing industry. He acknowledged that he had participated in these attacks and added, "In fact, I'm going to continue to do so today." He seemed to have no trouble absorbing the contradiction inherent in this proposition. He averred he was "no friend of contract brewing." He said contract brewing also confused customers. "The attention that has come to contract brewers in their 'truth in labeling' matter has undermined for all of us the credibility of our industry. . . . The contract brewers do not build breweries, or if they do, they are very small."

He did not name names. But he clearly was referring to industry leaders: Boston Beer, then brewing at Hudepohl-Schoenling and at Blitz-Weinhard, and Pete's Brewing Company, then brewing at Stroh. My company was also contract brewing, but we were probably not big enough to make Shipman's list. In addition to confusing customers, these contract brewers, he said, were helping "to preserve those breweries that would otherwise fail. Those old-line breweries—you know who I am talking about—whose existence is doomed and the closure of which would open up the new era in our industry. The new era of big breweries and small breweries. That's an era that will happen; it's been delayed."

Shipman reported that his vision of the future had compelled him to travel to St. Louis to seek a relationship with AB. "There I solicited them for the relationship that would open their distributors for Redhook products. This relationship really has worked out very, very well."[7] Indeed that year Redhook would grow by 45 percent, to 224,578 barrels. But after a few more years of growth Redhook's sales would begin to fall. In 2012 it would report sales of 191,000 barrels.[8] Many beer aficionados shunned Redhook as "Budhook." The partnership with AB has not worked out well for Redhook.

If there is a lesson in Redhook's experience, it may be that humility is a virtue. Shipman had been an important leader and voice in the craft brewing world until that speech. But it marked the beginning of the end for his leadership.

Shipman's talk prompted a retort from Fred Bowman of Portland Brewing Company, who served on the board of advisors for the Institute for Brewing and Fermentation Studies. "I think it was an interesting statement, that regional breweries should dry up and blow away," Bowman told the *New Brewer*. He added that one benefit of contract brewing is that it helps to preserve and repurpose the heritage breweries. "The Blitz-Weinhard Brewery in the heart of Portland is a beautiful building. I'd hate to see it go away."[9]

Boston Beer and Pete's Brewing Company also went public. Both were contract brewed. Both had experienced meteoric growth. Both used mass media, radio for Boston and radio and television ads for Pete's. The use of mass media—the tried and true vehicle of the national brewers—distinguished these two contract brewers from their microbrewing brethren. By brewing at large regional breweries, the contract brewers were able to ramp up production to meet the demand created by the mass advertising. Microbrewers like Sierra Nevada were constantly constrained by the capacity of their small brewing operations. To expand they had to invest in new equipment and personnel. Brewing is a very capital-intensive business. The nimbleness of the contract brewers only compounded the microbrewers disdain for them.

Boston Beer, by far the largest specialty brewer, selling 948,000 barrels in 1995, raised $86.1 million, selling 4.6 million shares in an offering that placed the company on the prestigious New York Stock Exchange. Koch came away with nearly 40 percent of the shares and 100 percent of the voting shares. That meant he controlled the board of directors and the company. Koch also angered institutional investors by offering regular beer drinkers thirty-three shares at $15 each with a coupon printed on the bottom of his six-packs. The first shares were priced at $20 each and opened at $27.[10]

Koch recalls that he received $65 million from the six-pack offering but had to return $50 million, because he had agreed to limit that part of the offering to $15 million.[11] Clearly Samuel Adams drinkers were willing to invest in their favorite suds.

For Koch it was the best of times and the worst of times. Not long after his triumphant public offering, AB unleashed a media campaign against

Boston Beer Company, calling Koch out for posing as a microbrewer while actually brewing his beer in big industrial breweries around the country. On a Sunday evening in October 1996, NBC's Stone Philips went after Koch on *Dateline NBC,* a lightweight investigative journalism program designed to compete with CBS's successful and long-running *60 Minutes.*

The segment introduced Koch, who told of his family's history in the brewing industry. It highlighted his medals in the Great American Beer Festival, his success in establishing the Samuel Adams Boston Lager brand in major cities across the country. A *Dateline* reporter visited the tiny brewery Koch had bought from Bill Newman and moved to the former Haffenreffer Brewery buildings in Jamaica Plans, Massachusetts. Then *Dateline* lowered the boom:

> But there's one small problem with this picture: At least 95 percent of Samuel Adams isn't brewed here, or anywhere even near Boston, for that matter. It's brewed here, at the Stroh's Brewery in Lehigh Valley, Pennsylvania. Here at Genesee in Rochester, New York. And at several other large industrial breweries throughout the country. And while it may be handcrafted, one single batch at a time like the bottle says, each single batch is brewed in a kettle that can hold up to one-hundred to two-hundred thousand bottles of beer. That's right—the Sam Adams you buy in the store is most likely brewed in the same place as more humble and less expensive brands, like Old Milwaukee, Stroh's or Little Kings. And Sam Adams is far from alone. Many of the expensive boutique beers that promote themselves as "handcrafted" and "microbrewed" are actually made in larger commercial breweries like this one; it's called contract brewing.[12]

Koch responded: "If Julia Child comes to your house, brings her own ingredients and her own recipe, goes into your kitchen and makes dinner for you, who made the dinner, you or Julia Child?"

Francine Katz, an AB executive, made the case against Samuel Adams and other contract-brewed beers in the *Dateline* report. "This comes down to honesty and truth in labeling. . . . All we're saying is, 'Hey, guys, let's agree on some basic rules of honesty, let's be truthful on our labels.'"

Many microbrewers across the country were also vehemently opposed to contract brewing, and some reveled in Koch's pain. The brewing industry is fond of *schadenfreude* because the misfortunes of brewers so often play out in real time in the trade and mainstream press. The craft brewers of Oregon were particularly incensed by Koch's decision to sell a contract brew in Oregon under the label Oregon Ale and Beer Company. The *Dateline* piece showed footage of Deschutes Brewery in Bend, Oregon, and interviewed Deschutes's founder, Gary Fish.

> *Dateline:* How do people out here in Oregon involved in craft brewing react when they look at a bottle of Oregon Ale and it says "microbrewed" on the label?
>
> Fish: I think they feel patently offended.[13]

The Oregon brewers joined AB in petitioning the Bureau of Alcohol, Tobacco and Firearms (ATF), which regulates the beer industry, to require breweries to say on their labels who made the beer and where it was made. The ATF did nothing, but Boston Beer Company began listing on its labels the city where its beer was brewed.

AB also ran ads in the *Boston Globe* and other New England daily newspapers asking, "Which of these beers is brewed in New England?" The caption below a bottle of Samuel Adams read, "This one isn't." And under a bottle of Michelob: "This one is." The Michelob was brewed at AB's New Hampshire plant. AB also ran a national radio ad around Halloween in which the ghost of Samuel Adams confronts an actor playing Jim Koch. "Time to stop tricking beer drinkers, Jim," says the ghost. "You're trashing my good name, and I won't stand for it." Thunder booms in the background, while the ghost explains that Samuel Adams is made in the same breweries that make "Schlitz, Schaefer and Old Style . . . beers costing one-half of what you charge." The Koch figure stammers that he is too busy making commercials to brew and bottle his own beer.

The plucky Koch did not back down, but he sounded defensive with ads repeating his Julia Child analogy. One of his ads thanked AB for its concern about the quality of his beer. He added that he had handpicked the breweries he worked with and made his beer with "our own more expensive ingredients."

"You guys at Budweiser still have that Sam Adams standard to keep reaching for," he teased.[14]

Pete's Brewing also went public, raising $62.1 million and promising to build a brewery at an undisclosed location in Southern California. Pete's had sold 347,800 barrels in 1995. The prospectus for the offering said Pete's would spend $30 million to build a brewery with an annual capacity of 250,000 barrels. But it was not to be. Stroh Brewing Co., which was brewing Pete's under contract, had options on 1.1 million shares, or 10 percent of the outstanding stock, and a Stroh executive was joining the board of directors. After the offering the cofounder of Pete's, Pete Slosberg, a former techie, owned 5.6 percent of the publicly traded company.

Slosberg had started the company with Mark Bronder, a teetotaler who had worked with him at the California tech company ROLM. Bronder had left ROLM in the 1980s to start a venture capital fund. He knew Slosberg was a homebrewer, and he suggested they start a microbrewery "to get [in] on the ground floor of a growing industry." The idea appealed to Slosberg—IBM had bought ROLM, and Slosberg was not looking forward to the corporate regimentation for which Big Blue was famous.[15]

They planned to call the company Mark and Pete's Brewing Co., taking a cue from Ben and Jerry's famous ice cream company. But Bronder realized his teetotaling was not a good angle for the company story, so they opted for Pete's Brewing Co. Bronder phoned Bob Stoddard, owner of the Palo Alto Brewing Co., one of the early microbreweries, and asked if Palo Alto could brew beer for Pete's.

"Bob was amenable and encouraged us to move forward with the idea," Slosberg writes in his memoir, *Beer for Pete's Sake*.

> This eliminated lots of planning and red tape for us. We didn't have to expend incredible amounts of energy deciding what equipment to purchase, what capacity to build, where to locate the brewery, or how we'd raise the large amount of capital required. Our back-of-the-envelope calculations indicated that we could start our own company with far less money than we had anticipated. Who'd have thought it? You didn't have to own your own brewery to make great beer! I guess some people have to hug their own vessels and pipes every day in order to feel good, but that wasn't a requirement for us.[16]

The two entrepreneurs eventually decided to produce a brown ale modeled on Nut Brown Ale, a malty dark ale, from the Samuel Smith Old Brewery in England. They had a friend do a sketch of the bearded Pete for the label. But they decided the sketch looked "like a Middle East terrorist," and they dropped that idea in favor of picturing Pete's dog Millie, an English bull terrier, on the packaging.

"Millie . . . was in my opinion the best-looking dog on earth," Slosberg writes. "Mark thought Millie was the silliest looking dog on earth. Together, we both thought putting an English bull terrier on the label would certainly get people's attention, whether they loved the dog or hated her." They named their ale Pete's Wicked Ale after Bronder heard a comedian use the adjective *wicked* repeatedly in his standup routine.[17]

This was the kind of kitchen-table brainstorming that had created many craft breweries and beers for three decades. The Pete's label had the kind of down-home feel that the marketing gurus would, years later, dub *authenticity*.

Pete was a natural at public relations. In an interview he mentioned Duff Beer, the fictional brew that is the favorite of the television cartoon star Homer Simpson, and it got Slosberg an invitation to a taping of the popular TV show. He met the actor/director Quentin Tarantino, a fan of Pete's Wicked, and presented him with a Pete's Wicked jacket. He did the same for then-governor of California, Pete Wilson. He also got a tour of the TOPGUN school in Fallon, Nevada, where fighter pilots are trained. The pilots were all fans of Pete's Wicked Ale, so the tour was easy for Slosberg to arrange.

Unfortunately for Pete and Mark, AB's highly paid marketing geniuses had also settled on an English bull terrier as the mascot for the world's best-selling beer, Budweiser. AB demanded that Pete's stop using the label depicting Millie. Use of the dog by Pete's Brewing Company predated AB's, but Pete's had established the trademark only in California.

"The absolute best we could hope for would be to prohibit the use of Spuds Mackenzie in California," Slosberg writes. "There were no guarantees that this would be the ultimate result. If anything, we could lose our company in legal fees. Did we want to be in the legal business, or the beer business? We were first, but what mattered was who had the most financial resources."[18]

Pete's then produced a series of television ads in which Slosberg is seated at a table on a San Francisco street and offers to give his autograph or pose for pictures with passersby. Of course, few passersby had ever heard of him and awkwardly turned down his offers. The ads ended with the tagline, "Not yet world famous." They were a hit, and the *New York Times* named the campaign among the ten best for 1994.[19]

The ad campaign and the media buy cost Pete's Brewing Co. a million dollars. The ad firm that produced the television spots was Goodby, Silverstein & Partners in San Francisco. After the *Times* applauded the Pete's ads, AB approached the firm with a $31 million contract to handle its Budweiser Ice Beer contract. Goodby Silverstein promptly dumped Pete's.

Three years after Pete's initial public offering, Pete's was sold to the Gambrinus Co., owner of Bridgeport Brewing Co. and importer of Modelo Brewery's Corona brand. Under the stewardship of Carlos Alvarez, CEO of Gambrinus, Pete's began a long decline that ended with the disappearance of the brand in 2012. Slosberg said Gambrinus made little use of Slosberg's marketing prowess in the two years that the founder was committed to promoting the brand. He said the two main markets for Pete's were California and Massachusetts, but the only appearances he made for Gambrinus were in Kentucky and Mississippi, two states not known for their craft beer markets. Alvarez failed with Pete's, but had great success with Corona Beer. He had also purchased the Spoetzl Brewery in 1989 and made its Shiner Bock one of the top-selling specialty beers in the country.[20]

The last of the IPOs was that of Hart Brewing Co., later renamed Pyramid Brewery. CEO George Hancock, a former Coopers & Lybrand accountant who had made money in a tech company before buying Hart, raised $49.4 million with his public offering. He announced plans to pay down debt and build a new brewery in Northern California and soon after began construction of a large brewery in Berkeley.[21] When Pyramid's earnings went down the stock tanked, an experience repeated by so many publicly offered breweries, which effectively closed the IPO window for the industry.

Hancock said the cash that Boston Beer Company got for its IPO was irresistible. "Everybody looked at the multiples that Sam Adams got, and we couldn't pass up that kind of opportunity," he said. "It was as simple as that. Would I rather run a private company? Absolutely. But we raised a lot of money and built a huge facility in Berkeley."

Hancock also had a plan to buy smaller craft breweries and bring them into his publicly traded company, which was brewing 117,000 barrels annually when it went public. He visited Brooklyn and talked to us about buying Brooklyn Brewery. But we wanted the same kind of multiple that he got, and Hancock was not willing to pay that kind of money for our company, which was hardly profitable.

The new brewery in Berkeley did not increase Pyramid's production potential as rapidly as Hancock planned. He said that immediately after completing the IPO, the company missed its first quarterly earnings target. A group of angry stockholders hired an attorney and sued the company. "Welcome to the world of public companies," Hancock said.

In the next few years Pyramid grew to more than 200,000 barrels, but production was still not growing as quickly as a public company needed to.

Hancock retired as CEO in January 2000 and turned the brewery over to his chief operating officer, Martin Kelly, a former Miller Brewing Company sales executive. Hancock became chairman of the board.

"I think we lost something at that point," Hancock said. "I think we didn't really understand what an impact those changes would have on the culture of the company. . . . It goes back to what I was saying about this being a movement, a kind of religious cult. It has to be run as a business, but the thing works best because everybody's bought into the mission. They fall in love with the company. They fall in love with the brands, the beers, the team. And they can do spectacular things. I think Pyramid did that in the '90s. We had a great team of people. We had some stiff competition in the Northwest from the Widmer brothers. We were both focused on our wheat beers."

Hancock eventually fired Kelly. Alan Newman at the Magic Hat Brewery in Vermont then hired Kelly. In 2008 Magic Hat bought Pyramid and took it private in what seemed to be revenge for firing Kelly. The Magic Hat team rebranded the Pyramid beers. They changed the name of the flagship Pyramid Hefeweizen to Haywire. They described the move as transforming the Pyramid brand into a lifestyle brand. But sales plummeted, and Magic Hat/Pyramid was sold to North American Breweries in 2010, whose anchor was the Genesee Brewing Co.

Hancock said Pyramid had to transform itself into a private company after the Enron scandal brought a new wave of regulation for public companies in the form of the Sarbanes-Oxley Act of 2002. "We were spending hundreds of thousands of dollars a year on compliance with Sarbanes-Oxley, paying consultants who used to work for the accounts who caused the Enron scandal in the first place. They were making millions cleaning it up. The small public company model basically became invalid at that time. Hundreds of small companies had to go private. If I could have taken it private myself, I would have done that. For the sake of the shareholders, all the shareholders, you've got to take a more dispassionate decision, and the right decision was to sell it at that point."

Hancock said the only brewer who had the size necessary to fulfill the obligations of a public company was Jim Koch's Boston Beer Company. "Jim's contract-brewing strategy gave him the marketing dollars to create a fast-growing company that wasn't limited by bricks and mortar, so he could expand his business much faster than the traditional craft brewers," Hancock said. "In the end he won that battle. He got out there faster, invested the marketing dollars to create the brand. He is one of the brightest guys in the industry and the most driven to succeed."[22]

Other large and small breweries joined forces at this time. In 1995 Miller Brewing Company bought the Austin-based Celis Brewery, the Belgian white beer brewery founded by Pierre Celis, a Belgian.[23] The label of his Celis White Beer pictured a cowboy lassoing a steer. Miller also bought a 50 percent stake in the Shipyard Brewing Co. of Portland, Maine, in 1995. Shipyard's cofounder Fred Forsley announced he bought it back from Miller in 1999.[24]

Bert Grant sold his company, Yakima Brewing and Malting Co., to Stimson Lane Ltd., owner of Chateau San Michel, Columbia Crest Wines, and US Tobacco, in 1995.[25]

The craft brewing industry found 1997 to be a heady but anxious year. Charlie Papazian opened the 1997 Craft Brewers Conference in Seattle by noting that the number of breweries operating in the United States had surpassed 1,200, more than in any other country in the world, including Germany. But not all was well. Hancock, CEO of Pyramid, said that distribution channels were flooded with new products. "The main challenge used to be to brew enough beer," he said. "Now it's to sell enough beer."[26]

When I think of this dizzying period of growth and decline and change, one really prophetic moment stands out: Full Sail cofounder Jerome Chicvara's speech at the 1997 Craft Brewers Conference. It remains, in my opinion, one of the most compelling speeches ever given at such a conference. Chicvara began his speech with a tribute to the mecca of craft brewing, the great Northwest; craft beer enjoyed a 10 percent market share in both Oregon and Washington State. He reminded the packed ballroom that Oregon's state motto was "Things Look Different Here."

He went on to explain that his standard speech about the craft brewing movement was a "gospel of bricks and mortar." He called that type of speech "If You Build It, They Will Come," a line taken from the sentimental baseball movie *Field of Dreams,* about a dreamer who builds a ballpark in the middle of a cornfield.

"I can think of no two better ways to burn significantly large chunks of money than building breweries or ballparks," Chicvara said. "I've never built a ballpark, but I think that building a brewery is good training for that. Maybe I will do that in my next career. The premise was simple. If you build it, they will come: beer seekers, enthusiasts and customers would flock to your brewing shrine and product, all in exchange for simply being Nike-esque, just building it, or just doing it."[27]

He showed slides of old and new baseball parks, from Ebbets Field to Camden Yards, and then slides of the large breweries being built by Sierra Nevada, Grants, Redhook, Pyramid, Full Sail, and Deschutes. But, he said, things had changed since the year before, when he had given an optimistic speech. In 1997 the title of his speech would be, "If You Build It, Will They Come?" Or, better yet, 'Why, and For Whom, Am I Building This?'"

"It is time to focus your vision, your vision for 1997 and beyond," he told the conference. "The twenty-first century: craft beer heaven or craft beer hell?" Chicvara said that Redhook's alliance with AB and the capital raised from IPOs set the stage for craft beer wars or a long-prophesized shakeout in the industry. He proceeded to show a clip from the first *Star Wars* movie that showed the Death Star annihilating other space ships. As if the imagery was not clear enough, he said, "That big one is Redhook."

Before digging into the *Star Wars* metaphor, he referenced the new confusion in the craft brewing industry. Up to now the enemy had always been the large domestic breweries and the imports. "I don't know about you, but on any given day, I am trying to decide who my real competitor is. Here is some food for thought on the players in this drama. Pardon the hyperbole. If you are a member of the cast in my satire, it's all in good fun."

Chicvara then showed footage from the film *Jurassic Park,*" with a ferocious *Tyrannosaurus rex* devouring smaller dinosaurs. It was a none-too-subtle reference to AB and its 100 percent share of mind policy. He then showed another cut of *Star Wars,* with Darth Vader as an empire builder. "If you can't beat them, buy them," Chicvara said, in another not so subtle reference to AB and Redhook.[28]

Darth Vader: What is thy bidding, my master?

Emperor Palpatine: There is a great disturbance in the force.

Darth Vader: I have felt it.

Emperor Palpatine: We have a new enemy: Luke Skywalker.

Darth Vader: Yes, my master.

Emperor Palpatine: He could destroy us.

Darth Vader: He's just a boy. Obi-Wan can no longer help him.

Emperor Palpatine: The force is with him. The son of Skywalker must not become a Jedi.

Darth Vader: If he could be turned, he could become a powerful ally.

Emperor Palpatine: Yes, yes. He would be a great asset. Can it be done?

Darth Vader: He will join us, or die, Master.[29]

He then discussed how competition in the craft brewing segment could get "downright nasty." He showed another clip of the T-Rex mauling a challenger, a shout out to AB's multi-pronged media attack on Jim Koch and Boston Beer Company.

"Jim, are you out there?" he shouted to the audience. "Big Jim. You are still living, right? This hasn't happened yet. My apologies for the undignified nature of this particular metaphor, but it is rather evocative, don't you think?" Koch was not in the audience.

Chicvara went on to describe the perils of getting noticed by the big players in the industry, and of becoming collateral damage in the war over market share. Using clips from *Star Wars,* he described Darth Vader's attempts to lure Luke Skywalker to his destiny, "the dark side." It was another not-so-subtle reference to Paul Shipman and August Busch III. "You know, at a certain point, I believe there is such a thing as an offer you can't refuse," he said. "But beware the dark side of the successful deal."

He may have been referring to the fees and other strings that were part of Redhook's distribution deal with AB. It certainly looked like a great deal at the time, what with AB pressing its 100 percent share of mind program and forcing distributors to drop brands that were not in some way allied with AB. "All marriages require trust," said Chicvara. "And all marriages entail compromise. But in some marriages, one spouse can be, shall we say, more compelling than the other?"

Another *Star Wars* clip he showed that day has echoed in my mind ever since. It is a scene involving Darth Vader and Lando Calrissian, a former ally of Skywalker's who has made a deal with Darth Vader.

Darth Vader: Take the princess and the wookie to my ship.

Lando Calrissian: You said they'd be left under my supervision.

Darth Vader: I am altering the deal. Pray I don't alter it any further.[30]

Chicvara was illustrating a peril implicit in any deal between two unequal parties: the stronger party could change the terms of the deal.

According to Chicvara, success in 1997 was simply a matter of surviving. "Success is what you can claim, if you are at next year's conference, in my opinion," he said. He compared the beer wars of 1997 to the beer wars of the 1880s. "In 1889 a British brewer—now get this—a British brewer of-fered $16 million for Schlitz, Pabst, and Blatz. That's $16 million in 1890s money. In 1890 small brewers began consolidating in response to this. And in 1892 the price of beer in the United States dropped 50 percent. The gloves were off."

Chicvara said, "The major brewers have taken a decided interest in the high-end specialty beer category from the production side as well as the dis-tribution side." To survive, he counseled, brewers should stay small and not attract the attention of the large brewers. He advocated regional markets and niches within niches.

"Don't try to be everything to everybody," he said. "Strange things hap-pen. Look what happened to my buddy Bert." He showed a life-sized card-board cutout of Bert Grant in a Scottish kilt. It was produced by the new owners of Grants Ales for point-of-purchase displays in supermarkets. It had been on display in the lobby of the conference hotel.

"Bert's got pretty nice legs for a kilt," Chicvara said in closing. "If you stay small, you'll never have to subject yourself to this sort of fun and games."[31]

It was a sobering assessment of a difficult time in the revolution.

Fritz Maytag offered similar advice at the 1998 Craft Brewers Confer-ence in Atlanta: "I have a passion for small," he said.[32] I remember hearing his talk and thinking: "Easy for you to say. You are brewing 100,000 plus barrels in that beautiful little brewery in that beautiful city on the Pacific Ocean. I'm here in a gritty neighborhood of Brooklyn struggling to grow beyond 30,000 barrels. When I get to 100,000 barrels, I'll decide whether small is beautiful."

My company and hundreds of others were still growing, despite the over-all malaise. The growth of the segment leader, Boston Beer Company, flat-tened out at just over a million barrels annually. Pete's Brewing Company had begun to lose ground. Many small brewers opined that the Nor'Wester brands, the contract brews like Rhino Chasers, and the red tide of beers from the large brewers, were confusing the consumer. Some blamed the divisions among craft brewers for the slump.

At the 1996 Craft Brewers Conference in Boston, David Geary of Geary's Brewing Company in Portland, Maine, had decried the infighting in the industry and applauded Jim Koch for teaching everyone how to sell beer. Geary's speech drew boos from the audience when he criticized efforts to exclude Boston Beer from the ranks of craft brewers. "So, Jim Koch is not a craft brewer? The man who taught us all to sell beer? Ridiculous!" Geary boomed.[33] The iconoclastic Geary also praised AB for making a great beer, a quality beer. More boos. Geary's talk was controversial, but I think it actually exemplified one of the great strengths of the craft brewing revolution: that the industry is made up of very strong-minded entrepreneurs, people who are used to rowing against the tide, people who are not comfortable with the easy way out, people who revel in telling it like it is. Throughout the history of the industry people have made speeches like Geary's, and I hope we never lose that quality of dissent. Craft brewers don't mind sticking their necks out. Sometimes they are wrong, like Paul Shipman in Seattle. But often they highlight a truth that many do not want to face; they keep us all from becoming too wedded to a prevailing orthodoxy, from believing our own bullshit. That is a great strength.

Having said that, I did not agree with Geary's declaration that Koch had taught us how to sell beer. Koch was selling beer the way the large brewers sell beer, with radio and television ads. So was Pete Slosberg. I was not selling beer that way, and neither were hundreds of other craft brewers. Maybe I should have been; Koch and Slosberg were selling a lot more beer than I was.

Geary's defense of Koch came at a dangerous moment. As I've mentioned, Koch had started a contract-brewing operation called the Oregon Ale and Beer Co.—selling an Oregon-branded beer that was being produced in the Northwest by Saxer Brewing Co. Chicvara, the chair of the Oregon Brewers Guild, was calling for Koch's expulsion from the AOB. The guild had developed a seal to put on its members' packaging to differentiate their products from Koch's Oregon-branded product. Chicvara was also promoting a plan to grab some headlines by throwing boxes of Samuel Adams Boston Lager from a ship in Boston Harbor, a kind of Boston Beer Party.

IT SEEMED TO ME THAT THIS OREGON FEUD WAS GETTING OUT OF HAND AND GENUinely threatening the unity of the movement. Did it really make sense to isolate the biggest player in the segment, a player who had done much to spread the word about craft beer, even though his sole aim was to sell Samuel Adams Boston Lager and now Oregon Ale?

During the 1996 conference in Boston I got Koch's home phone number and called to ask if he would attend a meeting with the Oregon brewers. The last time I had spoken with Koch was during the shouting match we had had about his misleading advertisements based on his victories in the Consumer

Preference Poll. We were not exactly friends. To my surprise he agreed. He drove from his home in suburban Boston to the conference hotel downtown.

Chicvara recalls that the meeting was attended by Gary Fish of Deschutes Brewery, Jack Joyce of Rogue Ales, Jamie Emmerson and Irene Firmat of Full Sail Brewing Company, Fred Bowman from Portland Brewing Co., and Mike Sherwood, the executive director of the Oregon Brewers Guild.[34]

The Oregon brewers took turns excoriating Koch for his faux Oregon craft beer. "Fish had a couple of frank and substantive comments," Chicvara recalled. "Jamie and Irene told him it bordered on fraud and he was denuding the value of real Oregon craft-brewed beer—even though the beer was brewed at Blitz Weinhard and Saxer and wasn't bad beer. It was pretty decent to good. The discussion centered around him undermining the value/pricing proposition of Oregon craft beers. Nobody liked it."

Koch listened intently, sometimes twirling the hair over his left ear the way I had seen him do before in similarly stressful situations.

"Koch said little—'Aw shucks, golly, what's all the fuss,'" Chicvara said. "Mr. Boston Consulting Group/Harvard MBA wanted us to believe that he was just like us. His Will Rogers persona didn't sell. This did not play well with the Oregon Brewers Guild members."

I recall that Koch did agree to consider phasing out his Oregon Ale and Beer Co., which he did a couple of years later. Chicvara believes the Oregon Brewers Guild's seal helped unmask Koch as a carpetbagger, and that was the reason Koch gave up. "The Oregon consumer figured out that there was no such thing as Oregon Ale and Beer," Chicvara said.[35]

However, the meeting did forestall any campaign to expel Koch from the AOB or stage a Boston Beer Party. And it brought Koch face to face with some of his most bitter detractors. Koch has always been sort of a loner in the industry. Many of us had our cliques of brewer friends whom we hung out with and drank with at the annual conferences. For instance, Gary Fish and I rarely missed an opportunity to play golf when we got together. While we enjoyed a day at the golf course, the intensely ambitious Koch was likely visiting customers or meeting with his distributors.

Koch later recalled the Boston meeting as a turning point in his relations with the other players in the industry. "When you reached out to me, that was a watershed that opened up a new future," Koch told me. "It wasn't much fun being attacked by everyone all the time. This was a way for me to join and be respected by my peers, a group of people who have been very capable and good competitors."[36]

The closing years of the twentieth century were a tumultuous time for craft brewers, and many commentators said craft brewing was undergoing a shakeout.[37] David Edgar of the AOB made the case against a shakeout in the May–June 1998 issue of the *New Brewer*. He pointed to a dictionary definition of *shakeout* as "an elimination of business concerns, products, etc., as a result of declining sales or rising standards of quality."

He then showed that the number of regional specialty breweries had increased from 395 to 451 between 1996 and 1997; the number of brewpubs had increased from 691 to 851 in the same period. Overall, 317 brewing concerns had opened in 1996, whereas 36 had closed; in 1997 the ratio was 231:61.

"While a true shakeout may still happen, it didn't in 1997 and doesn't seem to be happening in 1998," Edgar wrote. "The industry is maturing. Many entrepreneurs are waking up to the cold reality that you can't just put a clever name on a fancy package—and you can't just call yourself a brewpub— and expect to be successful. There are many important details to getting each concept right—some of which can only be learned from experience."[38]

BUT NO ONE COULD DENY THAT SOME FAILURES WERE DRAMATIC. THE RED BELL Brewing Co. in Philadelphia started brewing Red Bell Blonde Ale in 1993 at the Lion Brewery in Wilkes-Barre, brewers of the regionally distributed Stegmeir Beer. James Bell, a stockbroker, and his partner, Jim Cancro, an engineer, launched their beer with catchy billboards that proclaimed, "Philadelphia Is Putting Blondes Behind Bars." They got their beer into Philadelphia's Veterans Stadium, and a year later they opened a forty-barrel brewhouse in the city's old Brewerytown neighborhood, once home to many pre-Prohibition breweries like Schmidts and Ortleib's. Later that year Bell and Cancro opened a brewpub in the CoreStates Center, home to the Philadelphia Flyers and the Philadelphia 76ers. Bell and Cancro took their company public in 2002, revealing they had been hemorrhaging cash since its founding. The stock tanked, and the state revoked Red Bell's brewing license because of unpaid payroll taxes—a cardinal sin for any business. Red Bell closed later that year.

Steve Mason, a former physical education teacher, and Alan Davis, a Vermont businessman, and some other friends started Catamount Brewing Co. in White River Junction, Vermont, in 1986. Mason had apprenticed with a brewery in Hertfordshire, England, in 1983 and returned to the United States with plans to start a microbrewery. He cobbled together a brewhouse from a yeast tank salvaged from the Stroh Brewery in his hometown of Detroit and purchased conditioning tanks from the microbrewery supplier JV Northwest.

Mason's Catamount Gold, a hoppy golden ale, won a gold medal at the Great American Beer Festival in 1989. The company also made an amber ale, a pale ale, an oatmeal stout, and some seasonal beers. Production had ramped up to 12,000 barrels by 1993. Davis, the salesman, wanted to expand the company's marketing efforts, hire salespeople, and develop more sophisticated point-of-sale materials. But Mason wanted to expand the brewing operation and boost production of the award-winning Catamount Gold. The board of directors sided with Mason, and Davis left the company later that year.

Mason found a new brewery site in an industrial park in Windsor, Vermont, about fifteen miles south of White River Junction. The $5 million brewery, financed with bank loans, opened in 1997. *Inc. Magazine* quoted the marketing expert Paul Ralston as saying the new brewery was "a beautiful facility, a real Cadillac." But the year it opened was the year the craft brewing industry's growth flattened, and the company never generated enough sales to pay off the heavy debt it assumed to build the brewery.

"I think Mason felt that if he could keep making an excellent product, people would come," said Jack Shea, owner of Capitol Distributors Inc., adding, "When you are developing a brand, you need street presence. You need a sales force talking up the product. Catamount was late in the game to do that."

Inc.'s obituary for Catamount in October 2000 listed the causes of death as "tepid marketing; untimely expansion."[39]

Before the year was out, the Harpoon Brewery bought Catamount's Windsor brewery.

From 1995 to 1998 I kept a list of failed breweries pinned to the wall behind my desk in Brooklyn. I wish I still had that list. I recall it grew to more than forty, including about a dozen brewpubs and production breweries that popped up in New York. The Manhattan Brewing Company, where Brooklyn's brewmaster Garrett Oliver learned to brew professionally from Mark Witty, the former Samuel Smith brewer, failed with three different owners. Locations all over the city closed their doors. It seemed they all had trouble developing a team that could serve a quality meal and a quality beer at the same time. Maybe they underestimated the amount of money they had to invest to hire a top-notch chef and brewmaster.

In 1995 former wall streeter John Bloostein opened Heartland Brewery in Union Square. The food and the beer were quality. Finally a Manhattan brewpub that looked like it might succeed. But when Bloostein decided to expand his concept to other Manhattan locations, he started contract brewing his beer at Greenpoint Beer Works in Brooklyn, a strategy that continues to this day. Bloostein found Manhattan real estate to be too expensive to hold the vats and tanks of a microbrewery. The only Heartland brewpub that still brews on-premises in Manhattan is the Chelsea Brewing Company, in the massive Chelsea Piers complex on the West Side.

The most spectacular flop in the Big Apple was the Zip City Brewing Co., just off Fifth Avenue on West Eighteenth Street. Zip City was the fictional town in Sinclair Lewis's novel *Babbit*, a satiric depiction of small-town businessmen. Zip City was a beautiful brewpub. The copper-clad serving tanks were displayed in the center of a large room, with an oval bar enclosing them. The brewmaster, Jeff Silman, a veteran homebrewer, made very nice German-style lagers and wheat beers. For six years the pub did a booming business but slumped in year seven, and owner Kirby Shyer closed it down.

Unfortunately for the rest of the craft brewing movement, Shyer allowed the *New York Times* to witness him pouring 3,100 gallons of unsold beer down the drain. The *Times* story described the craft brewing industry as losing ground to cheap beers. "I don't go out to microbreweries as much as I used to," Mark Conrad, a financial analyst for a Wall Street firm and a former Zip City customer, told the paper. "I drink cheap beer, very cheap beer." He explained that the novelty of microbrews had worn off and that he now frequented only local bars or took home a six-pack of Ballantine.[40]

The article went on to quote Jim Parker of the AOB as acknowledging the phenomenon of a cheap beer backlash. "Part of it is our own fault in the craft beer industry," Parker told the reporter. "Some places charge $6 or $7 for beer that may not be worth it. . . . Or someone gets burned on a bad six-pack, so they may not be willing to take a chance next time."

Parker's comments played right into the *Times* reporter's thesis that the craft brewing industry's glass was half empty, that the fad had run its course. The facts did not bear out this pessimism. The story duly reported that the industry grew by 26 percent in 1996, but noted that it had grown 50 percent in both of the two previous years.

That article would haunt the craft brewing industry for many years. When assigned a story, most journalists immediately go to the library to look up recent stories on the same topic. So anyone writing about the microbrewing business would almost certainly see the piece about Zip City's demise.

Parker's gaff was a learning experience for the staff of the AOB. I am pleased to report that the marketing staff at the BA, the successor of the AOB, is much more adept at keeping the press focused on the positive aspects of the industry.

The brief spurt of public offerings was not repeated. Only Boston Beer Company would consistently demonstrate the kind of financial results that ring bells on Wall Street. The other public companies would struggle. Many companies failed, but many more companies with a novel approach to craft brewing started up and sowed the seeds for the boom that would come in the first decade of the new century.

CHAPTER SIX

THE SECOND GENERATION

INNOVATION

DESPITE THE MONUMENTAL FAILURES OF SOME CRAFT BREWERS IN THE MID-1990s, my company and many others continued to grow. Daniel Bradford, then chair of the Brewers' Association of America (BAA), patiently argued that no shakeout had occurred, that the core of the industry was progressing at the same clip it had for fifteen years. What the industry really had seen was just a few spectacular flops.

"Steve Mason [who started Catamount with Alan Davis] was a good guy, but you know he and Alan couldn't run a business," Bradford said. "And Rhino Chasers: Did you ever understand their marketing? Rhino Chaser is a surfboard, so why are you putting a rhinoceros on it?"

And then, referring to Jim Bernau of Nor'Wester and the Indian billionaire Vijay Mallya of United Brewers, Bradford added, "There were several people in that period, the '90s, who tried to do a national rollup . . . but the problem was almost all of them were bankers, money guys. They weren't beer guys."[1]

In retrospect I cannot believe the media got it so wrong. During the so-called shakeout—let's say between 1994 and 2000—the number of craft breweries actually grew by 1000.

The period could be more accurately characterized as a new wave of innovation, a second coming of craft beer. In Fort Collins, Colorado, New Belgium was just getting started, with Kim Jordan and her husband, Jeff Lebesch, betting their lives on making Belgian-style beers in the basement of their home. In Rehobeth Beach, Delaware, Sam Calagione, who had tended bar in New York City and worked as a male model, was concocting strong hoppy beers using unorthodox ingredients; Burkhard Bilger, writing in the *New Yorker,* later called Calagione's brews "extreme beers." In Sonoma, California, Vinnie Cilurzo and his wife, Natalie, were experimenting with beer aged in wine casks, with the dreaded *Brettanomyces* yeast, which yielded surprising sour flavors.[2] Brooklyn's own Garrett Oliver began a series of collaborations with British, Belgian, and German brewers after coming up with a rich black imperial stout called Brooklyn Black Chocolate Stout. Dale Ketechis started Oscar Blue's brewpub in Lyons, Colorado, in 1997 and five years later began selling his Dale's Pale Ale in cans, introducing a whole new set of packaging options for craft brewers. Meanwhile, Jim Koch pushed the envelope with high-alcohol-content beers.

Many among the first generation of craft brewers were strict adherents of the German Purity Law of 1516, the Reinheitsgebot, which restricts brewers to four ingredients—water, grain, hops, and yeast—but the second generation did not feel encumbered by any such boundaries. Tomme Arthur, head

Tomme Arthur of San Diego's Pizza Port and the Lost Abbey. Photograph courtesy of Pizza Port and the Lost Abbey. © John Schultz

brewer at Pizza Port in Solana Beach, California, writing in the *New Brewer* in 2000, said, "As brewers, we each have our own ideas and philosophies. And, like writers who belong to the community of artists, we belong to this community as well. Our recipes, like prose, exist on paper though ultimately they live and breathe in our customer's glass. Poetry may be formed from words on a page, but it comes alive when recited. If this is true, then our recipes are not merely words on a page. They are pieces of liquid art which evolve over time and provoke thoughtful discussions."[3]

The first brewery to base its beers on the quirky styles of Belgium chose the name New Belgium. Jeff Lebesch was an award-winning homebrewer working for an engineering firm in Fort Collins, Colorado. At that time the most exotic beers available in Colorado, home of Coors Brewing Company, were from Watney's, Samuel Smith Old Brewery, and Sierra Nevada Brewing Co. In 1985 his work took him to Europe, where he toured Belgium on a bicycle, visiting the amazing array of artisanal breweries in that tiny country. "Jeff became enamored of all these amazing styles of beer in Belgium," Kim Jordan said.

Kim Jordan and Jeff Lebesch of New Belgium Brewing Company at the groundbreaking of their brewery with their children Zack and Nick.

"He went back to Belgium in 1988 and visited a famous beer bar in Bruges, Café Brugs Bertj'e, on a Wednesday," she said. "The bar was usually closed on Wednesdays, but it was a holiday, the Day of the Procession of the Blood of Christ, and it opened that day at 4 p.m. There was no one there, and so he sat and talked with Jahn de Brunah, who owned the bar with his wife, Daisy Claeys. Jahn was in a good mood, which is not always the case. He was charmed that an American should have fallen in love with Belgian beers, so he pulled some special stock from his cellar, beers from Liefman's and the Trappists, lambics and others. He discussed the ingredients and the breweries. They toured Belgian beers from soup to nuts. Jeff was thrilled to receive this hospitality from a knight of Belgian beer."[4]

Lebesch returned to Fort Collins and began talking about starting a brewery to make Belgian-style beers. "The experience with Jahn was really seminal in the creation of New Belgium," Jordan said. (In fact, New Belgium still takes all its employees to Belgium, rents a room at Brugs Bertj'e, and re-creates the creation story.) Jordan met Lebesch later in 1988 at a friend's party in Fort Collins and they began to date. "Jeff, being a practical guy, I really think he thought I could help him start the brewery," Jordan said. "I could be the front of the house, doing the marketing and selling. He could be the brewer."

Back then Jordan was a social worker counseling troubled low-income families. She and Lebesch married in September 1990 and bought a 900-square-foot house in Fort Collins. The following March they began building a 300-square-foot addition to the house and digging a cellar. "The reason for the addition was we wanted to start a brewery," Jordan said. The brewery went in their new cellar. Jeff shifted to one day a week at the engineering firm; Jordan started working only four days a week for social services. Her son, Zack, was in the first grade. She would load her station wagon with cases of twenty-two-ounce New Belgium beers, pick Zack up at school, and make deliveries in the afternoons. She would get home about 6 p.m., make dinner, put Zack to bed, and then go to Kinko's to make table tents and copy labels for posters. They were selling five varieties, Fat Tire, Abbey, Triple, Sunshine Wheat, and Cherry. "We thought Abbey would be our flagship, but Fat Tire took off right away, particularly off premise," she said. "Fat Tire was pretty darn successful right away."

Like many craft brewers before them, Lebesch and Jordan were learning the beer business the hard way. Jordan recalled wheeling a load of cases into Aggie Liquors in Fort Collins and hearing the owner ask, "What's your price point?"

"I was thinking, 'What's a price point?' but I didn't want to sound stupid. So I thought he must mean the wholesale price, and that is what I said, and it was OK. I didn't want to blow it."[5] In the beginning most of their sales were COD (Cash on Delivery), because customers realized they needed the cash. But some insisted on 30-days credit, in accordance with Colorado law.

They operated their basement brewery for fourteen months and then bought an old freight depot on the outskirts of Fort Collins in August 1992 and started preparing it for a new brewhouse. The loading docks at the new property were on the north side of the building, a bad design for snowy Colorado. Lebesch fashioned a system to channel the steam from the brew kettles into a radiant heat system to keep the docks clear of snow.

They entered their beers in the 1992 Great American Beer Festival blind-tasting competition. Jordan was nine months pregnant, but she poured beers at the festival on Thursday, Friday, and Saturday. "The next Wednesday, I delivered a baby, Nick, and the following Monday I brought Nick to the brewery, set up a bassinet, and got to work. I don't think I would have the stamina to do that today. But, you know, that is what entrepreneurs do—you don't have any choice. Those are the things you do when you start out." For their first three years at the festival, it had no category for Belgian-style beers. New Belgium's beers were not even judged.

All the bottling at the depot brewery was by hand, using a filler Lebesch had made. The filler tube was attached to a peristaltic pump that was operated by touching two electrodes together. "You had to touch those wires just right to get the pump to fill the bottle to the correct level," Jordan said. Then a wicker roller applied the paper labels. "You rolled them on, and then you straightened them out by hand," she recalled. "It was pretty crazy."

Filtration and filling of bottles were accomplished by means of a long stainless steel tube stuffed with a muslin liner. Jordan sewed the muslin liners closed at one end and inserted them into the tube. "There was an eighth to a quarter inch of yeast in the bottom of all our beers," Jordan said.[6]

In the early 1990s the craft beer market in Fort Collins was highly segmented. Another craft brewery, Odell's, was doing kegs; CooperSmith's was a brewpub, and New Belgium was doing bottled beer, so New Belgium had a monopoly on the off-premises business. One of its first customers in Fort Collins was the Town Pump, a bar managed by J.B. Shireman, who would later become a key employee of New Belgium.

"Out of the blue came this guy, who not many people had heard of, doing these Belgian-style beers out of his basement," Shireman said of Lebesch.

"When Kim and Jeff started, the Town Pump and a bar across the street that Jim Parker, of Oregon fame, owned, called the Mountain Tap, we took the [New Belgium] beers first. And right away I thought it was pretty unique, between the labels that were water-colored by their neighbor and the very different styles of beer. I believe we carried Abbey and Fat Tire to start, and then very quickly along came Sunshine Wheat, Old Cherry, and Triple. That was a very diverse lineup for those days."

Shireman said neither he nor any of his customers had ever tried a Belgian-style beer. Few had even heard of it. Fort Collins had almost no craft beer scene and certainly no Belgian-style beer on the market. "The New Belgium beers had to be explained to us, via Jeff and Kim, because I didn't know anything about them," he said. "They had these odd names—Fat Tire with this old cruiser bike on the label—Abbey, you know I'm from the South so it looked to me like it had a preacher on the label. I didn't know what this story was, but when I asked and it was explained to me, it really helped, and it enriched the experience, and we started telling it to other people. It was based in authenticity, and I think that is critical for any brand."

He said he was impressed by the passion with which Jordan explained the beers and by Lebesch's commitment to quality. "I believe it was the first batch that Jeff released of Old Cherry," Shireman said. "It didn't turn out exactly the way he wanted it to. They were brewing in their basement on Frey Street and they couldn't afford to dump it, so I guess they went to Kinko's or whatever and printed up these little stickers, slapped them on the bottles, and basically said, 'Look, there is nothing wrong with this beer. It's not going to hurt you. It is not terrible, but it's not up to par. So stick with me, and the next batch will be better,' something to that effect. And I remember seeing that and thinking, 'Wow, this guy is really committed to what he knows he can do, and I think that is pretty impressive. Or he's just a brilliant marketer,' and I know from knowing Jeff over the years that is not the case. He was just amazingly honest and committed to quality from the very beginning. I thought, 'That is something really unique. This industry is pretty cool, and it's getting going.' There are really interesting beers, and here is somebody who kind of threw the whole industry a curve ball by going out on the Belgian-style limb.'"[7]

Shireman became a partner in the Town Pump in 1992, then quit to work for New Belgium in late 1995. At that time the company was selling about 20,000 barrels a year in Colorado and part of Wyoming. New Belgium had been shipping beer to Washington State, Minnesota, and Washington,

DC, where Jordan's parents lived, but those ventures had not worked, so they pulled back. Shireman wanted to get out of the relatively crowded cities of the Front Range of the Rocky Mountains, and Jordan hired him to sell in the ski areas of western Colorado.

"Fat Tire took off—big time," Shireman said. By 1998 they had sold the equivalent of a million cases in Colorado, Arizona, New Mexico, Kansas, and Wyoming, most of it in Colorado and Arizona. The company couldn't afford to put sales representatives in each state, so New Belgium organized crew drives—weeklong sales efforts in which four or five sales personnel worked with distributor sales representatives. "The team just sort of built up over time," he said. "We got bigger and bigger, and the nonproduction side of the business split into sales, marketing, branding, eventing, Tour de Fat, and field quality. All of those, with the exception of branding, fell into my lap."

The Tour de Fat was a bicycle festival with outrageous costumes that captured the *Guinness Book of World Records* title for the largest bike parade. It was held in big cities of the states where New Belgium sold its products, and proceeds from the festivals went to local charities.

"When we went into the Pacific Northwest, Washington State was pretty loyal to Washington beers, and Oregon was very provincial, too," Shireman

J.B. Shireman, formerly Sales Manager of New Belgium, Shireman now works as Vice President of the First Beverage Group, an investment firm that works in the beer industry. Photograph courtesy of Angela Shireman

said. "Short of Sierra Nevada coming in and making some inroads, to my knowledge no out-of-state brewer made a major impact in those markets. But New Belgium did. In California we sold a million case equivalents in very short order, and we didn't have full distribution in the state. We weren't in chain retail actively enough to get ads and displays, and we had no big-box store business." The big chain supermarkets dominate business in most West Coast states, but Colorado law does not allow chain stores to sell beer. "We thought that chains were something you put on your car when it snows," Shireman said. But he went on the road for New Belgium and learned the chain business. Eventually he took the company into twenty-six states. "Jeff was good at allowing his people to take control," said Shireman. "Kim was always front and center no matter who she had around her, and is to this day, it seems."[8]

It was a heady time at New Belgium, and a fissure developed over the question of how fast to expand.

"There was a 'Grow versus no-grow debate in the brewery,'" Shireman said. "There was a faction that said 'we gotta strike while the iron is hot. We gotta go, we gotta blow to the East Coast. We gotta double down.' And there was another faction that said, 'Look, we are barely keeping our hands on this thing as it is.' Words to the effect of, 'I'll lay myself in front of the first truck that tries to cross the Mississippi River in the next five years.' Through that conversation we developed a 'trickle to the market' strategy that said we won't cross the Mississippi River for five years. We started infilling some core states. . . . We opened Nebraska and some other[s] . . . Arkansas, and that really primed the waters in Chicago. That . . . allowed us to build the infrastructure that we needed to handle and manage California and the competitiveness that was emerging in the Northwest and to continue to take care of Colorado, where they still are an extremely solid player."[9]

Shireman said he favored a go-slow approach because there was so much to learn about each state New Belgium entered. Also, many distributors in New Belgium's existing markets were consolidating. New Belgium was handled by liquor distributors in many markets, but some of those were being bought by beer distributors. One beer distributor was expanding especially rapidly; Reyes Holdings was buying many small beer distributors across the country. Shireman said at one point more than 70 percent of New Belgium's business was in flux.

"We were either buying our brand from liquor distributors and moving it into beer houses, or beer houses were buying one another, and we were caught in the consolidation. . . . That was a crazy time," he said. So how did New Belgium survive?

"I've said forever that I would rather be lucky than good. . . . But I don't think it was all luck," Shireman said. He attributes New Belgium's survival to a combination of an approachable beer, an interesting name, and a colorful label with a bicycle hand painted by a neighbor. "And . . . beer is such an emotional thing, and it's such a visceral purchase for people that you just look at that and you remember, 'I had a bike like that.' Who doesn't like riding a cool old bouncy-seat bike?"

At the start of their venture, Jordan and Lebesch went hiking in the Rocky Mountains and wrote down the vision of their company in a spiral notebook: "That is New Belgium—amazing efficiencies and ingenuity, MacGyvering things together with this huge heart and soul behind it." Shireman said, they've "given away one dollar per barrel in philanthropy in every state they've done business in for years, and so they didn't become successful and then decide we're going to be green and we're going to be groovy—they had that in their DNA from the beginning."

To Shireman, the outdoorsy nature of Colorado, the bicycling culture, and the 300 days of sunshine that the state enjoys all add to the aura that surrounds New Belgium, but, he added, "At the end of the day, man, it's like catching lightning in the bottle—POW!"

He said the magic of a brand is something that cannot be identified in a focus group.

"You've sat in on these focus groups: 'Why do you like Brooklyn Lager?' 'Oh, I like the taste.' That's bullshit. There's something there. There's some other little connection that reminds them of a trip that brought them to Brooklyn, or something. It's way deeper and more emotional than that. The short answer is who the hell knows? It's rarely one thing. It's a number of things that just happen to create the perfect platform for the brand to launch. People sit in a room and try to recreate that. You have to understand that your brand is in the hands of the consumer, particularly nowadays with social media and everything like that."

In 1996 Lebesch went to Belgium and hired brewmaster Peter Boukhart away from the Rodenbach Brewery. Lebesch stepped back from day-to-day operations and sat instead on the board of directors. He and Jordan divorced and he eventually sold his shares in the company to Jordan. Shireman left New Belgium in 2009 and now works as an industry consultant for First Beverage Group.[10]

Writing in the *New Brewer* in 2000, Tomme Arthur celebrated the creation of New Belgium's La Folie, a sour ale that he said combined all the best aspects of various Belgian brewing traditions: the acidity of a young Rodenbach, the yellow haze of lambic, and the thirst-quenching tartness of Timmermans.

"I loved it," Arthur wrote. "For in it, I consumed the spirit of discovery and the experimentation wherein each of us can be a modern-day Columbus or Einstein in the brewing world. As history has taught us, greatness finds those who are not afraid to explore and experiment. We should not be afraid to fail. Even the greatest authors have failed more than once. Not all of Shakespeare's tragedies are considered successes. Remember, there is no substitute for experience and the best experience comes from experimenting."[11]

AS NEW BELGIUM TOOK HOLD IN THE WEST, ANOTHER BELGIAN-FOCUSED BREWERY was born on the East Coast. Rob Tod started Allagash Brewing Company in Portland, Maine, in 1994. He had graduated from Middlebury College in Vermont with a major in geology and a minor in music. He worked odd jobs in Colorado for a couple of years, mostly in construction. "I missed New England and came back to Vermont not knowing what I was going to do," Tod said. "I moved in with a friend, and another friend said he was working at Otter Creek Brewing in Middlebury, Vermont, and his boss said he was looking for a part-time keg washer.

"So I got in late one night, and the next day I was at the brewery at 8 a.m. I just fell in love with the place. It had tanks and pumps and electrical equipment—all the stuff I loved. I learned welding in high school, working on an old car the teacher owned. I just stepped into that brewery, and it was fascinating to me."

He said the brewery had both a scientific aspect and a creative aspect. "Beer and brewing," he said, "encompassed everything."

"In two days I went from not knowing anything about these little brewery businesses to knowing exactly what I wanted to do with my life. I called my parents and told them I knew what I wanted to do: I wanted to make beer. There was literally a thirty-second pause, and my mother said, 'One of these days you're going to have to stop living in a fantasy world.'"[12]

Nonetheless his parents cosigned loans to help him buy equipment and invested in the company, which he started in Portland, Maine. He focused on

Rob Tod of Allagash Brewing Company. Photograph courtesy of Alagash Brewing Company.

Belgian-style beers because he wanted to differentiate himself from the first wave of craft brewers, who were making ales and lagers.

He planned to keep things very simple, do it all himself. He didn't hire anyone for two years. "I didn't want employees. I wanted as few things as possible for me to screw up," he said. "I wanted to do something different, and it seemed to me the Belgian styles did that. The only people making Belgian beers were Unibrew in Canada and New Belgium in Colorado. I was in the business to give people a new experience with beer. We did that, but unfortunately no one wanted to drink it. I would pour it for bartenders in Maine, and they would see it was cloudy and say, 'What's wrong with it?'"

Tod said his approach to the brewery and to the product were naive, and his work ethic tested the patience of his wife and daughter. "I did everything myself. I am quite sure I could never do it again. I just wouldn't have the energy to do it again. I remember one Christmas Eve I had to go to the brewery to repair a pump. The next morning we opened presents with our daughter, and then I had to head back into the brewery to work on that pump. It was that way every weekend those first two years."

He started with a few draft accounts: The Great Lost Bear, Three Dollar Deweys, Brian Boru Public House, and Fore Street Restaurant, all in

Portland, Maine. "Those first retail accounts were very supportive, but they couldn't control what people ordered," he said. "They kept us on draft in spite of our being the slowest-moving, the most vulnerable, beer on tap. They said, 'It's not going to sell, but I'll put it on tap.' They were right. It didn't sell, but they kept me on tap, and eventually people learned about the beer. It sure sells now."

He said in the mid-1990s distributors were convinced that American craft beer was dying and Americans were moving to imports. He called all the distributors in surrounding states and they wouldn't even meet with him. "I would say, 'I'm going to be in your town next Friday, can you give me twenty minutes?'" he said. "They would reply, 'I'll meet you, but I don't have much time.' In the meetings the distributors would invariably say, 'Why don't you brew something more accessible so you can do some volume?'"

In the important Massachusetts market he went with International Beverages, a small distributor of British, German, and Belgian imported beers that was later acquired by Brooklyn Brewery's Craft Brewers Guild distributor. "I went with International Beverages because I knew you guys were going to buy it," Tod said. "I think I was the only American craft beer in the house when you took it over." Allagash is now one of the great success stories in the Craft Brewers Guild distribution network, now owned by Jerry Sheehan, one of the country's largest Anheuser-Busch (AB) distributors.

"Now wholesalers are eager to get Allagash beers," Tod said. "After fifteen years I became an overnight success."[13] Today many beer drinkers know that a Belgian-style wit, or wheat beer, is meant to be cloudy.

Allagash White now accounts for 80 percent of Tod's business, but the other 20 percent is just as important to his company. Allagash Black is a stout fermented with a Belgian yeast and has 7 percent alcohol by volume (ABV); Allagash Tripel is a Belgian-style tripel; Allagash Curieux (*curieux* means curious in French) is a tripel that is fermented in Jim Beam bourbon barrels and then supplemented with a small dose of tripel that enhances its bourbon character.

Tod also does many one-off beers every year: sour beers, beers brewed with cabernet franc and chardonnay grapes, beers brewed with red currants, beers aged in oak barrels, whisky barrels, rum barrels, beers inoculated with *Lactobacillus* and *Pediococcus*. "We do a ton of one-offs," Tod said. "We'll do a dozen this year alone. Innovation is a big part of our business culture. It keeps things interesting for our customers and our employees. It is a huge motivator."

"I think social media has been a huge driver for our category. Social media gives us a chance to open a little window into our brewery so people all over the world can see what we are doing," he said. "We can do 500 bottles of a one-off, and thousands of people know about it."[14]

BACK OUT WEST, ONE OF THE MOST QUINTESSENTIALLY ARTISANAL CRAFT BREWER-
ies was getting its start, fittingly, in a winery. Vinnie Cilurzo left college in San Diego to work in his family's winery in Temecula, California, in 1989. His father, a lighting director working in Hollywood, poured all his extra cash into the winery, which he operated with Cilurzo's mother. Cilurzo took up homebrewing as a hobby and took some brewing courses at University of California, Davis.

A few years later, in 1994, he and a friend, Dave Stovall, founded the Blind Pig, a microbrewery named for a Prohibition-era speakeasy in Temecula. But it was small and the equipment crude. "We made a lot of mistakes with the Blind Pig," Cilurzo said. "We were poorly financed, and though our beers were amazing when fresh, they had no shelf life. But all those mistakes helped make our success later at Russian River. You've got to learn from your mistakes."

The Blind Pig was a so-called Frankenbrewery, parts cobbled together from a defunct brewery—old dairy equipment, plastic tanks, and old pumps. The first beer made at the Blind Pig was a strong India pale ale that Cilurzo and Stovall called Inaugural Ale. "In general, I knew what I was doing because of my experience with the winery, but I had never really brewed a commercial batch of beer on my own," Cilurzo said. "The idea was, we would double the hops to cover up any flaws in the beer. In the end the beer turned out pretty nice."[15]

With that plan he invented the first double India pale ale. After struggling at the Blind Pig for three years, he sold his shares and moved on to work on a microbrewery that Korbel Champagne Cellars was starting. "Korbel was expanding, acquiring other wineries, so they left me alone at the microbrewery," Cilurzo said. "It was at Korbel that some of what are now considered innovative beers were born. I could do anything I wanted, so I got into making Belgian-style beers, aging some beers in wine barrels, and brewed a double IPA again."

The first version of his famous Pliny the Elder double IPA was sold only on draft. He would not bottle Pliny until 2008. They bottled the 8 percent

ABV Pliny in 500ml bottles, with a crown cap. "You have to drink Pliny when it is fresh," he said. "We use a cork for our Belgian-inspired beers as well as for our sour-barrel-aged beers. In general our crown-finished beers do not age well, while our cork-finished beers can handle some age, particularly the sour-barrel-aged beers."

He started using the wild yeast *Brettanomyces* in some of his concoctions in 1999, when he was still at Korbel. "Most winemakers don't want *Brettanomyces* in their winery because it can ruin the wine, but I wanted to make sour beers like the Belgians," Cilurzo said. He said that New Belgium's brewmaster Peter Boukhart, creator of New Belgium's famous sour beer La Folie, advised him on the processes. "I would ask Peter a question, and he could only give me a nibble of an answer," Cilurzo said. "It really made me think for myself and helped me create what became the Russian River sour program of today. I didn't want to copy New Belgium."[16]

Both Cilurzo and Tomme Arthur learned from Boukhart. "He was our mentor, a huge influence," Cilurzo said. Before they were married he and Natalie bought the brewery from Korbel and opened a brewpub named Russian River Brewing Company in 2004 in Santa Rosa, California. Cilurzo developed three year-round beers in addition to Pliny—Temptation, which is fermented in chardonnay barrels; Supplication, fermented in pinot noir barrels with sour cherries; and Consecration, fermented in cabernet sauvignon barrels with currants. Pliny sells for $4.50 to $5 per bottle wholesale and is 60 percent of Russian River's business. In 2013 the brewery expected to produce about 15,000 barrels. Another 10 percent of its business is sour-barrel-aged beers. Russian River's pub, which employs about sixty-five people, sells about 2,500 barrels of the sour beer. Seven or eight people work in the laboratory, brewing, and packaging operations. The brewers manage a twenty-barrel brewhouse at the pub and a fifty-barrel brewhouse at the production brewery, where about 600 wine barrels are used to age their beer. The wine barrels are used three times because repeated use drains the barrels of their vinous flavors and aromas. They keep the two original wine barrels as a reminder of their roots.

Twice a year Russian River makes a 10.5 percent ABV triple IPA called Pliny the Younger (PTY), a draft-only beer. "It is available for two weeks at our pub starting the first Friday in February, so people can always count on the release date," Cilurzo said. "The recipe is a bigger version of Pliny the Elder with the emphasis on Simcoe and Amarillo hops, both of which have a strong, fruit-driven character, which helps balance the beer's higher ABV.

One of the unique qualities of PTY is that it is dry-hopped four times. [A process in which hops is added to the fermenting beer, providing the beer with its pronounced hop aroma.] PTY has become a giant deal for Russian River. For two weeks straight we have a line to get into the pub. It is really incredible. People come from all over the United States, and even the world, each year to drink the beer."[17]

The Sonoma County Economic Development Board is working on an economic impact study of those two weeks. Preliminary results indicate that the occasion generates more than $1.5 million in economic activity for the area.[18]

"It's crazy to think what is going on in the American craft beer movement today," Cilurzo said. "Natalie and I were just in the Midwest visiting Bell's and New Glarus. We are planning to get out to Brooklyn to see what Garrett is doing. We are on a fact-finding mission to figure out how much we want to grow. We are thinking maybe we want to grow to 25,000 or 30,000 barrels. We don't want to get much bigger than that. I'm not sure we buy into the mind-set that you have to keep growing."

Vinnie and Natalie Cilurzo of Russian River Brewing Company.

Cilurzo said he and Natalie think more like winemakers than brewers. They distribute their own beer locally and sell in four states. Eighty percent of their beer is sold in California. Their most famous beers are high-alcohol beers, but a lot of the beer sold in the pub is less than 6 percent alcohol.

Innovation is in Russian River's DNA, but Cilurzo says it is not a deliberate process. "I don't think a brewer can be innovative if they are trying to be. It just happens, kind of spontaneously. You just follow your instincts. Natalie and I feel blessed that we have been able to make these double IPAs and barrel-aged beers. . . . Growing up in a small business environment helped."

AS EVERY STUDENT OF BEER KNOWS, HOPS ARE THE SEASONING OF THE BEER, THE wonderfully alluring green cone-like flowers that impart bitterness and aroma to the sweet barley porridge that is the meat of beer. Brewers on the West Coast worship hops, and their enthusiasm for this pungent cousin of marijuana has spread across America to make the most traditional hop-forward style, the IPA, the number one style of craft beer in the country.[19]

In 1849 California became the epicenter of the gold rush; today, it is ground zero for the hop rush.

It all started with Sierra Nevada Pale Ale, the first beer brewed commercially by the pioneering Ken Grossman and still his best-selling beer. Grossman's pale ale put the Cascade hop on the map. But the West Coast brewers who followed Grossman have taken hops, as measured by International Bitterness Units (IBU), a measure of the hop flavors in a beer), to dizzying heights.

Vinnie Cilurzo acknowledged he had overhopped his first India pale ale in an attempt to mask any off flavors from his primitive brewing system. In doing so he accidentally created the first double IPA.

Experimentation also proved serendipitous for Greg Koch and Steve Wagner, when they were putting together the Stone Brewing Co. in Escondido, California, north of San Diego. It was destined to become one of the most successful brewing startups of the 1990s. In *The Craft of Stone Brewing Co.* Koch and Wagner confess that the home-brewed ale that became Arrogant Bastard Ale and propelled Stone to fame in the craft brewing world, started with a mistake.

Greg Koch recalls that Wagner exclaimed "Aw, hell!" as he brewed an ale on his brand spanking new home-brewing system. "I miscalculated and added the ingredients in the wrong percentages," he told Koch. "And not just

*Greg Koch and Steve Wagner, founders of Stone Brewery. Photograph ©
Stone Brewing Co.*

a little. There's a *lot* of extra malt and hops in there." Koch recalls suggesting
they dump it, but Wagner decided to let it ferment and see what it tasted like.

They both loved the resulting hops bomb, but they didn't know what
to do with it. Koch was sure that nobody was "going to be able to handle it.
I mean, we both loved it, but it was unlike *anything* else that was out there.
We weren't sure what we were going to do with it, but we knew we had to do
something with it somewhere down the road."[20]

Koch said the beer literally introduced itself as Arrogant Bastard Ale. It
seemed ironic to me that a beer from southern California, the world of laid
back surfers, should produce an ale with a name that many would identify
with New York City. But such are the ironies of the craft brewing revolution.

Arrogant Bastard was relegated to the closet for the first year of Stone
Brewing Co.'s existence. The founders figured their more commercial brew
would be Stone Pale Ale, but its first-year sales figures were not strong, and
the company's board of directors decided to release Arrogant Bastard.

"They thought it would help us have more of a billboard effect; with
more Stone bottles next to each other on a retail shelf, they become that
much more visible, and it sends a message that we're a respected, established
brewery with a diverse range of beers," Wagner writes. Once they decided to
release the Arrogant Bastard, they decided to go all out. The copy on the back
label of Arrogant Bastard has become famous in the beer world:

ARROGANT BASTARD ALE

Ar-ro-gance (ar'ogans) n.

The act or quality of being arrogant; haughty;
Undue assumption; overbearing conceit.

This is an aggressive ale. You probably won't like it. It is quite doubtful that you have the taste or sophistication to be able to appreciate an ale of this quality and depth. We would suggest that you stick to safer and more familiar territory—maybe something with a multi-million dollar ad campaign aimed at convincing you it's made in a little brewery, or one that implies that their tasteless fizzy yellow beverage will give you more sex appeal.

The label continues along these lines for a couple of hundred words. Some call it a brilliant piece of reverse psychology. But Koch insists he was just listening to the beer that had emerged from a mistake in Wagner's kitchen.

In addition to innovative beers and marketing, Koch and Wagner have also made their San Diego brewery a tourist destination, with the Stone Brewing Bistro & Gardens, with plans to add a hotel to the Stone empire.

SAM CALAGIONE OF DOGFISH HEAD BREWERY IN MILTON, DELAWARE, TOOK HIS EX-perimentation in a different direction. We met in the early 1990s, when he was tending bar at a craft-focused restaurant on Manhattan's Upper West Side, Nacho Mama's. "You were one of the first microbrewers to come in and do a beer promo for us," Calagione said. "That was where I learned about beer outside the light lager juggernaut. I really started enjoying your beers and New Amsterdam, New England, Celis, Pike Place, Sierra Celebration—those were the beers that I cut my teeth on." He bought home-brewing equipment at the Little Shop of Hops in the city and started making his own beer. He reasoned that the first and second generation of craft brewers were all making beers based on traditional Old World styles, albeit using fresh local ingredients and no corn or rice adjuncts. He wanted to do something different.

"I said I am not going to stand out in that crowd, so instead I went the culinary route and started looking at what Alice Waters and James Beard were doing with American cuisine," he said. "We don't have to genuflect to Old World culinary traditions. America grows these beautiful ingredients, so let's celebrate that. So 'Off-centered ales for Off-centered people' was built around 'let's look at the whole culinary landscape for potential beer ingredients' instead of existing traditional beer styles."

Sam Calagione of Dogfish Head Brewery. Photograph courtesy of Dogfish Head Craft Brewery.

Calagione purchased a ten-gallon brewing system and crafted his own fermenters from used beer kegs. His first beer was Indian Brown Ale, a rich dark ale fortified with brown sugar. The next beer was Aprihop, an IPA with apricot flavors. Then came Immort Ale, which used maple syrup from his family's farm in western Massachusetts, peat-smoked barley, juniper berries, and vanilla, and Chicory Stout, made with roasted chicory, coffee, and licorice root. He always introduced beers in pairs to gain some economies of scale and to reduce the chance that a single introduction would flop. "That's what we opened with at the restaurant in 1995," Calagione said. "Shelter Pale Ale—that was our concession to tradition for when people came in and asked for a Bud Light." With this eclectic and unusual portfolio, they struggled.

Two years later he cobbled a thirty-barrel brewery together from old yogurt and cannery equipment. From 1997–99 Calagione lost money on beer production. "Dogfish would have been bankrupt if it were not for our restaurant," he said. "It took all the profits from our restaurant to keep our production brewery going. Bankrupt because, in that era, trying to sell a $12 six-pack of maple syrup–infused, oak-aged Immort Ale—there were hardly any takers, but we never dumbed down our beers, we never discounted our beers."[21]

Then, sometime around the millennium, Calagione's "off-centered ales" caught the attention of *Food & Wine* magazine and then NBC's *Today* show. Calagione's engaging personality and rugged good looks didn't hurt. Shortly thereafter his Raison D'Etre, brewed with beet sugar, green raisins, and a Belgian yeast, won *BeerAdvocate*'s Beer of the Year. "Those little moments sort of changed our trajectory, and I think we have had double-digit growth every year since 2000," Calagione said.

Calagione's best-selling beer is his 60 Minute IPA, part of a series that also includes a 90 Minute IPA and a 120 Minute IPA. These beers are born of a special technique of hopping that Calagione developed himself.

"I was watching a chef show on TV, and the chef was talking about adding little bits of pepper, little pinches, the entire time the soup simmered," he said. "The chef said if you added that same volume all at once, it would have been crushingly bitter and with dislocated flavor. And that was what got me thinking: What if I applied that chef's technique to hopping? Because traditionally hopping happened in a few big increments, one early for bitter, one late for aroma."

Ever the tinkerer, Calagione rigged up one of those old-fashioned toy football games that sets the plastic players in action by vibrating the metal playing field. He dumped hops onto the field and allowed the vibration to slowly feed the hops into the brew kettle during the boil. Instead of dumping hops in early in the boil for flavor, and then later for aroma, he slowly boiled the hops into the wort. This went on for ninety minutes, producing a beer that was 9 percent ABV and 90 IBUs. In 1999 he released the 90 Minute IPA in draft only, along with Midas Touch, a wine and mead concoction made with ingredients found in drinking vessels from the tomb of King Midas.

He started bottling the 90 Minute the next year and called it an imperial IPA on the label, thus creating a new beer style. He started brewing 60 Minute IPA in 2002 because he reasoned that he needed a less alcoholic beer for people who wanted more than one.

"I learned that, by doing those tiny doses, we could make a beer that was incredibly hoppy but didn't have that crushing end bitterness that a lot of IPA drinkers, and particularly West Coast brewers, love, so ours was well differentiated, and continual hopping also led to a flavor profile that was pretty unique in the context of West Coast IPAs," he said.[22]

He was not copying the west coast brewers but rather was reviving an IPA style that had been championed at the Ballantine Brewery in Newark, New Jersey. I recall drinking Ballantine India Pale Ale in the 1970. It was one of the few mass-produced beers that had a pronounced hop flavor. It seemed to be stronger than most light lagers, too.

"Ballantine also did a beer called Burton Ale, which they never even sold," Calagione said. "It was only for VIPs and distributors, and they would age it in wood tanks. It was something like 10 ABV, huge IBUs, Ballantine Burton Ale, so if you talk about the birth moment of the American extreme beer movement, Dogfish gets some credit for the modern version, but Ballantine was doing wood-aged 100 IBU high-end beers that they didn't even sell—talk about white whales. If there was a *BeerAdvocate* in that era, that would be the holy grail."

Dogfish now brews Burton Baton, an IPA aged in wood tanks. "That is our way of saying we want to take the baton from this once-mighty, hoppy East Coast, wood-aged beer brewer [Ballantine]. We are defending our heritage against the West Coast hop snobs. We want to give credit where credit is due."

Calagione has a good-natured rivalry going with West Coast IPA brewers like Russian River's Cilurzo, Pizza Port's Arthur, and Stone's Koch and Wagner. The rivalry came to a head when Dave Alexander, owner of the beloved Brickskeller and RFD (Regional Food and Drink) in Washington, DC, proposed a Lupulin Slam, with a team of West Coast brewers meeting a team of East Coast brewers to determine who makes the best and biggest IPA. (Lupulin is the active ingredient in hops.)

The west was represented by Pizza Port, Oggi's, and Avery. Calagione enlisted Old Dominion and Capitol City breweries to represent the east and designed a secret weapon for the slam. He found a strange-looking filter that he suspected was pharmaceutical equipment at a food-grade scrapyard near his brewery. He redesigned it to be a pressurized hop filter and ran a finished 120 Minute IPA through it. He called the contraption Randall the Enamel Animal (*enamel* in honor of the gritty feel that excessive hops give your teeth) and brought it to the Lupulin Slam. "And we ended up beating all these West Coast brewers with [a] Randallized 120 [Minute IPA]," Calagione said. That night Alexander ordered one of the devices for RFD, and Tom Nickel, owner of O'Brien's in San Diego, ordered two. Calagione since has sold about 300 Randalls to bars and restaurants, and 1,000 smaller versions, called Randall Juniors, for home use. "It's great because you can use it for spicing and hopping," Calagione said. "And beer lovers get to see how hops affect their beer, so it is great for demystifying the beer process. It's a good educational tool."

Calagione has done much to educate Americans about craft beer. His Discovery Channel television series *Brew Masters* aired from November 2010 to March 2011. He routinely does tastings and dinners with his wine-beer hybrids and his ancient ales line of historical revivals. Dogfish planned to package thirty-seven different beers in 2013, but Calagione is planning to step back a bit in the future.

"My coworkers pretty much staged an intervention and said this is just not scalable," he said. "So they asked me to hiatus five or six of [the beers], and just do them every two or three years because inventorying all that packaging and those ingredients means the cost side of our business is pretty different than most breweries.'"[23]

60 Minute IPA represents 48 percent of Dogfish's volume, but Calagione does not want it growing beyond that because the soul of Dogfish is innovation. "We like to push the envelope and create niches where we see opportunities," he said. "Niches that get us closer to the highest culinary and wine communities, because we are always trying to prove that beer deserves to be in that world. I give Garrett a lot of credit for doing a lot of work in that realm as well. But for us, that is why we opened as a brewpub, because we were brewing these complex wine-like beers. We wanted to have that direction conversation, that yes, this doesn't exist as a style, but here is why we did it."[24]

AT THE BROOKLYN BREWERY THE DRIVER OF INNOVATION IS GARRETT OLIVER, WHO joined the brewery in 1994 and introduced Brooklyn Black Chocolate Stout, a Russian imperial stout with 10 percent ABV. At the time this traditional style, first brewed for the court of Russia's Catherine the Great, pushed the envelope of taste and alcohol content, and it remains one of the brewery's most popular and well-known beers. The beer writer Michael Jackson noted it was the first beer to connect with chocolate, although its chocolate flavors came from roasted malts, not from cocoa.

Oliver also undertook a series of collaborations that were among the first ever by an American brewer. The first was Brooklyn Bridge Bitter, brewed with W.H. Brakspear & Sons at Henley on Thames, a regional brewery made famous by the patronage of the Beatle George Harrison. Oliver also did collaborations with the Kelham Island Brewery and JW Lees in England, La Chouffe in Belgium, and the Schneider Weisse Brewery in Bavaria.

"More than anything else it was an idea that we wanted to be out there in the world," Oliver said of the collaborations. "I kind of felt like, as American brewers . . . when you went traveling—and we went traveling all the time— you would tell people, 'Hey, I'm an American brewer,' and if anything they just looked sorry for you. The collaborations were a way of showcasing the invention of America's craft beer revolution."[25]

Oliver shook up the British brewing world in 1994 with a speech on IPAs in Whitbread's Porter Tun Room in London. The event was sponsored by the British Guild of Beer Writers. Oliver was still working at Manhattan Brewery. He served a strong IPA called Rough Draft to the audience of more than one hundred brewers and beer writers, representing most of the UK beer industry.

"I kind of knew they had brought me there to roll a grenade into the room, and I was happy to oblige," Oliver said. He told the gathering that he had fallen in love with beer on his first trip to England but added that the 3.5 percent ABV IPAs that were being brewed in England were nothing like the strong beers first brewed by the British brewer George Hodgson in the 1820s. Those were closer to 6 to 7 percent ABV and very strongly hopped. Oliver told the gathering "'Nobody in the UK is making IPA. We make IPA in America,' and there was great harrumphing in the room. People tasted the beers and said, 'Well, this is very interesting and amusing, but no one is ever going to drink something like this.' But then within a year, maybe two years, very quietly, the IPAs started to come out of England from some of the old-line brewers, particularly Samuel Smith's. They were pretty early in with their SS India Ale, which maybe wasn't quite as assertive as an American IPA. Whether or not the speech was a trigger for this, it really made an impression on them."[26]

I am reminded of what Madonna once said about the American rock band Green Day: they sound like Americans trying to sound like Brits trying to sound like Americans. "It's a British style, taken up by Americans, and then British brewers have taken up the American style of IPA, which they then sell back to us," Oliver said.

When Oliver joined Brooklyn Brewery, we were still distributing most of the great beers of Belgium, and we often talked about brewing Belgian-style beers in Brooklyn. We visited many of these breweries in the 1990s. In 2004 we decided to buy a bottling line to do 100 percent bottle-conditioned beers like those brewed by some of the Trappist breweries in Belgium. Oliver attended a seminar on bottle conditioning at the Craft Brewers Conference and learned that Bert Van Hecke, the young brewer at the St. Bernardus monastery in Belgium, was the only one doing 100 percent conditioning in the bottle. Others were starting with partially carbonated beer.

Oliver tried to find literature about bottle conditioning, but there was none. "When I started looking around, I couldn't find anything about how to do it," he said. "There was lots of stuff on homebrewing, but this was clearly different. I started to ask brewing professors at Weihenstephan and Doemens in Munich and at Catholic University of Leuven, 'Well, do you have materials that you teach this from? I'll have it translated.' They said no, we don't teach this, like nobody teaches this. This stuff is . . . passed down in families and in companies, and there is nowhere to learn about it. To me this was completely fascinating. I have never really seen anything like this."

During one of his trips to Belgium locals invited Oliver to tour St. Bernardus, but he was rebuffed by the managing director, who told him, "We find that American brewers are coming to Belgium, and they are stealing all our ideas, and they are ripping us off."[27]

Oliver contacted Van Hecke in 2003 and found he was leaving St. Bernardus to go to work for a large industrial brewery called Martin House Brewing Company. "I said, 'Have you ever been to New York City?'" Oliver recalled. "He said no. I said, 'How about this? You come over here, spend four days with us, teach us this stuff, and I will take you around New York City and show you a good time and pay you for your work.'"

Oliver prepared his brewing staff for a descent into the unknown world of bottle conditioning. "I told the brewing staff, 'We are going to go from being competent to being incompetent. And this is going to make you and me and all of us really unhappy. And in a certain way, it is going to be awful. But here is the thing: Everybody be nice to each other. Everybody try to help everybody else get along. Realize the guy next to you doesn't know what he is doing, either. And it is going to mess with our heads. But on the other side of this, we are going to become competent again, and once we arrive there, we are going to be in a whole different place. And I need you to trust me on this. We are taking a leap out into thin air, but we are going to make it.' And we did. It was in a way the coolest thing we ever did. You talk about entrepreneurship—I don't have that experience, but that is my version of it."

The result was Brooklyn Local 1, one of the few beers ever to be rated A+ by *BeerAdvocate*.

"People often ask me what is my favorite beer, and I have a different answer every time," Oliver said. "But for me, Local 1 was a turning point for the brewery. It's when we became who we are now. You spend your professional life trying to be the person who you have been pretending to be all along. I felt we were a really good brewery and we were pretending to be a brilliant brewery. We puffed ourselves up and we filled that space—we're not the only ones, everybody did it. I kind of felt like when we did Local 1, that is when we started to get at least somewhere close to who we believed we were."[28]

Boston Beer Company's contribution to innovation has been the production of extreme beers, like Samuel Adams Utopias, a beer that CEO Jim Koch describes as somewhere between a vintage port, a fine sherry, and an old cognac with a nose that "explodes into the room." At 27 percent ABV, it is, he says, "the strongest naturally fermented beer ever made." He introduced Utopias in 2002. It is a blend of beers chosen from a library of oak-aged beers first brewed in 1994 as an 18 percent ABV beer called Samuel Adams Triple Bock. He calls it "the lunatic fringe" of the beer world. It is released every two years and packaged in a copper-clad bottle shaped like a brew kettle. Koch continues to push the envelope.[29]

ONE OF THE GREAT SUCCESS STORIES AMONG THE 1990s STARTUPS IS OSKAR BLUES, a restaurant high up in the Rocky Mountains, founded in 1997 by Dale Katechis, who describes himself as a restaurateur and a mediocre homebrewer. Katechis had the courage to do what no craft brewer had done before: package all his beer in aluminum cans. In 2013 Oskar Blues will sell 125,000 barrels at breweries in Colorado and North Carolina. And Katechis is the first to acknowledge that much of his success can be attributed to chance encounters and good old luck.

"In November 2002 we sold our first can of beer," Katechis said. "At the time no one was marketing canned craft beer. There is a list of people (Brooklyn Brewery included) who had done some contracting of cans. At the time there was nothing on the market and I think the industry even—we saw cans as an opportunity to market the restaurant. I really had no ambition of, you know, having a brewery and packaging canned beer, other than to market the restaurant. We could buy this little machine, this two-at-a-time can machine, and package some of our beer and drive it up to liquor stores and beer stores, and it would drive people up to our restaurant, because being in a town that

Dale Katechis of Oskar Blues on his original canning line. Photograph courtesy of Oskar Blues Brewery.

was at the time 1,600 people, we needed to create a destination, a reason for people to come up to Lyons. That was one thought."[30]

His customers loved it, and people flocked to Lyons, as he had hoped. Katechis said he learned that the canned beer was superior to bottled beer. It kept out the light, and it got cold more quickly. So he bought a bigger canning line and a truckload of cans and signed up some distributors. Dale's Pale Ale, based on his home-brewing recipe, took off, "and the next thing we knew, we had created this beer company. That is how it happened," he said.

"Dale's Pale Ale is a beer I first brewed in a bathtub as a home brewer in college," Katechis said. "I had gotten a home-brew kit for Christmas 1990 and just fell in love with the whole art and science of it. I would say I was probably a mediocre home brewer at best, at my peak, but I was intrigued by the business side of it. . . . I've never been accused of being meticulous about anything, and . . . brewers need to be meticulous. And so it was important that I go out and find brewers that were much better at it than I. I guess I am a restaurant guy, and that is always where my passion had been. But there were a lot of things about the beer business, and making beer, that kind of translated."[31]

Katechis now runs three restaurants in Colorado and the brewery in North Carolina, employing fourteen people on the brewery side and 200 in the restaurants.[32] It wasn't a career he would have predicted for himself. After he graduated from Auburn University in Alabama in 1993, he and his then-girlfriend, Christy, headed to Montana. "My dream was to be a fly-fishing guide, but we landed in Boulder to visit a friend . . . ran out of money, and got jobs." He worked at a backpack manufacturing company and tended bar at the Old Chicago restaurant. He and Christy married and now have four children.

"One day I was riding my bike from the backpack company to the restaurant, and I smelled beer brewing," Katechis said. "I was homebrewing at that time, and I stopped into this little storage shed, and there was a guy in there by the name of Gordon Knight, brewing beer. We struck up a friendship, and I think that was probably . . . the first time I thought, 'That might be something I would want to do for a living,' because it looked like a great job."

Gordon Knight is well known in Colorado for winning gold medals at the Great American Beer Festival for three different breweries—High Country, Estes Park, and Wolf Tongue. "Knight brewed a beer called Renegade Red, and it was kind of an inspiration for a beer that we ultimately ended up naming after him, which is still in our lineup," Katechis said. "It's called G'Knight." Originally, it was named Gordon's, until Gordon Biersch Brewing Company objected.[33]

MANY FIRST-GENERATION CRAFT BREWERS ARE LOOKING TO VERTICALLY INTEGRATE their breweries by cultivating their own malted barley and hops—a practice that addresses the consumer's desire for local beer and builds connections with local farmers, who are always looking for customers for good cash crops. Anchor, Sierra Nevada, Rogue, Brooklyn, and many others are growing hops, barley, and wheat or commissioning crops from local farmers in their regions.

Larry Bell, CEO of Bell's Brewery in Kalamazoo, Michigan, started buying local hops for some of his beers in the late 1980s. In 2008 he bought a farm and started growing barley. In 2013 he planted 160 acres of barley. Each acre yields fifty barrels of beer.

"I was contacted by a farmer who was growing grain for Busch Agriculture [an AB subsidiary], and he kind of got frustrated working with them and called me and said, 'How about I grow for you instead?' I checked him out, and he sounded good, and then a farm became available next to his, and he said, 'Why don't you buy it, and I will manage it?' So we did that and adapted it for barley, and we are growing two-row barley up there."[34]

Larry Bell of Bell's Brewery. Photograph courtesy of Bell's Brewery.

One problem many craft brewers have encountered is the absence of a malting facility to process the raw barley. That is not a problem for Bell's, which has its malting done at Briess Malt & Ingredients Co. in Chilton, Wisconsin. Oberon, a wheat beer, is Bell's biggest brand and accounts for 45 percent of their sales volume. Next comes Two-Hearted Ale at 25 percent. So far, the local ingredients are used in seasonal and specialty beers but that could change if the quality and quantity of the local grain increases.

"Our Christmas Beer is 100 percent of the Michigan-grown malt," Bell said. "We converted our pale ale to be called Midwestern Pale Ale, and we are using a little bit of the homegrown barley in that. We have a picture of the farm on the label now. . . . We make a Harvest Ale in the fall with 100 percent Michigan malt and 100 percent Michigan hops. I think last year we made, like, forty-five barrels of it." The Harvest Ale is sold at Bell's brewpub in Kalamazoo.

Bell makes some hoppy beers, like Hoptimum, but he says his hoppy beers are not aiming at bitterness but rather strong hop flavors. "I think we have always been more about balance than the indiscriminate use of hops. We're making a Berliner Weisse style that is slowly catching on. It's hard to find the hop in that thing. We like doing other styles. We are in the bread-basket of the country; let's do some things that feature malt, too. For us it's about balance; the old three-pint rule."[35] A good pint should make you want to drink three more.

At Brooklyn Brewery, Mary Wiles, the assistant brewmaster who oversees our production at the Saranac Brewery in Utica, is growing hops and barley on her farm near Syracuse. In June 2013 we did a wheat beer with GROWnyc, the company that oversees New York City's fifty-six farmers' markets. Brooklyn Greenmarket Wheat Beer is made with 70 percent New York-grown wheat. The wheat comes from the third-generation farm of Peter Martins, of Penn Yan, New York. Some proceeds from sale of the beer go to GROWnyc.

Innovation is a hallmark of the craft beer revolution. The excitement that craft beer has brought to the American brewing industry has spread around the world. Craft brewers can be found in virtually every country in the world today, even the pariah state of North Korea. All are struggling against the domination of their home markets by light lager beers produced by large breweries, many of them owned by the four largest brewing companies in the world—AB InBev, SABMiller, Heineken, and Carlsberg.

Fritz Maytag and Ken Grossman at the 2011 Craft Brewers Conference. Photograph © Jason E. Kaplan.

The 2009 Beer Institute board of directors: President Jeff Becker, Dan Tearno of Heineken, Carlos Fernandez of Modelo, Steve Hindy of Brooklyn, Tom Long of MillerCoors, Dave Peacock of AB InBev, and Bill Hackett of Crown Imports (Modelo). Photograph courtesy of the Beer Institute.

Matthew Reich, founder of the New Amsterdam Brewery, and brewing chemist Joe Owades.

Charlie Papazian at the "Beer and Steer" in the 1970s. Photograph courtesy of Charlie Papazian.

Jack McAuliffe, New Albion founder, and Jim Koch, Boston Beer founder, recreate New Albion Ale. Photograph courtesy of the Boston Beer Company and Modern Brewery Age.

Charlie Papazion, president of the Brewers Association, and Daniel Bradford, publisher of All About Beer. *Photograph courtesy of the Brewers Association.*

British beer writer Michael Jackson and Brooklyn's brewmaster Garrett Oliver. Photograph courtesy of the Brewers Association.

Jerome Chicvara, cofounder of Full Sail Brewing Company.

Photo © Tom Dalldorf

Jerry Sheehan, owner of L. Knife and Son distribution.

The Brewers Association Staff with Chief Operating Officer Bob Pease front and center. Photograph courtesy of the Brewers Association.

Reyes Holdings first warehouse in Spartanburg, South Carolina. Photograph courtesy of Reyes Holdings LLC.

Todd and Jason Alstrom of Beer Advocate. *Photograph by Taylor Seidler (*Beer Advocate*).*

Henry King, former president of the US Brewers Association and the Brewers Association of America.

Howard and Robert Hallam of Ben E. Keith Distributing Company.

CHAPTER SEVEN

BEER AND THE MEDIA

IN THE WAKE OF THE CRAFT BEER REVOLUTION CAME A PROLIFERATION OF BEER publications, first on paper and later on the Internet. These publications have played a central role in spreading the word about artisanal beer.

Indeed only one player in the craft category, Boston Beer Company, has succeeded by using the same traditional media—radio and television advertising—that the national brewers used to monopolize the US beer industry for most of the twentieth century. Boston Beer's nearest rival in sales is Sierra Nevada Brewing Co., but it's a distant second. Boston sold 2.7 million barrels of beer, flavored malt beverages, and apple cider in 2012, beer accounted for 2.1 million barrels. Sierra Nevada sold just under a million barrels of beer. New Belgium was next at 764,741 and so on down the line. But Sierra Nevada and all the others sold their brews without radio or television advertising.

This represented a big change in the way beer was sold in the United States. Before Prohibition the United States had about 2,000 breweries. After Prohibition only about half came back. Between 1933 and 2000 the US beer industry underwent a massive consolidation; the result has been that two national brewers, Anheuser Busch (AB) InBev and MillerCoors, today sell more than 70 percent of the beer Americans consume. AB InBev and MillerCoors did that largely by television advertising. The messages they aired repeatedly are burned into the memories of many Americans: "For all you do, this Bud's for you," "More taste, less filling," "Miller Time." The baby boom generation can probably sing some of the regional breweries' jingles of their youth, but their children, the Gen Xers and the Millennials, most likely have no memory of those beers. Of course the younger Millennials may not recall the Budweiser and Miller ads, either, because television now has many more channels, and Millennials likely spend more time on their computers, cell phones, and tablets than they do in front of a television.

The Internet has arguably been the greatest ally of the craft beer revolution. Daniel Bradford, the former marketing director of the Association of Brewers (AOB) and now publisher of *All About Beer* magazine, recalls surveying *Zymurgy* readers in 1986.

"I sent out a survey to try to figure out, other than homebrewing, what hooks did I have—how could I talk to these people, how can I find more people like them to read *Zymurgy?*" he said. "And other than [that the overwhelming majority were] white, middle-aged guys, twenty-five to forty-five, [the survey showed] almost 100 percent had a personal computer. This is in the eighties. I don't think Apple had even been invented. And there were even stories that [said that] at the computer exhibit at the Smithsonian, on the blackboard, was a home-brew recipe. I'm not sure if that is true. The home-brew revolution was simultaneous with the personal computer revolution, and I'm convinced it continues to this day with all these bloggers and social media."[1]

Today nearly every craft brewer has a website and someone to talk directly to its customers and fans through social media. "I think social media has been a huge driver for our category," said Rob Tod, founder of Allagash Brewing Co. in Portland, Maine, who uses it to keep fans apprised of what his brewery is doing.[2]

THE MOST REMARKABLE EXAMPLE OF THE POWER OF SOCIAL MEDIA IN THE CRAFT brewing category is *BeerAdvocate*.[3] Brothers Todd and Jason Alstrom started the website as a hobby in 1994. Today it gets about 2.5 million unique visitors a month, or 20 million a year. That means in the last nineteen years many millions have read news, gossip, commentary, opinion, tasting notes, and gripes about craft beer and beer in general on the Alstroms' site.

Todd and Jason have always been into computers. Their father was a buyer for a clothing company that provided him with a Timex Sinclair computer to track sales. The brothers went to school on the Timex. "We later graduated to a Commodore, and then I think an Apple 2+, and then a PC with a 286 Intel chip," Todd said.

He graduated from Monson High School in Massachusetts in 1987 and joined the Air Force. He trained in Maine and was shipped off to Newbury,

England, forty-five miles west of London. It was the final days of the Cold War, and Todd and his detail were preparing for World War III. They drove a convoy of four trailers—pulling four medium- and long-range ballistic missiles topped with nuclear warheads—to wooded areas to simulate what would happen if thermo-nuclear war broke out. If war had broken out, the missiles would have been a "final F-U" to the Soviet Union, he said. Todd finished his three-year stint but re-enlisted for two more years when the first Gulf War broke out in 1991.

Jason visited him in 1989 after he graduated from Monson High.[4] "I was just becoming aware of good beer," Jason said. He and Todd began to explore the quiet delights of an English pub in Newbury. They recall drinking Marston's Pedigree bitter and Courage Directors' bitter. "I fell in love with English ales, and my brother and I bonded over beer," Jason said.[5]

When Todd left the Air Force in 1993, he returned to Boston and got a job with an advertising firm, where he built websites for large corporations like General Motors. Jason took a few computer courses at Newbury State College in Massachusetts, got married, and moved to his wife's hometown, Savannah, Georgia. There he worked on a ground crew for Delta Airlines, then moved back to Boston in 1996 to take a similar job with Delta at Logan International Airport.[6]

The brothers became beer geeks and sought out every interesting import and microbrew they could find. They entered discussion groups about beer on the Internet. "In 1996, there were not a lot of people on the Internet," Todd said. "We used to battle it out with other beer geeks on Usenet. We had epic battles with people . . . very heated arguments over what beer was the best, and what was the worst. We didn't realize at the time, but we were laying the groundwork for discussion groups. In 1998 beer forums began to appear on the Internet."

In 1996 they began developing a discussion group called *Beer Guide, Advocates for Beer*. Todd said people found the name confusing and eventually they changed it to *BeerAdvocate*, hoping they would not be challenged by companies like *Wine Advocate*. They were not. In Todd's view "*BeerAdvocate* was more a call to action than just a website."

"It was just Jason and I sharing our views about different beers up to then. At some point, people asked, 'Why don't you let us post our reviews, post our notes?' And we said sure. We were very encouraged by the response. We started tasting and writing about anything we could get our hands on."

Todd was making six figures designing websites, but his heart was not in the corporate world. "We always had a sense of working for ourselves. We got it from our mom and stepdad, who ran a store in Faneuil Hall selling men's accessories like belts and suspenders."[7]

They drew tens of thousands of users to their website. Then, in 2001, CNN reached out. "They came and interviewed us for about five minutes. They cut it down to a two-minute segment, and then they ran it over and over. Things blew up. The response almost killed our website. We had to upgrade our server. Since then, we have upgraded four or five times, maybe more."[8]

In 2003 the Alstroms sponsored their first beer festival, the Art of Beer Festival, at the Boston Center for the Arts, also known as the Cyclorama on Tremont Street. The one-day festival drew more than 1,000 people—not a complete sellout but a big success. In January 2004 they did their first Extreme Beer Fest at the same location, drawing 2,000 participants and about thirty breweries.

Todd quit his cushy job in 2003 and took the plunge. Jason left his job at Delta in 2006 to join his brother. Today their main sources of revenue are festivals. The Extreme Beer Fest is a two-day event that draws 2,500 people. They also do a Belgian Beer Fest that draws a similar number. Both are held at the Cyclorama and enlist the participation of about thirty breweries. Their American Beer Fest is held at the Seaport World Trade Center in Boston and draws 15,000 beer lovers sampling beers from 135 breweries. They do a smaller event, Beer for Beasts, for the benefit of local animal shelters at the Bell House, a music club in Brooklyn, New York, that holds 1,200 people.

The Alstroms also make money from banner ads on the *BeerAdvocate* website and publish a magazine that circulates 50,000 print copies and is hosted by Google online. "We are at the point now where we need a solution for the future," Todd said. "Fifty percent of our business now is on mobile devices like iPhones and Droids."

The brothers are modest about their success and the tremendous influence they have had on the craft beer revolution. "We were one of the first ones to give people a way to talk to each other about beer," Todd said. "If you are a beer geek, chances are you are a geek about other things too, like computers and food. We came along at the right time, and so did microbrewers. Today there is a market for craft beer, and newcomers don't need to spend money on advertising. They've got us."[9]

On the West Coast, Joe Tucker of Santa Rosa, California, runs *RateBeer*, an online site with consumer ratings of beers, breweries, and bars that gets 1.2 million unique visitors per month. The site was started by software engineer

Bill Buchanon and a few friends in Atlanta in April 2000 with $1,500 in seed money. Tucker got involved a few months later, in July. He had worked for software companies in Europe and the United States until the "dot-bomb stage," when his last company, a $53 million project called www.comedy world.com, imploded.

"I was living in Berkeley, doing the home-brewing thing," Tucker said. "I had spent time in Oregon and knew about the microbrewing revolution."

Traffic to the site grew rapidly, leading to repeated server crashes, usually at midnight. Buchanon had children, and he grew impatient with the late-night work. The original plan was to sell ads to fund the site, but they had no sales team and no business plan.

"Bill asked if I wanted the site, and I said, 'I don't know if I want it. I don't have any money.' Bill said, 'You don't get it. I'm giving it to you.'"[10]

Tucker took it over, revamped the interface, and eventually sold advertisements and premium memberships that enabled members to see the site without ads and to access special features like data about beers or bars. "The funny thing is, I have never met Bill," Tucker said. "We have talked on the phone, but that is it."

Tucker is the only full-time employee. He quit his day job with a computer company in 2006. He has a part-time ad sales rep, volunteer coders, and 119 volunteer administrators around the world who guard against people who try to game the system to unfairly promote their beers or bars or denigrate others.

"It's a great thing for craft beer," Tucker said. "When we started, a lot of people saw it as us against the world. . . . We didn't see it that way. Rather than seeing it as a fight, we saw it as an inevitability. Everything was going in that direction."[11] First came wine, then coffee. It was only natural that beer would be next.

"I thought it was important to keep ratebeer.com going," he said. "I saw myself as one of the stewards of the craft beer movement. We didn't build anything, but we brought people together and let people communicate and share their ideas."

PRINT MEDIA ALSO HAVE PLAYED AN IMPORTANT ROLE IN THE CRAFT BEER REVOLUTION.
The *New Brewer*, published by the Brewers Association, is flourishing, and *Zymurgy* is read by more than 50,000 members of the American Home-brewing Association (AHA). *Draft* magazine is the most polished of the lot.

Malt Advocate started out doing a lot of craft beer coverage but has become more focused on whisky. (The big liquor companies spend far more on advertising than do craft brewers.) The *Real Beer Page* is another great resource, as is *Brewbound*.

The oldest of the publications devoted to beer is *All About Beer*. The magazine was started in 1978 by Mike Bozak, a printing company sales representative in Southern California, and several partners. Bozak was not a beer geek, just a businessman who saw an opportunity. "He was walking down the street and noticed a display of imported beers," said Bradford, who purchased the publication in 1993. "He realized that imports were taking off, and there was no place to learn about them, so he started *All About Beer*. The microbrewing thing was just getting started in California and the Northwest, so he also covered that emerging scene."[12]

The first cover of the magazine featured a photo of the actor Paul Newman, a known beer lover, with the Budweiser racing car. Other early covers featured Clint Eastwood, Burt Reynolds, Willie Nelson, and Rodney Dangerfield. Clearly Bozak knew how to get people's attention at a newsstand. *All About Beer* also employed the British beer writer Michael Jackson and the Oregonian Fred Eckhardt, both key opinion shapers in the early days of the craft beer revolution.

Bradford left the AOB in 1991, married Julie Johnston, an academic working at Duke University, and moved to Durham, North Carolina. His relationship with Charlie Papazian had become strained. He said it was "not exactly true" that Papazian fired him but "it amounted to the same thing. It was time for me to go."

Papazian had done a great job establishing the AOB and keeping it in the black financially. Bradford had done a great job running the festivals and conferences and getting attention for the growing craft brewing industry. "We were a perfect fit for the microbrewing industry," said Bradford. "We had our differences, but I always had a respect and appreciation for the role Charlie played. The industry benefitted from our different contributions. We both did our jobs and the industry was better for it."

Bradford had earned an MA in American history from the University of Colorado in Boulder and did graduate work at the University of Michigan. He got "about halfway" toward fulfilling the requirements for a PhD. He had always wanted to teach history and brought this high-minded educational approach to *All About Beer* when he bought the magazine two years after moving to Durham.

"I envisioned *All About Beer* as a catalyst to create a community to educate the public about beer appreciation and beer quality," he said. "Even our festivals are organized around beer appreciation and education." Bradford said the local brewers' tent is the most popular one at the annual World Beer Festival, which the magazine sponsors in Durham. People are more interested in the local scene than they are in the regional breweries or European breweries that are pouring their beers. In Bradford's view the second most popular part of the magazine is the "Art of Beer" section, which focuses on beer and food pairings, cask ales, and beer equipment.

Based on his experience with the World Beer Festival, he moved *All About Beer*'s focus from being a lifestyle magazine featuring people making beer to focusing on both the makers of beer and the beer itself.

One of its more popular features is the tasting panel, a group of experts who taste new beers and write about them. Among the tasters are Papazian, Charlie Finkel of Merchant du Vin, Garrett Oliver, the Alstroms, Roger Protz of Britain's Campaign for Real Ale, and the beer writers Stephen Beaumont and Fred Eckhardt.

"I changed the rules of the professional tasting panel," Bradford said. "I told the writers, 'I'm not interested in your opinions. I want you to describe in words what you are tasting. I want you to paint a picture of the beer in front of you.'"[13]

Bradford's *All About Beer* has a circulation of about 40,000, and it is increasing rapidly. "Our social media presence has soared over the past few years, and so has our circulation." But the stories that *All About Beer* tells cannot be told in 140 characters, like a tweet. "We're the long form. People buy our magazine because they want to read about beer."

"I'm fascinated by the role social media has played in the craft beer revolution," he said. "I'm of the opinion that the explosion of micro-, pub-, and nano-breweries is closely related to the growth of social media. The problem is, you can create a buzz with 140 characters, but you cannot create any content. The result is that a lot of small breweries that really suck can be very popular at the same time. There is a craving for the new and exotic. That works against brands and in favor of styles. Everyone wants an IPA, any IPA, or they want a beer with Citra hops, any beer."

All About Beer runs an online tasting using Google Hangout where participants taste six beers from the same brewery to develop a sense of that brewery's personality and house character.

Bradford praised the role of weekly newspapers devoted to craft brewing in the craft beer revolution. "The brewspapers were like the early days of social media," he said. "They keep the local buzz going. Their job is to tell people what was going on with beer in their communities. Our job is to educate people about beer."[14]

The granddaddy of the newspapers dedicated to the craft beer revolution is *Celebrator Beer News,* based in Nevada City, California. *Celebrator*'s editor and publisher is the energetic, irrepressible, omnipresent, bearded, bespectacled, and often top-hatted Tom Dalldorf. Dalldorf is the media member of the Class of '88, a reconstructed wine geek and a legend in the annals of innovation in California's branch of the US Postal Service.

Dalldorf was a letter carrier in Hayward in the 1970s and early 1980s. He noticed that mail carriers in Florida were wearing shorts on their steamy delivery routes, and he cut off his trousers to make his rounds in Hayward. The postmaster called him in for a reprimand, but Dalldorf convinced the boss that shorts were as necessary in California's heat as they were in Florida's. Dalldorf had already won acclaim for editing the best local newsletter in the USPS, a venture that derailed when the Postal Workers Union discovered he was having the paper printed at a nonunion shop.

While making his rounds he earned a master's in political science with a focus on China. In 1979 he opened a wine shop in Hayward, learning the finer points of wine tasting, and he judged at the state and national levels. "I met up with Bret and Julie Nickels, two Canadians from Vancouver, at the one beer event that I did at my shop," Dalldorf said. In 1988 the Nickelses wanted to start a newspaper about the fledgling microbrewing business in the West. Dalldorf credits them with coining the term *brewspaper.*

Dalldorf learned that the Nickelses were typing out all their stories and feeding them into a scanner to set type for the paper, which they called *California Celebrator* (after the wonderful double bock produced by the Ayinger Brewery in Aying, Germany). Bret Nickels wanted to print 5,000 copies for the first issue, but the printer insisted on a minimum of 10,000. Bret Nickels drove all over the state to drop off copies of the bimonthly. According to Dalldorf, all 10,000 copies were gone in three weeks.

"I told Bret that I had a Mac that could make this work much easier," Dalldorf said. "For $3,000 I could buy a Mac laser printer and do the job much quicker and cheaper than the Nickels were doing it." The Nickelses decided to pay Dalldorf to layout the paper, and he became a partner in the venture.

When Bret Nickels announced he was heading back to Canada and shutting down the paper, Dalldorf countered, "You can't do that. You have created something significant here. You've got readers all over the state and advertisers who are committed to *Celebrator*." Dalldorf then made a proposition: "You should let me take it over." When the Nickelses agreed, Dalldorf bought them out.[15]

Now Dalldorf had the arduous task of peddling the papers all over California, a state that takes as long to travel as the trip from New York to Miami. Dalldorf started using UPS to deliver the papers. By 2013 the paper's per-issue circulation was 55,000, mainly to locations west of the Mississippi, but with some presence in every state and many foreign countries.

Celebrator has published some legendary beer writers, like Eckhardt and Beaumont, Jay R. Brooks, Don Erickson, Mike Pitsker, Steve Shapiro, and Gail Ann Williams, as well as Jack Curtin and Lucy Saunders. Michael Jackson is still listed on the masthead as consultant, a tribute that I am sure the Bard would appreciate.

"Michael Jackson took Bret and me under his wing and guided us along," Dalldorf said. "Kim Jordan [of New Belgium] set the bar pretty high in New Orleans in 2003 when she said craft beer could be 10 percent of the market. But we all dove into the cause with the intention of making great beer, not making money. We made what we liked and the consumers followed us. This thing called flavor, and this thing called character, which Michael Jackson insisted on, is what drove us. Writing about this dynamo has been an exhilarating experience."[16]

Tony Forder and Jack Babin started the bimonthly tabloid *Ale Street News* in 1992. The 20,000 copies of its first run were distributed in New York City by Brooklyn Brewery's distribution company, the Craft Brewers Guild. Forder, born in Uckfield, England, was a fan of Jack Kerouac's novel *On The Road*. Forder's fascination with Kerouac brought him to the United States at eighteen to hitchhike to California. In San Francisco he met and married Sue, Jack Babin's sister, and got a journalism degree from Humboldt State College in Arcata.

"I got into the beer newspaper business the same way a lot of people got into the craft brewing industry—homebrewing," Forder said. "I was into homebrewing in California and before that in England. Jack visited us in California and we started homebrewing together."

After the birth of their daughter, the Forders moved to New Jersey, and Tony and Jack started a home-brewing club, the North Jersey Wort Hogs.

Other members of the club went on to found a home-brew store in Teaneck. Forder worked for community newspapers in California and New Jersey. He knew and admired Tom Dalldorf's *Celebrator* and even wrote some pieces for Dalldorf.

Back East, imports from Belgium, Germany, and Britain, as well as American microbrews, were coming into the market. "People didn't know anything about these beers, and we thought a newspaper could serve a good purpose," Forder said. He met Tom Potter and me at Company B's in Orangeburg, New York, just north of New York City in 1992. Company B's was one of those pioneering craft beer bar-restaurants that shocked the restaurant world by refusing to carry Budweiser, Miller, or Coors products. It was an instant success.

Ale Street News was an instant success too. Tom Potter and I bought the back page of *Ale Street News* to promote the great beers we were distributing through the Craft Brewers Guild. The paper grew rapidly. Today it prints 80,000 copies and circulates up and down the East Coast and in some Great Lakes markets. Forder has been full time since 1994. Copublisher Jack Babin splits his time between *Ale Street News* and Micros, the restaurant software company. In addition to publishing the newspaper, Forder and Babin sponsor beer dinners, festivals, and excursions to the Great American Beer Festival and the great brewing nations of Europe.[17]

The biggest player in print beer media is Bill Metzger, who publishes seven regional newspapers with a combined circulation of 275,000. The Syracuse, New York, native found himself in Austin in the early 1990s when his partner landed a job with the Texas Department of Education. Metzger was teaching high school science and editing an environmental newspaper. A home brewer, he started writing for the *New Brewer* and Bill Owen's *American Brewer.*

"On our vacations we traveled the world seeking out breweries, and I knew that craft brewing was going to come to Texas," Metzger said. "There was no beer publication in Texas, so I got the idea to start a newspaper." He said Billy Forrester, owner of the Dog and Duck Pub in Austin and founder of the city's first brewpub, wrote him a check for ads in the first three issues. Jim Koch also committed to ads. The first issue of *Southwest Brewing News* appeared in 1993.

Metzger and his partner moved back to the upstate New York city of Buffalo in 1996, and he started *Great Lakes Brewing News* that year. It was a tough time for the industry. *Southern Draft,* a newspaper covering the southeast, went out of business, and so did New York City's *Beer and*

Tavern Chronicle and *Barleycorn,* focused on the mid-Atlantic states. The next year Metzger bought the struggling *Yankee Brew News,* a New England publication.

In 1998 Metzger started *Mid-Atlantic Brewing News* with help from *Barleycorn* regular contributors Jim Dorsch and Greg Kitsock. Later came *Northwest Brewing News, Rocky Mountain Brewing News,* and *Southern Brewing News.* Metzger, copublisher Jamie Magee, and two other full-time employees run the show. The papers are printed in four states and distributed to brewpubs, production breweries, and beercentric retailers by mail. Metzger said his only misfire was *Mississippi Valley Brewing News,* which he started in 2003 and folded three years later.

Metzger said the regional focus has been the key to his success. "I thought the regionality of the movement was very important, and I had a lot of faith in the passion and creativity and drive of the craft brewers I met."

Not content with writing about beer, Metzger recently bought a bar in Buffalo, Gene McCarthy's Brewery and Kitchen, and has broken ground on a new brewhouse with a 3.5-barrel brewing system.[18]

Beer Marketer's Insights, a forty-year-old newsletter covering the US brewing industry, started an e-mail newsletter called *Craft Brew News* in 2010. Publisher Benj Steinman, whose father, Jerry, began *Beer Marketer's Insight,* said he had been covering craft brewing in the main newsletter for years. But when he attended the 2010 Craft Brewers Conference in Chicago, Benj was stunned not only by the size of the conference but by the number of wholesalers in attendance. Beer distributors are one of his main audiences.

"That vitality of that CBC [Craft Brewers Conference] was a startling contrast to the big brewer conventions, which were unexciting by comparison," he said. "Total beer sales were down, and yet craft was up double digits. Craft looked very much like the future that evening. We had a couple of new product ideas, including a craft newsletter, but that evening made our decision a no-brainer. . . . Three years later, it is still a growth story."[19]

Steinman's competitor, *Beer Business Daily,* published in San Antonio, Texas, by the witty, entertaining, and often provocative scribe Harry Schumacher, also started a craft publication.

"There was so much information coming out about craft brewers and craft beer that *Beer Business Daily* was becoming a craft beer newsletter," said Schumacher. "We thought it was time to give craft beer its own publication because the big brewers were getting short shrift in *BBD*. They are 80 percent of the volume, but they were only getting 20 percent of the ink."[20]

He hired Jen Litz to write the craft newsletter and is thinking of hiring a second writer soon. Schumacher said he was somewhat jealous of Litz because she got to cover the news about growth while he was stuck reporting on down numbers for the large brewers.

The proliferation of beer publications means there is a daily stream of information about brewery startups, brewery sales, and brewery acquisitions. *Beer Marketers Insights* and *Beer Business Daily* compete vigorously for news about craft brewers and distributors. The industry is thoroughly covered on a daily basis. For the beer consumer, there is a constant flow of news about new beers, events, and festivals. Any startup brewery, no matter how small or remote, will find its beers reviewed on *BeerAdvocate* or *RateBeer*.

CHAPTER EIGHT

CRAFT BREWERS RESUSCITATE THE BREWERS' ASSOCIATION OF AMERICA

THROUGHOUT THE EARLY AND MID-1990s, CRAFT BREWERS BECAME INCREASINGLY aware of the need to organize politically. Just about every annual Craft Brewers Conference had a session or two devoted to the problem of managing relationships with distributors.

In all but a few states, brewers are prohibited from distributing their own beer. They are required to sell their product to a distributor, who then sells it to a bar, restaurant, or retail store. Typically a distributor will buy a case of beer for, say, $20, and mark it up by 40 percent, to $28. The $8 covers the distributor's delivery and sales costs and profit. In most states distributors are protected by franchise laws, which stipulate that the brewer creates a franchise with a distributor when they sell and deliver a brewer's beer. So a brewer cannot take the brand back, or assign it to a new distributor, without the agreement of the first distributor unless the brewer shows that the distributor is not doing the job or is doing something illegal, behaviors that would be considered just cause for termination. But just cause for termination is very difficult to prove.

Typically, a brewer attempting to divorce a distributor is in for a big legal battle. Large brewers have large legal departments and budgets. Small brewers don't. Hence the frustration of many small brewers when they find that their distributor is not in fact selling their beer.

I recall seminars at the Craft Brewers Conference on managing distributors, primarily gripe sessions, with speaker after speaker describing their dysfunctional relationships with wholesalers. In those years motivating a distributor to focus on a microbrewed beer seemed to be an utter impossibility. Distributors were supposedly independent businesses, but in practice they were quite beholden to the large brewers. They dutifully pushed whatever the large brewers produced, whether light beer, dry beer, or ice beer, all styles that emerged in the 1990s—even though none of these beers was substantially different from the light lager megabrands that had dominated the beer market since the inception of modern craft brewing. Most markets had a Miller distributor, a Coors distributor, and a Budweiser distributor. The Budweiser distributor was often 100 percent focused on Anheuser-Busch (AB) brands. Indeed August Busch III, with his 1996 "100 percent share of mind" campaign, seemed determined to enforce that restriction with all his distributors. The Miller and Coors brands, a fraction of the size of AB's, had less influence with their distributors. Miller and Coors distributors usually carried many imports and were more willing to pick up a microbrewed beer.

Only Jim Koch and Pete Slosberg seemed able to attract the attention of these distributors. I think this was because they were advertising on radio and television, like the big boys. Distributors understood radio and television advertising, but they did not appreciate the word of mouth marketing that was propelling most craft brewers. I recall distributor sales managers' advising me to do what Jim Koch was doing. They said, "Why don't you do some radio or television ads? Or put up some billboards around New York City?"

They didn't seem to understand that those strategies were way beyond my means. And I didn't want to do that sort of marketing anyway. If I had an extra $50,000, I would hire a sales rep or two.

Fritz Maytag was constantly reminding us that the three-tier system—the constructs put in place by most states after the passage of the Twenty-first Amendment to the US Constitution, which abolished Prohibition—was the only thing that stood in the way of allowing the large brewers a complete monopoly of the US beer market. Prohibitionists thought brewery ownership of bars was a primary reason for the overconsumption and abuse of beer and other alcoholic beverages. The three-tier system specified that a brewer could not own a distributor license or a retail license.

But if, as Maytag said, the three-tier system prevented concentration of the industry in the hands of large brewers, why did the large brewers seem to control so much of the US market? At one Craft Brewers Conference Maytag went so far as to advise all of us to go home and hug our distributors. I found this difficult to accept. Was I supposed to go back to New York and hug William "Wild Bill" Pflaumer, owner of Midway, a distributor on Long Island that had lost almost every customer I had ever handed it?[1] Pflaumer's people also went to great lengths to avoid paying me. Our contract specified payment in thirty days. But typically the check would be mailed on the thirtieth day. It was drawn on a Philadelphia bank, so it took a few days to clear. Once, I received an unsigned check that Pflaumer's accountant insisted I mail back to Philadelphia for a signature.

Or maybe I should hug Carmine Stella, the distributor who closed his doors and disappeared a week after ordering a trailer of Brooklyn Lager and telling me he had mailed the check for the previous trailer? That disaster cost me more than $40,000, at a time when Brooklyn Brewery was struggling to make a profit. A hug was the last thing I had in mind for Carmine Stella.

The only way to address these problems was to become politically active and push for state legislation that would make it easier for small brewers to work with distributors. One way to do it would be to exempt from the franchise laws brewers that represented only a small percentage of a distributor's business. Or perhaps a state legislature could require distributors to pay for beer in a shorter time frame.

Here I think it is necessary to describe some of the organizations that represent the various segments of the beer industry. They have similar names and are therefore easy to confuse.

> *The Brewers Association (BA)*—The trade association established in 2005 upon the merger of the BAA and the AOB.
>
> *The Brewers' Association of America (BAA)*—A trade association of small regional breweries established in 1942 to ensure that small brewers got their fair share of tin and barley, materials that were being rationed during World War II.
>
> *The Association of Brewers (AOB)*—Founded by Charlie Papazian in 1978, the AOB was an educational organization that began to evolve into a trade organization. The American Homebrewers Association publisher of the *New Brewer*, was a subsidiary of the AOB, as was the Institute for Brewing and Fermentation Studies, publisher of *Zymurgy*, and Brewers Publications. The AOB also ran the Great American Beer Festival and the Craft Brewers Conference.
>
> *The National Beer Wholesalers Association (NBWA)*—A trade association representing America's 1,000 beer distributors in

Washington, DC. Distributors have similar organizations in
every state to lobby state legislatures because every state has
different laws and taxes for beer.

The Beer Institute (BI)—A trade association purporting to represent
all brewers, but primarily represents the larger brewers. The
BI was established in 1986 after the demise of the US Brewers
Association.

In the mid-1990s the Institute for Brewing and Fermentation Studies,
forerunner of the AOB, was becoming more active in politics, but only in
an informational way. In May and July 1994, for example, the institute sent
out "Brewers Alerts," warning of two bills before Congress that would almost
certainly bankrupt most small brewers. Both bills are still under consideration as I write. The first measure promotes equivalency, that is, taxing beer
the same as whisky. This is a change that the liquor industry has long advocated, for obvious reasons. But beer is not like whisky. Beer is made by naturally fermenting grain and is limited in alcohol content. Whisky is made by
brewing and then distilling grain to concentrate alcohol. Brewers have always
presented beer as the "beverage of moderation," and characterized whisky as
hard liquor.

The second issue is slotting fees. These are fees suppliers pay to grocery
stores to obtain favorable placement on store shelves. This is a common practice for soft drinks, which may explain why Coca-Cola and Pepsi fill virtually
all of the soft drink sections in grocery stores. Slotting fees are illegal in the
beer business because only large companies could afford such fees. The grocery industry is committed to changing that.

I would guess that when these alerts went out twenty years ago, many
small brewers did not fully understand the importance of opposing these
changes. In May 1995 a number of small brewers attended their first joint
brewer-distributor legislative conference in Washington, DC. The BI and the
NBWA sponsored the three-day lobbying effort. Four craft brewers attended:
Ken Grossman of Sierra Nevada, Pete Slosberg of Pete's Brewing Company,
Bill Cross of Willamette Valley Brewing Company, and Peter Egelston of
Smuttynose Brewing Company. The brewers made known their opposition
to higher beer taxes, government warning labels, and revoking the deduct-
ibility of advertising expenses. They also made the case that alcohol abuse was
declining, and brewers were part of the solution to that problem.

The small brewers got a great reception. "With all the congressmen I visited, as soon as I said I was from a microbrewery, their ears perked up," Egelston said. "It's like I'm sort of this exotic thing they've heard of and want to know more about."[2] In subsequent years the agenda for the joint legislative conference would tilt toward distributor issues, like abolishing estate taxes or fighting proposals to tighten the rules of the Occupational Safety and Health Administration or seeking relaxation of the rules for obtaining a commercial driver's license. The agenda was set by the BI and the NBWA. We microbrewers were, at most, window dressing, with no say in developing the agenda. However, we all had the same experience as Egelston: members of Congress and their young staff members would light up when we told them about our fledgling companies or similar outfits that were popping up and hiring people right in their districts. Here was something unusual: a manufacturing concern creating jobs at home, not moving its operations to Mexico or China.

Despite our minor role, I found these conferences fascinating. We were witnessing how public policy is influenced in Washington, where the federal excise tax and many of the regulations that govern the beer business are promulgated. The head of the BI was a back-slapping former US representative from Long Island, Ray McGrath. He seemed to think it was funny that he preferred white wine to beer. I never understood why August Busch III tolerated that. *He* would never be seen without a Budweiser in his hand, and he enforced the same discipline on his lieutenants and his distributors.

The Anheuser-Busch (AB) delegates to the joint legislative conference were unmistakable fit men with short neatly parted hair; they wore dark blue suits and red ties and seemed to move in phalanxes. They did not really mix with the other delegates. When August III or August IV deigned to appear at one of the lavish receptions held for the conferees and the members of Congress and their staffs, the AB distributors scrambled for a few words with them. A pack of aides and security personnel with wires sticking into their ears always attended the Busch men, who never stayed long.

Peter Coors was often at the receptions too, minus the entourage. Tall, tan, and trim, with silver hair and a chiseled cowboy jaw that seemed to embody the Rocky Mountains and the sunny west, Coors, too, was besieged by distributors. I had met Coors at Cornell during my freshman year, but it was not a moment he recalled when I reintroduced myself at a conference.

He was a member of Psi Upsilon, a prestigious jock house that also counted the son of then-Secretary of State Dean Rusk among its brothers.

I believe Coors was a senior that year. He was wearing a beautiful tan suede sports coat. I recall thinking I would almost certainly ruin that coat if I were to wear it just once. In retrospect, I am surprised Psi U even afforded me an audience. In addition to celebrities, Psi U counted football, basketball, and baseball players among its membership. I was a member of the golf team—not quite on the same level.

I did join Sigma Alpha Epsilon, also a jock house, but with no celebrities. I got in on the coattails of some of my friends on the football team. Coors married a Cornell co-ed, Marilyn Gross, who was a "little sister" of SAE—a member of a sort of ladies auxiliary.

At one legislative conference, I literally pulled on Coors' coattail to get his attention in a circle of distributors. "Hey, Pete, I'm Steve Hindy from Brooklyn Brewery. I was a member of SAE at Cornell. I think your wife Marilyn Gross was an SAE Little Sister," I said.

"Really?" he said, sort of glancing in my direction before returning to the attention of his obsequious distributors. It was probably about the same amount of attention I got when I first met him, three decades before. Maybe being a microbrewer in this league was the equivalent of being on the golf team at Cornell.

The one muckety-muck at the BI who seemed to have some interest in the microbrewers was Jeff Becker, its spokesman. Becker was a handsome guy; he looked a lot like the actor Michael Douglas. He had dark hair with silver highlights and seemed comfortable with the brewers and the distributors. He was the man who presented the BI platform at the big opening meeting of the conference. He was a great speaker, funny and at home on the big stage. He had personal relationships with many members of Congress. If McGrath was the political insider, the backroom dealer, Becker was the front man, the voice of the industry. He was an able spin doctor and a consummate diplomat, one of those guys you couldn't help but like, perhaps because he took an interest in other people. He once asked how I had gotten into the brewery business and was intrigued by my journalism background. As we chatted, we soon realized that we both loved golf. Becker belonged to a couple of golf courses in the DC area, and he started hosting me and my friend Gary Fish, founder of Deschutes. Becker was a great golfer. He had a two handicap and a sweet swing.

The spring legislative conference became an annual tradition for me, as well as about twenty-five other small brewers. We all knew that it was not our agenda that was being promoted, but we were learning from the big brewers and distributors. Gary Fish and I began to say that small brewers had to get a seat at the table where the agenda was written.

Sometime in the mid-1990s the AOB began to organize a meeting of the few state small-brewer guilds that were active. I recall attending one of these meetings and raising questions about how the AOB could promulgate a political agenda when it was not run by brewers. The Institute for Brewing and Fermentation Studies had had an advisory board made up of brewers since the early 1980s, but it was not the governing board of the AOB. The real power of the association clearly rested with the people who were defining its purpose and mission. At some point the association changed its legal status from educational organization to trade organization. The latter status usually reflects an intention to lobby state legislatures and Congress, like a real trade association.

"I think the problem was that the AOB was starting to behave like a trade association, but the board of directors was made up of Charlie [Papazian's] friends—an insurance guy, some attorneys, a realtor," said Kim Jordan, CEO of New Belgium.[3] There had been meetings with John Hickenlooper, founder of the Wynkoop Brewing Company and a good friend of Papazian's, about developing a board of brewers for the AOB, but the talks had gone nowhere. Jack Joyce of Rogue Ales, a member of the Institute for Brewing and Fermentation Studies advisory board, said the change in status was a head fake designed to give the appearance of a trade association.

"My point of view was that the BAA's role was the legislative role, the role on Capitol Hill," Joyce said. "Charlie had no interest in that. He wanted to run the conference and the beer festival and the educational programs of the industry."[4]

The AOB stumbled badly in 1998, when it attempted to stage the Great American Beer Festival in Baltimore. The date of the event conflicted with a big sporting event in that city, resulting in poor attendance and a major loss of money. Papazian also drew fire for staging the World Beer Cup, a blind-tasting competition for beers from all over the world, in Rio de Janeiro that year.

Some small brewers were members of the BAA. Fritz Maytag had been involved with the BAA for many years, as had Ken Grossman and Ted Marti of August Schell Brewing Company. Other small brewers, like George Hancock of Pyramid Brewery, Rich Doyle and Dan Kenary of Harpoon Brewery, Fred Bowman of Portland Brewing Company, and Kim Jordan of New Belgium, had even joined the BAA board. They began to encourage other small brewers to get involved with the BAA. Grossman recalled that the BAA was a barely functioning trade association. For many years the main event for BAA members was the annual meeting and dinner dance in Fort Lauderdale, more a tax-deductible vacation than a business meeting. Henry King, the long-time president of the U.S. Brewers' Association (forerunner of the BI), was head of the BAA. He set the agenda.[5]

I ATTENDED THE 1997 ANNUAL CONVENTION OF THE BAA AT THE FAIRMONT COPLEY Plaza Hotel in Boston. It was the organization's fifty-sixth annual meeting, and ninety-seven breweries were represented. I was among the many small brewers who were wondering whether the BAA could develop a political and public relations agenda for us. The meeting was kicked off rather inauspiciously by Michael Laybourn, the president of the Mendocino Brewing Company, which had only recently been sold to the Indian billionaire Vijay Mallya. Some of us wondered how the BAA could allow a foreign-owned company to be a member of the board. (Laybourn's company was later removed from the board and the organization.) Laybourn forgot to introduce the meeting's host, Rich Doyle, who had planned to introduce the guest of honor, Walter A. Sullivan, head of the Massachusetts Alcohol Beverage Control Commission.[6]

Joyce was aware that many brewers were unhappy that the AOB was dabbling in political issues. He organized what became known as the Rump Session, an informal meeting of many of the malcontents, including me. Aware that passions were likely to run high—Jim Koch of Boston Beer Company would be attending, along with some of his detractors—Joyce asked the beer writer Jack Ericson to moderate the session. It was held in a wood-paneled room with a thick blue carpet and a big meeting table with a dozen or so chairs. Joyce and Koch were smoking, so the room became stuffy right away. I bummed a cigarette from Koch. The room also held a cart with cold beer— never a good addition to a serious meeting.

Gary Fish recalls that Koch gave an opening statement, saying the problem with the industry was too many companies and some were making "crap beer." This got a quick and bitter response from Irene Firmat of Full Sail Brewing Company, who criticized Koch for contract brewing. Joyce recalls that Larry Bell also unleashed an attack on Koch for contract brewing and also for allegedly giving away beer in exchange for market share.[7] "He almost made Jim cry; he really hurt Jim's feelings," Joyce said. Kim Jordan recalls going after Koch, too, and that she pointed out that she was kicking his ass in the Phoenix market. Ericson was helpless to contain the acrimony. As the meeting verged on chaos, Fish recalls Ericson whispered to Joyce: "Is this what you had in mind?"[8]

Joyce recalled that the "Charlie [Papazian] haters" and/or "the East Coast mafia" were bent on getting rid of the AOB or taking it over. He refused to further identify the AOB's detractors, but I assume he meant me and Rich Doyle. I did not hate Charlie. I simply wanted a trade association that truly represented the interests of my company and the microbrewing industry. George Hancock of Pyramid Brewing insisted that because of the BAA's long track record of representing the industry in Washington they offered the best chance of developing an effective trade association. I came away from that meeting agreeing with him.[9]

The next day F.X. Matt, who chaired the BAA, agreed to allow an open meeting of all brewers attending the BAA conference. Jordan facilitated the meeting. "I recall I was way too hung over to be doing this," she said. "I stumbled through a speech about the need for a trade association to represent the interests of small brewers and develop a unified voice in the media." Larry Bell gave a somewhat convoluted talk in which he pleaded for the group to follow Robert's Rules of Order for the session. Jerome Chicvara of Full Sail said the small brewing industry needed a media campaign like the "Got Milk?" campaign to promote awareness of craft beer. Doyle and Hancock urged everyone to get involved with the BAA and turn it into an effective trade organization.[10]

It wasn't pretty, but that meeting was an important turning point for the industry. Doyle said the BAA board had known for some time that the organization's management needed an overhaul. Henry King was suffering from cancer, and Gary Nateman, the general counsel of the BAA, was no administrator. Doyle recalled one board meeting when a "considerable amount of time was spent trying to balance the organization's checkbook." Another problem was that the main funders of the organization were the large brewers—AB, Miller, and Coors. We knew that a truly independent trade association representing small brewers would have to be funded and run by microbrewers.

The job of easing Henry King out of the BAA presidency fell to Fritz Maytag. "Telling him [King] it was time to go was a hard thing," Doyle said. F. X. Matt asked Doyle to run a search committee to find a new president. Doyle tapped Maytag, Matt, and King to serve on the search committee. "I was the junior guy on that committee with the real lions of the small brewing industry," Doyle said. Maytag took a suite at a midtown Manhattan hotel, and the committee interviewed Gary Galanis, the public relations man for the NBWA; John Carlson, the president of the Colorado Brewers Guild; David Edgar, the director of the Institute for Brewing and Fermentation Studies; the journalist Harry Schumacher; and Daniel Bradford, cofounder of the Great American Beer Festival and publisher of *All About Beer*.[11]

Galanis got the job, mainly because of his experience with the NBWA, one of the most effective trade associations in Washington, DC. The board that chose Galanis was composed almost entirely of the new generation of craft brewers. F.X. Matt was its chair, Rich Doyle of Harpoon was vice chair, and Chuck Lawson of the Lion Brewery was secretary-treasurer. Board members included Bowman, Grossman, Hancock, Jordan, Marti, Maytag, Firmat, David Heidrich of Oldenberg Brewing Co., and Mark Stutrud of Summit Brewing Company. The next year the board added Fish, John McDonald of Boulevard Brewing Company, and me.

After surveying its members, the 1998 board developed a five-year strategic plan. The main objectives were "preserving the small brewers' tax differential; gaining fairer access to the marketplace; development of a public relations/media program focusing on the goodness of American beer; developing market behavior guidelines; working closer with other industry beer organizations at all levels."

To these ends the BAA developed a position paper in December 1998 on one of the most contentious issues of the day: the so-called equity agreements that Miller and AB were forcing their wholesalers to sign. The agreements were an attempt by the large brewers to ensure that their distributors concentrated their efforts on selling the large brewers' products. For AB it was an attempt to codify the "100 percent share of mind" policy that August Busch III had outlined in 1996. For Miller it was an attempt to catch up with AB.

The BAA position paper said in part:

> The Brewers Association of America, the trade association which represents small brewers who produce fewer than 2 million barrels of beer annually, is deeply concerned about the distributor contracts issued by Anheuser-Busch and Miller brewing companies. Both contracts would inevitably interfere with the independent wholesaler's ability to distribute the products of small brewers. These contracts bode ill for competition in the beer industry and ultimately for the American beer drinker. [In 1996] Anheuser-Busch unveiled its distributor contract that introduced the "100 percent share of mind" program. Under

this program, wholesalers were rewarded, through various financial and promotional incentives, for expelling small brewers, importers and others. They were given incentives to make their distributorships exclusive to AB products. Last month, Miller introduced a new contract with "Fair Share" provisions with objectives similar to the "100 percent share of mind" proposal. These contracts are restricting growth possibilities for all other brewers and especially small brewers. Ultimately, they will reduce consumer choice.[12]

The BAA paper analyzed Miller's contract in detail, noting that it required per-case sales incentives for Miller brands to be equal to or greater than those for non-Miller brands; that the distributor notify Miller of any acquisition or divestiture of any business, thus allowing Miller to approve or disapprove of any new brands the distributor might take on; that Miller approve of any general manager before hiring; that the distributor waive the right to jury trial in the event of any contract dispute; and that the distributor maintain certain debt-to-equity ratios.

"These contracts weaken the competitive position of the small brewer and limit their access to store shelves," the paper continued. "They undermine the independence of the wholesaler and thereby threaten the . . . essence of the state franchise laws that define the relationship between a brewer and a wholesaler. They severely limit competition among breweries, reduce consumer choice and lead to further big brewer domination of the marketplace."[13]

At last, small brewers were speaking up. It was a clear message to the large brewers that we were not going to stand idly by while they trampled our rights. Many distributors privately told me they were impressed by the BAA position paper and were very much in favor of its strong support for wholesaler independence. But none of them issued any public defense of the BAA. A few weeks after the BAA published the paper, Galanis was informed that Miller and AB were withdrawing their financial support for the BAA. We knew we wanted to be independent of large brewer money, but we didn't expect independence to come so quickly.

I recall asking Jeff Becker of the BI about the large brewers pulling their cash out of the BAA. "Hey, pal, you think these guys aren't paying attention to you?" he replied. "Your actions have consequences."

In early 1999, about a year after Galanis had taken over management of the BAA, he called me to say he had been offered a job as spokesman for Diageo, the giant liquor distributor and owner of the Guinness Brewery. He said he was conflicted and didn't want to leave the BAA. I said, "Gary, you have a wife and a small child. We are paying you $60,000 a year. I am sure they are doubling that. What is it about the offer that you have to ponder?" Galanis took the job.

A hiring committee of the BAA soon brought Daniel Bradford, the veteran cofounder of the Great American Beer Festival, on board as the new president of the BAA. With his knowledge of the cast of characters at both the big and small breweries, Bradford was the right guy at the right time. At the same time the NBWA dismissed its president, Ron Sarasin, and replaced him with the very aggressive lobbyist David Rehr. And the BI announced the retirement of its wine-drinking president, McGrath, and replaced him with the smooth-talking Jeff Becker. The new, younger leadership of the three trade associations seemed to herald a new era for the industry.

Undeterred by the BI's financial slap-down over our position paper, the BAA proceeded to outline its position on state franchise laws, the legislation that effectively allowed distributors to own beer brands entrusted to them, even in the face of poor performance. This put the fledgling organization at odds with the state beer wholesaler organizations that existed in all fifty states and were buttressed by the powerful NBWA in Washington, DC.

> The Brewers Association of America believes that small brewers represent a small portion of their wholesalers' business. Unlike the large domestic brewers, small brewers are not in a position to dictate unfair contractual terms to their wholesalers. Thus, small brewers and wholesalers should be free to enter into arms-length contractual agreements unfettered by state laws. State beer laws should provide a framework of regulation for the orderly conduct of the industry but need not and should not confer unfair commercial advantages upon either party.
>
> The BAA strongly supports an amendment to state laws that would exempt small brewers [using the Federal Government definition of 2 million barrels per year] from state 'franchise' laws. State laws should presume that contracts freely entered into by small brewers and wholesalers are fair.

The BAA went on to assert the right of any small brewer to self-distribute, an exception that already existed in several states.

The three-tier structure

> does not adequately cope with modern conditions in the brewing industry. "In particular, the three-tier system does not cope with the vastly increased

number of shipping breweries and the reduced number of wholesalers. The result is a severe curtailment of the distribution options for small brewers to the detriment of the consumer and the economy. Small brewers are being denied access to new markets and in some cases being eliminated from existing markets because they are not able to command the attention of a traditional beer wholesaler. The problem is exacerbated by the two largest domestic brewers who are attempting to preclude their wholesaler networks handling the products of other brewers.

The paper went on to advocate for self-distribution rights in the name of economic growth, consumer choice, the environment, and the three-tier system.

To overcome the problems inherent in those states that currently adhere strictly to the three-tier system, the BAA supports an amendment to state laws that would give small brewers the right in any and all states to obtain a wholesale license and distribute directly to retailers.[14]

The BAA was laying down a platform based on core issues that would endure for decades. Indeed, as I write in 2013, the BA continues to pound away at these issues, with some small successes.

The BAA was clearly filling the need of small brewers for representation in state and national affairs. During the next five years, under the leadership of Daniel Bradford, the BAA would provide a forum for small brewery owners to exchange ideas and hone their political and public relations skills.

"One of the consequences of having access to market issues is brewers come together to share stories, and create solutions and work through this sort of stuff," Bradford said. "It was the most unifying thing I have ever seen, and it went well into the '90s and the twenty-first century. So for the first two and a half decades of the craft beer renaissance, brewers had their backs to the wall. And I think that was the critical ingredient that turned, I mean, it could have been an incredible competitive situation, but it wasn't, except for a few individuals who came out of more of the world of business than the world of brewing."[15]

The annual BAA meetings became educational, with media training sessions in which members were asked difficult questions—"Isn't alcohol a drug that should be banned like other drugs?"—on camera and had their answers critiqued. Entrepreneurs from other industries, like Howard Schultz of Starbuck's Coffee and Chris Martin of Martin Guitars, discussed their companies and answered questions. And the board of directors reported on the programs of the various committees—Nominating, Membership, Public Relations and Marketing, Government Affairs, Wholesaler Relations, and Convention and Finance—and took questions from the membership.

The BAA leadership was also active in the annual legislative conference financed by the BI and the NBWA. But small brewers were still being relegated to the kids' table. We had no role in developing the agenda for lobbying on Capitol Hill. We were still looking for our piece of the action. Still, we found some members of Congress and their aides to be interested in our stories, and we did not hesitate to tell them.

The BI and the NBWA were paying attention. Becker in particular began to take an interest in the small brewing movement. He visited many BAA board members in their home cities. He came to Brooklyn around the turn of the century, and we had dinner at Peter Luger Steak House and then drank beer at Blue Ribbon, not far from my home. Becker told me about growing up in Saginaw, Michigan, and I told him about my early life in southeastern Ohio. In 2000 the BI invited a number of small brewers, including Jordan, Fish, Joyce, Koch, Grossman, and me, to attend its annual meeting as ex-officio, or nonvoting, board members.

The ex-officio board included the CEOs of Heineken and Modelo and industry suppliers of malt, hops, glass, and cans.

In 2000 the BI had only two voting members—Miller and AB; their heads served alternating two-year terms as board chair, and both companies contributed more than a million dollars annually to the budget. The institute's staff included Becker, a lobbyist, a lawyer, and a statistician. Only Becker and the AB and Miller CEOs attended the voting board meeting.

At the full board meeting, which included all the ex-officio members, Becker presented the annual report on the state of the industry and then the chair for that term said a few words. Then Becker asked if anyone had questions. When August Busch III was presiding, you got the clear impression that questions were not welcome. Busch was coming off an incredible era of expansion that took AB from a 20 percent share to a 50 percent share of the US beer business. There was no question of who was King.

I recall that at the first meeting to which the new craft brewer ex-officios were invited in Orlando, Kim Jordan piped up, "We small brewers are concerned that the large brewers' domination of the distributor tier makes it difficult for us to get our beers to market."

You could have heard the proverbial pin drop.

Busch raised his hooded eyes in Jordan's direction. "Don't you believe in the three-tier system?" he asked.

Kim said she did, but it was not working well for small brewers. End of discussion. That was August Busch III's first direct encounter with this new breed of brewer. It would not be his last.

Soon after that meeting the large brewers introduced a bill rolling back the huge beer excise tax increase that President George H. W. Bush had signed in 1991, which had doubled the beer excise tax from $9 a barrel to $18 a barrel for brewers making more than two million barrels annually.

At the next year's BI meeting in Naples, Florida, Jordan, Fish, and I approached AB CEO Pat Stokes and asked if he would include a sweetener in that bill for small brewers. We requested that the tax on the first 60,000 barrels be reduced from $7 to $3.50.

"No," said Stokes. "Ours is a rollback bill. You are asking for a tax reduction. We are simply asking for a rollback of the 1991 increase."

Oh, well, it was worth asking.

In 2003 the BAA did its first holiday beer tasting on Capitol Hill. About twenty-five small breweries poured their Christmas beers and their flagship brews, serving a room full of congressional staffers. We were not surprised to find that the young staff members were big fans of our beers. The NBWA funded the room rental and we donated the beers. It was a huge success—the importance of which was not lost on the NBWA and the BI. Jeff Becker and David Rehr were there.

We were beginning to learn that the craft beer revolution was about more than making and selling great beer. The beer industry, like the wine and liquor industry, is regulated by the federal government and by each of the states. In every state the distributors have an association that hires lobbyists and runs political action committees that dole out campaign donations to elected officials who write laws that regulate the industry. These associations have worked for decades to fashion the franchise laws that create competitive advantages for their business models and so vex craft brewers. Large brewers have lobbyists in every state too. This is why institutions like the BAA are so essential to the success of the beer industry.

Both the NBWA and the BI have long-standing relationships— meaning they have given political contributions and have access—to every leader in Congress and to the president, as well as to key state legislators and every governor in the nation.

We were learning that political action and influence are essential to shaping alcohol beverage policy in America, just as armies of lobbyists represent many other interests in Washington and state capitols. You might hate politics, but ignoring politics is perilous. You could make great beer and still fail if you did not understand the politics of the beer industry.

That fact had been dramatically demonstrated early in the twentieth century when a determined bunch of religious zealots and activists convinced the federal government and the states to institute a prohibition of alcoholic beverages, shutting down hundreds of breweries across the country. The US Brewers Association was not unified when Prohibitionist forces mobilized. It was divided between the big city brewers of the nation, who were mainly focused on their rich home markets, and the rising national "shipping" brewers like AB and Pabst, who were exploiting mass transportation and mass marketing to project their brands across the country.

In the twenty-first century, craft brewers needed a voice in Washington and in every state capital. Breathing new life into the BAA was an important step toward creating that voice. But it was only the first step.

CHAPTER NINE

JAILBREAK

BIG DISTRIBUTORS EMBRACE CRAFT BEER

ONE OF THE MAIN REASONS FOR THE INCREDIBLE GROWTH OF CRAFT BEER SINCE THE mid-2000s has been the willingness of large distributors across the country to acquire craft brands and educate their sales forces to sell those brands. This is nothing short of a sea change in the US beer business. For decades the large brewers dominated their distributors' businesses by selling their beer through the mass media, which they could afford to use to maximum effect. Beer sales reps in those days made their money by developing relationships with their customers. A free keg here, a one-free-keg-on-five deal there, tickets to the baseball game, football game, basketball game, t-shirts, hats, golf balls, and in some cases televisions, video cameras, stereo systems, a trip to the Super Bowl. The light lager beer they were selling was almost incidental to the transaction. The sales reps knew nothing about the beer except that it was light and crisp and drinkable. They took orders for a product sold through slick ads that promised the beer drinker would be the life of the party, that he (and the ads were overwhelmingly aimed at men) would attract the pretty woman, that he was a man's man.

Then in the late 1990s the audience for big media became splintered, no longer concentrating its attention on three channels—ABC, NBC, and CBS—and instead watching scores of channels, limiting the effect of mass media marketing. Imported beers led the way in educating the American beer drinker. Some bar and restaurant owners came to see carrying imports (which in the 1980s accounted for only about 3 percent of the US beer market) as a way of differentiating themselves from their competitors. They served a German beer or a Dutch beer that was somehow more sophisticated than the mainstream light American lager. And those pesky microbrewers that had been hanging around for years slowly went out into the market like beer evangelists, preaching that there was more to American beer than light lager, that many different kinds of lager were available. Even more radically, they preached that lager was only *half* the beer family—the other half was ale.

Some retailers embraced this new religion. They found customers who were homebrewers or who had traveled to Britain, Germany, or Belgium and knew there was more to beer than light lager. They showed their customers something special, something local. In many cases their customers already knew about these beers. In fact, in those early years customers often knew more about microbrewed beer than the bar and restaurant owners.

Among the big distributors, those carrying Miller and Coors had taken on many imported beers and now took on the microbrewers' beers. But that did not mean they promoted small beers aggressively. They essentially said to the brewers, "I will deliver it—but *you* have to sell it." As for the Anheuser-Busch (AB) distributors—who represented roughly 50 percent of the national market—most had no interest in the microbrews. The microbrewers had no money for marketing and their beer was expensive, more expensive than the imports in many cases. The result was that many microbrewers landed at wine and liquor distributors, represented by salespeople who basically knew how to sell wine based on the stories behind the wineries. And a small number of microbrewers distributed their own beers, though only a few states allowed it.

My company, Brooklyn Brewery, reluctantly went into the distribution business in New York City in 1988. My partner, Tom Potter, and I did it on the advice of Sophia Collier, the entrepreneur who created SoHo Natural Soda. She said she had tried to sell SoHo through health food distributors, soda distributors, and beer distributors. All those efforts had failed. "Your stuff doesn't sell," the distributors told her. So she bought a van, had her logo painted on the sides, and went out to sell SoHo Natural Soda herself. And she proved them wrong. When we met Sophia, she was selling her company to Seagram's for $20 million. (Seagram's then screwed it up, but that is another story.)

We took her advice and shelved our plan to build a small brewery in New York City. Instead we contracted with Matt Brewing Company to brew our first beer, Brooklyn Lager, and we put it in a van with our logo painted on its sides, and went out to sell our beer. Most people thought we were crazy.

Our beer was dark. It had a big aroma. It was expensive. And we needed to be paid in cash because we could not afford to give credit. In retrospect I cannot believe anyone bought it. But some people did, and after customers tried it, they placed more orders. A couple of years went by before the big distributors in New York noticed Brooklyn Lager. They could see that we were gaining ground in some of the city's best bars and restaurants. But by the time the distributors came calling, we had gotten over our fear of self-distribution. Now we could see the value in having those direct relationships with bars and restaurants and stores. We were educating our customers about our beer, and they appreciated it. It helped them differentiate themselves from their competitors. It made them special. And when we hosted beer tastings and dinners in their places of business, it strengthened their bonds with their customers.

A handful of other microbrewers and importers who were floundering in the portfolios of New York's big distributors came to us and asked us to take on their beers. Some of our bar and restaurant customers also asked us if we could get particular brands of beer that they had heard about but weren't able to order. By then I was familiar with Michael Jackson's *World Guide to Beer,* and I saw that Jackson had profiled many of the breweries approaching us for distribution. We decided to take on other brands and become the go-to guys for good beer in New York. We took on Charlie and Roseann Finkel's Merchant du Vin line, which included Samuel Smith's, Orval, Lindemans, and Ayinger, and Don and Wendy Fineberg's Vanberg & DeWulf line, which included Duvel, Saison Dupont, and others. We took on Paulaner and Hacker-Pschorr from Germany and Chimay from Belgium. We took on Sierra Nevada from California, Dock Street from Philadelphia, and Geary's from Maine.

Of course we got some criticism that we favored Brooklyn Brewery beers over the others. I won't deny it, but we wanted our distribution arm to be seen as having a larger mission. So we renamed the distribution company the Craft Brewers Guild, and our designer, Milton Glaser, crafted a cool logo that pictured a lovely beer glass and a lion figure found on a lyre uncovered in the excavations at Ur, the ancient Sumerian city where some of the earliest records of beer making had been found.

In 1996, when we opened a microbrewery in Brooklyn, we struggled to grow our brand and our distribution company at the same time. Both demanded cash. Tom Potter began to envision a little empire of Craft Brewers Guild distributors, and, to that end, in 1994 we bought a small craft beer distributor in Boston, Massachusetts, International Beverages, which was owned by one of our suppliers, Bill Erskine. We also hired Robin and Eric Ottaway, sons of one of my journalist friends, David Ottaway, to run the distributorship. What we were trying to do was develop a network of craft beer distributors in New York. But it didn't hold together. Some of our partner-distributors ran out of cash. And others just didn't want to follow our lead. Who were we to tell them which beers to distribute?

We tried an experiment. We blew about a million dollars on an ill-conceived plan to sell our Craft Brewers Guild portfolio directly to consumers in metropolitan New York. It was called totalbeer.com. This gross violation of the three-tier system was actually legal because a loophole in the New York statute gave us the right to be both a wholesaler and a retailer of beer. But it didn't work.

Sometime in the late 1990s we received an invitation to lunch from Jerry Sheehan, the Massachusetts-based Budweiser distributor who had bought the AB distributorship in Brooklyn, Union Beer Distributors. Sheehan was a fit, broad-shouldered man in his sixties, just over six feet tall, with a full head of silver hair and a strong Boston accent. He wore a tweed jacket and a tie. At an Italian restaurant about a block from our brewery, Sheehan told us about buying Union Beer from Joe Lomuscio, a man who had expressed interest in distributing Brooklyn Lager years before.[1] (Lomuscio told us that in the end St. Louis wouldn't let him do it.) I recall thinking that Sheehan must be quite a confident guy to think he could waltz into Brooklyn and run a big distributorship.

At lunch Sheehan quickly got to the point. "You have more draft lines here in Brooklyn than I do," he said. (I recalled from our earlier dalliance with Lomuscio that Union Beer kept a big wall chart of all the tap handles in all the bars and restaurants in Brooklyn.) Sheehan continued, "I want to distribute your beer."

It was flattering, but Tom and I had no interest in selling our distribution company at the time. Until that lunch I hadn't realized we had more tap handles than Budweiser. I knew that Budweiser was the number one beer in Brooklyn and that Heineken, distributed by Phoenix/Beehive, was number two. I began to wonder if all the big distributors had our Brooklyn Lager tap handles in their crosshairs. It got us thinking.

Then came the September 11 attacks on the World Trade Center, which effectively shut down many of the bars and restaurants we distributed to in Manhattan. We abandoned our Internet startup, totalbeer.com, which was struggling, and resolved to sell our distribution companies and focus on

Brooklyn Brewery. We were selling a little more than 70,000 barrels a year at the time, and we felt that the Craft Brewers Guild was actually impeding the growth of Brooklyn Brewery beers. The Craft Brewers Guild had served its purpose in making our brand desirable to the large distributors. Now we felt it was time to focus exclusively on our brewery. So Sheehan bought our operation in Boston. Though the portfolio there was not as extensive as the one in Brooklyn, he could still sell about 200,000 cases annually. And Sheehan believed in the business of the Craft Brewers Guild. So he hired all our staff to start educating his team about the beers in the portfolio.

After lengthy negotiations with Sheehan, Rod Brayman of Phoenix/Beehive, and Simon Bergson of Manhattan Beer distributors, we sold the New York distribution rights to the Brooklyn Brewery brand to Brayman and the New York rights to the rest of the portfolio to Sheehan. We got $12 per case for just under a million cases in annual sales, then used the money to reward our original investors and expand our brewery. To this day Sheehan thanks me for getting him into the craft beer business. And he often laments his decision not to buy the distribution rights to Brooklyn Brewery beers. He regrets listening to people in his company who thought it was too big a gamble.[2]

Sheehan has three sons who are active in his distribution businesses. Chris runs the Brooklyn operation, John runs Wisconsin, and Tim runs Massachusetts. They roll their eyes when their father talks about expanding the Craft Brewers Guild, but Sheehan has proved his doubters wrong, time and time again. Sheehan has since expanded the Craft Brewers Guild to fourteen states. His success has won the attention of AB distributors from coast to coast, not only because he has set up Craft Brewers Guild distributors in many of the AB InBev distributors' backyards. He is bold and fearless, some would say reckless. And he is a huge defender of distributors' rights, especially their right to franchise protection. If not for his outspoken defense of franchise laws, he would be a champion of craft brewers. I have fought him for years over this issue in New York, but I have to admit I really like the guy. You cannot help but like someone as bold and independent as he is.

Many other AB distributors have described to me how Sheehan challenged August Busch III and August Busch IV at their private distributor meetings. As part of the "equity agreements" that AB demands of its distributors, AB grades them on their adherence to the "100 percent share of mind" rule. The grades run from A to E, with an A distributor getting financial and other benefits denied those less committed to the AB line. All of Sheehan's AB distribution companies, from Brooklyn to Syracuse, New York,

Massachusetts, and Wisconsin, are rated E. All carry imports and American craft beers. At the AB distributor meetings Sheehan is the guy challenging the giant brewery's demands that his distributorships carry certain brands and meet certain quotas. More than once I have heard other AB distributors say, "Jerry is fighting the fight for all of us."

At the Brooklyn Brewery we feel we are good at managing our distributors. The reason is that we were a distributor and hence we feel their pain. We know what it is like to have a brewer come in and complain about the way we failed to focus on her brand, and we have experienced the frustration when that brewer offers no support for our efforts. We know what it is like for a brewer to come in, introduce a sales rep who is supposed to be working our market, and then watch that sales rep disappear after a day or two of getting beaten up in the New York market. We know what it is like for brewers to pull their brands and move to a competitor with no compensation to us.

Our approach is to focus on what we—that is, we and the distributor—both need to do, working cooperatively, to improve things.

Daniel Bradford, publisher of *All About Beer*, said he believes that craft brewers have made no difference in the three-tier system of distribution or how distributors do business. Craft brewers have simply learned to work with distributors. Consumer demand for craft beer is what forced the AB InBev distributors to open up to craft brewers. "We didn't really change the game. We just learned to play the game."[3]

Harry Schuhmacher, publisher of *Beer Business Daily*, sees the opening of the AB InBev network to craft brewers as a significant change in the structure of the beer distribution business. "The jailbreak substantially changed the industry on the distributor side more than anything else that happened in the last 20 years," Schuhmacher said. Before the AB InBev distributors opened up to craft, said Schuhmacher, craft brewers had two choices only: the MillerCoors distributor or a wine and spirits distributor. "There was a kind of malaise because the distributors didn't have to work that hard. There was no competition for brands. Now the competition is tremendous and the distributors are committing real dollars to marketing the craft brands. I would say the jailbreak definitely added a few tenths of a percent to the craft brewers' market share."

I think it is important for craft brewers to understand the perspective of distributors. I have talked to distributors who have told me about the bad old days before they had franchise protection. They lived in fear of the big breweries. The breweries could terminate their contract with a distributor for any reason or for no reason, and it could happen at any time. The distributors said they used to hide photos of their families on vacation or signs of golf or tennis if a brewer was coming to visit for fear the brewer would conclude the distributor was wasting time away from the job. I have heard stories of distributors being terminated by a giant because they took on a competing brewery. I have heard big brewers sneer, "We made these guys millionaires and now they are turning against us." No doubt the big breweries have done much to build their brands, but so have their distributors. And those distributors are the big brewers' representatives in the communities they serve. They are also the eyes and ears of the big brewers, and that relationship is a precious one for the brewers.

For me, getting to know Jerry Sheehan was important. It helped me understand that the history of the distribution business sometimes reads like a family saga. And their relationships with the big brewers—often decades old—can have a profound influence on family fortunes.

Sheehan was born in 1931 in Jersey City, New Jersey. His paternal grandfather, John Sheehan, had emigrated from Ireland in 1910. Sheehan's father was educated by Christian Brothers Academy and managed a company that employed 450 men servicing the rail lines for the Lehigh Valley Railroad. They called the workers "gandy dancers" because the mechanism that operated the carts they got around on looked like a teeter-totter, and the two men at the handles bobbled up and down like ganders dancing. Sheehan recalled that the men were paid every two weeks, and on payday many would head to the Bowery in Manhattan with the sole intention of getting blind drunk.[4]

When he was a student at Holy Cross College in Boston, Sheehan met Maureen Cortelli, a student at Newton College, at a tea dance. Her paternal grandfather was a shepherd who emigrated to America from Italy's Emilia Romagna region when he was sixteen. He sold peanuts on the streets of Plymouth, Massachusetts, after a stint making rope for the Plymouth Cordage Company like most Portuguese and Italian residents of the area. "When he got enough capital, he bought a horse and wagon and went out peddling in the countryside," Sheehan said. "Then he got enough money to build a grocery store. Whatever he made, he reinvested in real estate. He owned tenements and land."

At one point Luigi changed the family name to Knife after a banker warned him that no one would loan money to someone named Cortelli. Maureen's father, Domero Knife, became a wholesaler, selling flour to bakeries and hay, grain, and fertilizers to farmers, as well as cigars and playing cards to interested customers. Using the name Tim Knife, Domero became a beer distributor in 1935 and got the distribution rights to Budweiser Beer through AB's national sales manager. When Sheehan got out of the Marine Corps in 1957, he joined his father-in-law's business, L. Knife and Son. Domero Knife had a total of fourteen employees. Sheehan soon observed that Domero had no desire to grow the business. In fact, his father-in-law turned down Jim Beam Bourbon and other beverages that wanted him to distribute for them. When Sheehan argued for expansion, he was met with a shrug.

"Jerry, what do we want to get bigger for?" his father-in-law would say. "You can only drive one car." What Domero cared about was a lifestyle that allowed him time to enjoy his family and friends. "You have enough," Domero would tell Sheehan. "What do you want more for?"

This didn't sit well with Sheehan, who recalls, "I was always chasing him down to get Heineken's or this brand or that brand."

Sheehan can draw a vivid picture of the days before franchise laws when the breweries were king. "Every letterhead that came in said, 'There are no exclusive territories, franchises. Everything is order to order,' right on the letterhead. And they would do a one-day check up on you. . . . A guy in northern Massachusetts took on Rheingold [the New York City brewery]. He never sold another case of Budweiser. Sometimes people would pay the regional manager to get a territory from another distributor. The manager would just walk in and say, 'You're not performing,' and that was that."

In the 1960s Gussie Busch, the father of August Busch III, established a national distributor panel to write a contract for all AB wholesalers nationwide. "We sat there for days, with guys saying we want this and that," Sheehan recalled. "I said, 'Guys, we just want one thing, the right to sell your business as a going business.' That was the greatest thing we ever got. Before that they had the right to terminate you at will. If you want to terminate me, I can't sell it as a going concern."[5]

Before that contract was negotiated, distributors had no right to sell their business without the approval of the brewer. That meant they were completely dependent on the brewer. Sheehan worked as a route salesman for his father-in-law. "He would throw me out of the office every day," Sheehan said. "I ran a route until I became a ride-with supervisor. I never worked in the office. If I didn't make 10,000 retail calls, I will eat my hat. It was day in and day out for ten years until he died, and then I became general manager in 1967."

He said the company had four sales reps year-round and one extra in summer. His father-in-law was right to throw him out of the office, he said. "I scream when I see my men in the office drinking a cup of coffee in the morning. 'Go buy a cup of coffee and take it to a customer. Don't drink that coffee here.'"

Sheehan has three rules for selling beer: "Fresh beer sells beer. Distribution drives volume. Volume covers all sins. . . . I tell my guys, when they deal with suppliers, 'Consistently exceed their expectations.' Those are the keys to the beer distribution business."

His distributorship was selling other brands, like Pickwick Ale, Harvard Ale, Haffenreffer, and Utica Club, before it got Budweiser, so it was never an exclusive AB distributor. The distributorship was selling 100,000 cases a year in 1967. A case of returnable twelve-ounce bottles of Budweiser cost the retailer $3.73 plus a bottle deposit of 60 cents.

The Busch family lorded their market share over their distributors, but also shared some of the luxuries of their life with them.

Every year, Gussie Busch and his wife Trudy would pick up Sheehan and ten other distributors and their wives in Cape Cod in his yacht, "The *A & Eagle*," and take them to the Jockey Club in Fort Lauderdale, to Bimini, and to Walker's Key. Every morning they would take "bull shots," vodka and beef bouillon concoctions. All day they would play gin rummy, break for drinks and then dinner, and then drink all night. Sheehan said his wife Maureen, who doesn't drink, hated the trips and would retire to her stateroom to read. "It drove my wife nuts," he said. After six years, she stopped going on the cruises. The other wives couldn't believe it, saying, "Your wife is blowing Gussie Busch off!"

The 1970s were big years for AB. Sheehan's sales went to 300,000 cases and continued to grow 20 percent a year. He started buying other AB distributorships in the 1980s. The first was in Syracuse, New York; then he scooped up nearby distributorships in Rome and Utica and Little Falls. In 1988 he bought the distributorship for Wisconsin, Miller's home state, although the business was losing $1.2 million a year. It took a decade for Sheehan to make a profit in Wisconsin. All of the new distributorships were what Sheehan describes variously as basket cases or turkeys. (Syracuse had gone through three owners in three years.) Meanwhile, Sheehan noted, Busch favorites and family members were getting distributorships in places like Palm Beach and Washington State.

Also, Sheehan realized that by staying loyal to AB, he was losing ground to his competitors, who were taking on important craft brands that were growing rapidly. In Syracuse, for instance, he watched his competitor gain a 45 percent market share while Sheehan's share declined to 17 percent.

Sometime around 2000, Sheehan decided to aggressively pursue non-AB brands for all his distributorships.

When he first started selling Craft Brewers Guild brands, Sheehan focused on expanding their distribution and targeting craft-friendly customers. Later he recognized the importance of teaching his sales force the stories behind the various craft breweries. He recalled that Joe Lipa, the irrepressible eastern sales rep for the Merchant du Vin line of beers, was one of the best teachers for Sheehan's fledgling sales force. Now Sheehan requires all his sales reps to take Ray Daniel's "Cicerone" beer education program, the most widely respected program in the United States, and Sheehan invites luminaries like Garrett Oliver to address his team.

Educating salespeople has become so important to Sheehan that he has his representatives make regular visits to breweries like Wachusett, Smuttynose, Allagash, and Brooklyn to work with their brewers in the brewhouse. In Sheehan's view, these visits not only help his employees develop a sense of camaraderie with the brewers, it gives the sales reps a real feel for what goes on in the brewhouse. "When you pick up a bag of grain and pour it into the mash tun, you feel it and you see it and you smell it," he said.

As of this writing, Sheehan operates Craft Brewers Guild distributors in New York, Connecticut, Massachusetts, Rhode Island, Maine, Vermont, New Hampshire, New Jersey, Maryland, Virginia, California, Wisconsin, Kentucky, and the District of Columbia. He has at least one warehouse in each of the states, four in New York and three in Massachusetts. His biggest craft brand is New Glarus, which famously sells only in Wisconsin.

In Massachusetts the Craft Brewers Guild showed a 14 percent increase between 2012 and 2013, selling 1.5 million cases in all. In New York sales are projected to be more than double that, at 3.3 million cases for 2013. At the same time his Budweiser franchise in Brooklyn has fallen from sales of 5.3 million cases in 1996, the year he bought it, to 3 million in 2013. He said part of the problem in Brooklyn is that other Budweiser wholesalers are selling beer in his territory, violating his exclusive territory agreement with AB InBev. This practice, called transshipping, is the bane of all distributors. Sheehan's craft brands have higher profit margins than his AB InBev products, making up for the loss of AB volume.

AMONG THE AB INBEV DISTRIBUTORS WHO HAVE FOLLOWED SHEEHAN'S LEAD IS THE Ben E. Keith Company distributorship in Fort Worth, once the country's largest distributor of AB InBev beers. As a Dallas-area Bud distributor, Keith sold nearly 40 million cases annually. Howard and Robert Hallam, owners of the distributorship, bought a small craft beer distributor, C.R. Goodman, in 2008 and set up a statewide distribution network to sell craft beers outside their Bud territory footprint.

The company's affiliation with AB goes back to the Prohibition era, when it started an ice cream parlor that became a social center for Forth Worth. Ben E. Keith, who had been a top salesman for what was then a produce company and who had bought the majority of its shares in 1918, went to St. Louis and started buying malt syrups from Adolphus Busch to mix with ice cream. Gaston Hallam, whose first job with the company in 1924 was unloading boxcars, recalled that Keith salesmen also cautioned customers about another use of malt syrup. "Be careful," they would say. "If you put yeast and water in the malt syrup, it will turn into beer." The history of Ben E. Keith states, "Naturally, that's exactly what they did."[6]

When one of the founders died in 1926, the company changed its name to Ben E. Keith Company. When Prohibition ended, it began distributing AB beers. Ben E. Keith's first order of AB beer was for fifty-seven rail cars on September 15, 1933. On December 5 Ben E. Keith sold its first case of Budweiser.

Hallam, meanwhile, rose in the company and purchased its stock every chance he got; eventually he gained control. Ben E. Keith is now run by his two sons, Robert and Howard Hallam. On their watch Ben E. Keith has become one of the largest AB distributors in the country, selling more than 39 million cases of beer annually. Their food distribution business spans the states of Texas, New Mexico, Oklahoma, Kansas, Arkansas, and Louisiana.[7]

"We had been an exclusive Anheuser-Busch distributor ever since we became an AB distributor at the end of Prohibition in 1933," Howard Hallam said. "We had a long history with AB and never sold another brand of beer. But things began changing in 2006–2007. AB began making acquisitions and import arrangements for brands such as Rolling Rock, Grolsch, Stella Artois, Beck's, Bass, and others, and these brands were already assigned to other distributors in our marketing area. Thus, while we remained exclusive with AB . . . they were not exclusive with us."[8]

The Hallam brothers set out to expand their portfolio, but they found it difficult to acquire new brands. Their competitors had taken on every import and American craft beer entering Texas. The Hallams sought out top craft brands that were not yet in the state. They introduced Brooklyn Brewery from New York and Harpoon Brewery from Boston. Then C.R. Goodman, a statewide craft beer distributor, came up for sale.

"We saw that the growth of the craft segment was explosive, and so we paid a high price to acquire C.R. Goodman," Howard Hallam said. "We believed in the tremendous growth of the craft beer segment, and frankly we didn't want our competitors to get them. Over the years, we had watched our competitors take on many brands that we refused to take because of exclusivity—Modelo, Shiner, and many others. We were never offered these brands, or declined them, because of our commitment to exclusivity."

In 2013 AB is projected to sell about 35 million cases in Ben E. Keith's territory. But the statewide craft beer distributorship run by Ben E. Keith is projected to sell 3.8 million cases of craft beer, at margins higher than the AB brands.

"We have never looked back [with regret] on our venture with craft beer," Howard Hallam said. "It has been a lot of fun. It almost changed my life. We are very excited by these brands, and we like selling them based on their flavors and the people behind them. It has put fun back in the beer business."[9]

The breach of exclusivity by Sheehan and Ben E. Keith emboldened other AB InBev distributors to take on craft brands. The beer media began referring to this trend as a *jailbreak.* This led an AB InBev executive to criticize as insidious the practice of AB InBev distributors' selling other brands and competing against Bud outside their Bud territory.[10]

The AB InBev network in recent years has called for alignment of its wholesalers with the AB InBev-owned and -allied brands, like Goose Island, Redhook, Kona, and Widmer, but this has not stopped AB InBev distributors across the country from aggressively courting and acquiring other craft brands. This has opened up the country's largest beer distribution network to craft brands and in my view is a major reason for the rapid growth of craft beer since the mid-2000s.

Craft beer has grown by double digits since 2009. At the same time the large brewers, AB InBev with a 46 percent market share and MillerCoors with a 28 percent market share, have lost 17.6 million barrels of production.[11] In the late 1990s the industry analyst Bob Weinberg was predicting that the US beer market would increase by 10 percent in the first decade of the twenty-first century because the children of the last of the baby boomers were turning twenty-one.[12] Craft brewers enjoyed rapid growth in that period, but overall beer consumption fell significantly. Americans just are not drinking beer like they used to. The large brewers have blamed the recession, bad weather, and wine and spirits taking market share from beer. I believe a big reason is stricter enforcement of drunk-driving laws. People are far more careful about drinking and driving these days. And it is clear that some beer drinkers are looking for something a little more interesting than the light lager beers that built the empires of the national breweries.

THE LARGEST DISTRIBUTOR IN THE UNITED STATES IS REYES BEVERAGE GROUP, A MillerCoors distributor. Reyes has also developed a strong craft beer program. Reyes distributes more than 100 million cases of beer annually with operations in South Carolina, Georgia, Illinois, Virginia, California, Washington, DC, Florida, and Maryland. Reyes Holdings also operates a vast distribution network for the McDonald's Corporation.

The Reyes family story should be the subject of a book of its own. It begins in 1976 when brothers Chris and Jude Reyes, along with their father, Joe, purchased a Schlitz beer distributorship, Dixie Systems of Spartanburg, South Carolina. Dixie was a modest operation, with dirt floors and beat-up trucks. But Dixie became the foundation for a list of acquisitions that would reshape the American beer and food distribution world.

Reyes was an early distributor of Boston Beer Company and helped put Samuel Adams Boston Lager on the map. It was also an early distributor of Sierra Nevada. But for many years Reyes's distributors had a poor reputation among the smaller craft brewers. Many complained that Reyes's minimum delivery requirements for retailers and impatience with small-volume craft brands made it a poor choice for craft brewers.

My company moved our brands from DOPS, a small wine distributor in the District of Columbia, to Reyes in that territory in 2005. But after a few months of falling sales and Reyes cutting our portfolio, we went back to the wine distributor, cap in hand. Brooklyn was a small brand in the eyes of Reyes Holdings, but the company did not like losing the brand. Bob Johnson, president of Reyes's Premium Distributors of Washington, DC, started trying to bring us back, saying the company was changing its ways.

"We've always been selling the bigger crafts, but I think it was about 2004 when we said, 'You know, this thing is going to continue to grow. . . . We thought this [craft beers] is clearly going to be a very big thing for a very long time," said Jimmy Reyes, a director and senior vice president at Reyes. "And nine years later I still think it's going to be a very big thing for a very long time. The genie is out of the bottle, and variety is what the consumer wants."[13]

Jimmy Reyes said that craft brands now represent 14 percent of Reyes Holdings's annual sales of 105 million cases. That 14 percent in volume is almost 20 percent in gross profit. "I see that being 25 or 30 percent three years from now," he said. "I am a big believer that the category is going to grow, and it would be a good thing. . . . The beer category hasn't been that good since 2007. These things are growing in a tough economy. If the economy does get good at some point, they're going to grow even more."

He said today's craft beer consumers are looking for more than just seasonal beers. "They want a change more than once a season; they're going to change three times a season," he predicted. Reyes has developed technologies to handle the proliferation of brands, or SKUs (stock keeping units). "[But] the number one thing is just making sure that the beer is fresh."

Asked about the 1,500 breweries in the planning stages across the country, he said: "I think it's great; I would never tell an entrepreneur not to go after his dreams. That's not my job. There's been a million brands that you thought were going to do well that didn't and ones you thought weren't going to do anything that did well. You just don't know."

In his view the weak players will fold, but Jimmy Reyes believes the growth of new breweries will continue. Having seen how the Internet and social media have created awareness of craft beers all across the country, Reyes regards the change as permanent. "The whole country has opened up; people want choice and variety."[14]

Benj Steinman, publisher of *Beer Marketer's Insights,* said Reyes and L. Knife and Son are "the most influential beer distributors in the United States." He said the Reyes group has the best distribution systems in the business and "changed the game" when it acquired the Chicago craft-centric beer distributor Windy City Distibution in 2012, paying $70 million for annual sales of fewer than 1 million cases. "Sales of Windy City are up 40 percent in the first year," Steinman added.[15]

According to Steinman, L. Knife has one of the most developed non–AB InBev portfolios although it remains one of the largest AB InBev distributors in the country.

"L. Knife is what many AB InBev distributors these days long to be: less dependent on AB InBev," he said. "The average AB InBev wholesaler gets over 90 percent of its sales from AB InBev products. . . . L. Knife is one of the only AB InBev distributors that sells a high percentage of its volume in non–AB InBev products. . . . L. Knife began to get serious about craft beer over a decade ago, and it has paid off."[16]

CHAPTER TEN

THE BREWERS' ASSOCIATION OF AMERICA AND THE ASSOCIATION OF BREWERS MERGE

IT IS NOT HAPPENSTANCE THAT THE CURRENT BOOM IN CRAFT BREWING OCCURRED after the Association of Brewers (AOB) and the Brewers' Association of America (BAA) merged and became the Brewers Association (BA). The merger marked the first time in the history of the craft beer revolution that nearly all of the nation's small brewers were working together to promote and protect America's craft brewers. That is not to say that the craft brewing community was in lockstep on all issues. Getting 2,600 brewers to agree on every issue would be impossible. But the BA, with its elected board of directors representing packaging brewers, pub brewers, and homebrewers, was widely recognized as the legitimate representative of the American craft brewing community.

The negotiations that led to the merger were difficult. In the late 1990s and the early years of the twenty-first century, the BAA developed a solid political agenda for small brewers. Its members, which included most of the top fifty small breweries in the country, were working to develop their political and media skills through their interaction with the large brewers, represented by the Beer Institute (BI), and the distributors, represented by the National Beer Wholesalers Association (NBWA). The Christmas beer tastings in Washington, DC, organized by the BAA and sponsored by the NBWA, were the first time the small brewing community had presented itself to Congress in any organized way. But in that first year, 2003, the BAA had barely one

hundred brewery members, and its budget was $200,000. It was tiny com-
pared to Charlie Papazian's AOB, which had 625 brewery members and a
budget of $2.54 million that year. The AOB had two great money-generating
events, the Great American Beer Festival, which showcased 386 breweries in
2003, and the Craft Brewers Conference, which drew 905 participants that
year.[1] And BAA members were paying dues to both organizations and send-
ing employees and free beer to the events of both organizations. In 2001 craft
brewers also became active in the BI, which tapped a number of craft brewers
that year to serve as nonvoting members of its board of directors.

Members of the BAA, like me, were attending board meetings and events
for three trade associations. Martin Kelly, then CEO of Pyramid Breweries
and a member of the BAA board, said, "With only 3 percent market share, we
cannot hope to grow while supporting two competing trade associations."[2]
Kelly was referring to the BAA and the AOB, both of which claimed to represent small brewers.

But the AOB remained largely in the hands of Papazian. His board of
directors was more like the Boulder Chamber of Commerce than the governing board of a trade association. The Institute for Brewing and Fermentation Studies had always had a board of advisors. The first issue of the *New
Brewer,* dated November 1983, listed the advisors as Stuart Harris, Papazian's
computer-savvy friend who coined the term *microbrewery,* and William S.
Newman, the pioneering founder of the Wm. S. Newman Brewing Co. and
brewer of Albany Amber. Over the years Papazian added more brewers to
the advisory board, American and Canadian, along with some suppliers and
even some retailers and state association executives like John Carlson of the
Colorado Brewers Guild.

Chuck Skypeck, founder of Boscos Restaurant & Brewing Co., a brewpub
in Nashville, said the board of advisors became quite active in steering the Institute for Brewing and Fermentation Studies in the late 1990s. In 2002, when
merger talks between the AOB and the BAA got going, Skypeck chaired the
board of advisors. John Hickenlooper was vice chair.[3] Ken Allen of Anderson
Valley also joined the AOB's board of directors, the first brewer to do so.[4]

Sitting on the BAA board were the largest of the small breweries. The
chair was Kim Jordan of New Belgium Brewing Company, vice chair was
Gary Fish of Deschutes Brewery, and the secretary-treasurer was Chuck
Lawson of the Lion Brewery. Some early efforts to bring the AOB and the
BAA together went nowhere—the leaders of the AOB and BAA, Papazian
and Bradford, were barely even on speaking terms. The mistrust between

the two organizations was great. The AOB saw the BAA as a clubby association of the largest craft brewers. The BAA saw the AOB as a festival and conference promoter run by nonbrewers. During the years of competing organizations "we struggled getting along," recalled Jordan, chair of the BAA. She said she considered skipping the AOB's Craft Brewers Conference every other year to demonstrate her dissatisfaction with the situation.[5]

Hickenlooper tried to broker talks between the two organizations. His efforts failed, even though he was a close friend of both Papazian and Bradford.

"It was crazy to have two organizations competing with each other, particularly when both did different things very well and some other things not so well," Hickenlooper said. "It was a matter of getting two organizations to look beyond their narrow self-interest to the broader interests of the craft brewing community."[6]

One of the first informal efforts to discuss a merger took place at the Craft Brewers Conference in New Orleans in April 2003. The BAA team—Fish, Jordan, and I—pressed the AOB team—Allen, Skypeck, and Carlson—to agree to the concept of an organization run by and for brewers. We agreed, but neither board had officially sanctioned the meeting. The AOB board of directors took the initiative and invited Jordan to join its board. She agreed, on the condition that the board be informed that her purpose was to work toward a merger of the two associations. But when she announced her intention at her first board meeting, she got a cold reception. Clearly no one had told the other board members of her determination to work for a merger.[7]

Late in 2003 the BAA and AOB boards established the One Voice Task Force to work on a merger. The BAA team included Jordan, Fish, Rich Doyle of Harpoon Brewery, Kelly, and me. The AOB team was Papazian, Skypeck, Carlson, Jack Joyce of Rogue Ales, and Randy Mosher of the American Homebrewers Association (AHA). Word of the talks quickly spread through the industry.

But the effort got off to a rocky start. Joyce recalled that Bradford visited the Boulder headquarters of the AOB at one point and told the staff that the BAA was going to take over the AOB.[8] Bradford said that was not the message he sought to convey. He said Jordan had asked him to go to Boulder and meet with the AOB staff to assure them that any merger would not endanger their jobs. But the painful meeting backfired. "It was a noble gesture that scared the crap out of everybody," Bradford said.[9]

Despite that hiccup, the task force soldiered on. "This was such an exciting first step," Jordan said. "We had all of this potential to focus our industry's resources, and we were actually going to be able to work together to forge an agreement. Naively, I was sure this was going to be a terrific process."[10]

Intense and sometimes heated negotiations were held in 2003 and 2004 at industry meetings.

"At the outset, the challenge was that Charlie Papazian and his organization [the AOB] had a way of operating, and they didn't see any reason to change it," Jordan said. "The AOB was working well, and he felt the threat of losing control. And of course, there was the enmity between Charlie and Daniel Bradford."[11]

Among the difficult discussions were what the dues structure should be, how the new organization's board could be representative of the packaging brewers, pub brewers, homebrewers, and members of allied trades. How would Papazian work with Bradford? There were countless phone calls and emails. Fires erupted and were put out.

"It was a culture clash," Mosher said. "Both parties had long eyed the other with suspicion. Part of the merger process was a real discovery, on one side, of the intentions and professionalism of the other. I think it's fair to say that the BAA approached things very much from a tactical, business point of view, along the lines of a traditional trade association. The AOB approached things from a wider perspective. With its programs and activities of festivals, competition, and publishing, and the inclusion of homebrewers, AOB sought to promote beer as a cultural resource, a position important to the continued success of craft brewing."[12]

Many of the packaging brewers questioned the participation of homebrewers. What role could a bunch of hobbyists play in a brewing industry trade association? Complicating the discussion was that the AHA was losing money. The AOB was subsidizing it. Mosher and Joyce argued that the homebrewers were the biggest fans of craft brewers, the first line of defense in any attack on the industry.

The hydra-like organization that Papazian developed was on trial. Two of its elements, the AHA and Brewers Publications, were losing money. Were they important to the mission of a trade association?

As with any negotiation, it was a process of breaking down suspicions and building trust. At one point a rumor spread that the BAA was considering boycotting the AOB if the merger did not work out. While the BAA discussed that possibility, a boycott was never under serious consideration. Jordan, the former social worker who had counseled troubled families, was the peacemaker. She was a member of both boards and repeatedly urged both camps to avoid "making up stories" about each other. Because she was based in Fort Collins, Colorado, she was close enough to keep tabs on the AOB in Boulder.

"We worked hard, but no one worked more diligently than Kim," said Fish, who was chair of the BAA when it merged with the AOB.[13]

At a certain point, Jordan recalled, "Charlie [Papazian] just flipped a switch. I was wildly impressed with his sudden ability to get on board. I think the reason was [the AOB's chief operating officer] Bob Pease. Bob saw that the BAA board members had experience with running a trade association and they had experience with other not-for-profit organizations and governing boards. He realized, 'This is how a board should operate.' Bob saw it and helped bring Charlie to it. He saw that the BAA folks did not want to micromanage the AOB."[14]

The agreement was reached during two days of meetings in August 2004 at the Oxford Hotel in Denver's LoDo neighborhood. The two organizations agreed to merge into a new organization known as the BA. Nick Matt, CEO of Matt Brewing Company, distilled the mission of the new organization to, simply, "promote and protect" craft brewers. The organization would use the AOB offices in Boulder and retain the AOB's twenty-two employees. Papazian would become president of the BA. Bradford was offered the position of legislative director, but he declined and went back to serving as publisher of *All About Beer.* Pete Johnson, a former congressional aide who worked with Bradford on legislative affairs, became the head of the BA's Government Affairs Program.

The agreement provided for graduated dues for larger brewers, and static low dues for microbrewers and pub brewers. A strong committee system, modeled on the BAA system, would be put in place. The membership would elect seven packaging brewery board members, four brewpub members, and the AHA would choose two board members. And the full board could elect two at-large members to ensure geographic distribution and that breweries of various sizes were represented. An interim board was chosen to serve for a one year term and the merger became effective January 1, 2005. The idea that first took shape in the mid-1990s had led to the creation of a potentially powerful trade association.

"WE MET AS A TRANSITIONAL BOARD FOR THE FIRST TIME AT THE BAA'S FINAL conference in New Orleans in November 2004," recalled Steve Bradt of

Free State Brewing. "I thought it was a somewhat contentious meeting, and I felt we were moving forward with a very tentative sense of trust between the two sides."[15] Bradt recalled that during the first year of the new organization, "I was relieved and impressed with how the group came together to shape the vision and mission of the new organization. We disagreed, but there was respect and willingness to compromise. A lot of the credit for this has to go to Kim Jordan who shepherded us through the process with determination, patience and grace. Equal credit for the success of the first year has to go to the BA staff who responded to the needs and challenges of a new organization and a new board with energy, enthusiasm and a positive outlook, making our first year a huge success in every respect."[16]

The job of managing the new organization fell to the former day-to-day manager of the AOB, Bob Pease, now Chief Operating Officer of the BA. Pease said it was a very exciting, challenging, and scary time. "Looking back nine years later, I think it's clear that the merger was one of the seminal moments in the rise of craft brewing," said Pease in an interview. "I am very proud to have been involved every step of the way, from the due diligence period when the two organizations exchanged foundational documents to the very first board meeting in New Orleans."

The new board of directors was charged with the stated purpose of the BA, to "promote and protect" craft brewers and the community of brewing enthusiasts. But who were the craft brewers we were going to promote and protect? How did we define a craft brewer? These had been contentious issues for years. The BA's Public Relations and Marketing Committee, chaired by Vinnie Cilurzo of Russian River Brewing Company, finally recommended appropriate wording, and the board approved the following definition:

An American craft brewer is small, independent and traditional. Craft beer comes only from a craft brewer.

Small—Annual production of beer less than 2 million barrels. Beer production is attributed to a brewer according to the rules of alternating proprietorships. Flavored malt beverages are not considered beer for purposes of this definition.

Independent—Less than 25 percent of the craft brewery is owned or controlled (or equivalent economic interest) by an alcoholic beverage industry member who is not themselves a craft brewer.

Traditional—A brewer who has either an all malt flagship (the beer which represents the greatest volume among that brewer's brands) or has at least 50 percent of its volume in either all malt beers or in beers which use adjuncts to enhance rather than lighten flavor.

The definition would disqualify some long-time BAA members from using the designation of *craft brewer*—among them, the August Schell Brewing Company, D.G. Yuengling & Son (whose flagship brands used corn adjuncts), Redhook Brewery, and Widmer Brothers Brewing Company (both were partly owned by Anheuser-Busch [AB]). Such exclusions would lead to hard feelings and a nagging, sometimes bitter, controversy. But the merger led to a stronger organization financially and organizationally. Within a few years the AHA and Brewers Publications were growing and contributing financially to the BA.

"Once we had the right mix of people on the BA board, we were able to help focus and drive the very professional group of people that Charlie had assembled on the AOB staff," Jordan said. "The Great American Beer Festival got better, with more founders and owners attending, and the Craft Brewers Conference got better, and we knew what we had to build from this incredible base."[17]

ONE OF THE MORE INTERESTING MOMENTS FOR THE NEWLY FORMED BA WAS A meeting with August Busch IV during the 2007 joint BI–NBWA meeting in Washington, DC. As far as I know, this was the first time a Busch ever agreed to a meeting with the small brewers of America.

Stories of the rather tortured personal struggles of the fourth-generation heir of the world's largest brewery have been well-documented in several books: *Under the Influence* by Terry Ganey, *Dethroning the King* by Julie MacIntosh, and *Bitter Brew: The Rise and Fall of Anheuser-Busch and America's Kings of Beer* by William Knoedelseder. For the BA board of directors, meeting "the Fourth," as he was known, was a big deal. We viewed it as a step in our quest for a seat at the table with the large brewers and distributors.

I was chair of the BA when the meeting was held. Some members of the BA huddled in advance to talk about our approach. I said I would do an introduction and ask the first question of the young Busch. Then I would open the questioning up to others. Jim Koch said he wanted to hear Busch's explanation of AB's media campaign against Boston Beer Company in the mid-1990s. I told Koch I did not think it would be helpful to rehash that old dispute, and I thought Koch had agreed not to bring it up.

The meeting was held in a small conference room at a hotel near Capitol Hill. Busch was flanked by Dave Peacock, who would become president of AB InBev, Mark Boback, the general counsel for AB, and Bob Lackey, chief marketing officer of AB.

I opened the meeting by welcoming August Busch IV, noting that "We all have grown up drinking the beers that your family brews." Then I added remarks along these lines: "We have great respect for your company and your products. We came to the beer business in ways very different from you. You are the latest in a long line of Buschs to run your company. We all fell in love with beer and set out to brew special beers with special flavors and varied styles. I wonder if you could tell us what you think of our contribution to the brewing industry."

Busch responded in a respectful, low-key manner, telling us he had closely followed the development of the craft beer segment and thinks our beers have brought a great new vitality to the industry.

When he finished, I waited for one of my BA colleagues to follow up with the next question. Several seconds passed as an awkward silence developed.

Busch looked disconcerted. "Did I say something wrong?" he asked.

"No, certainly not—I am waiting for one of my colleagues to follow up," I said, laughing. He then fielded a few questions about distribution and the "100 percent share of mind" policy of his father. Then Koch launched into a long tirade against AB for the attack on his company in the mid-1990s. Busch listened patiently and replied, "Jim, that was in my father's time. I had nothing to do with that."

The meeting was important because it allowed AB to express its respect for what craft brewers were bringing to the industry. It was short on substance, but long on symbolism. I think it was an important step in the BA's development as a national trade organization. It moved us closer to that seat at the table.

CHAPTER ELEVEN

A SEAT AT THE TABLE

ON MAY 9, 2008, THE BREWERS ASSOCIATION (BA) FINALLY GOT ITS SEAT AT THE table—a seat on the voting board of the Beer Institute (BI) alongside the CEOs of Anheuser-Busch (AB), Miller Brewing Company, Molson Coors Brewing Co., which had earlier announced a joint venture called Miller-Coors, Heineken USA, and Modelo Brewing Co. (brewer of Corona Beer). The BI, not the BA, got to choose the new board member. And I was the choice. I assume that Jeff Becker, president of the BI, chose me because we had gotten to know each other pretty well during the previous ten years while playing golf and dining and drinking beer together many times. I was painfully aware that I would be performing a balancing act, since I also had to clearly represent the interests of the BA to maintain any credibility within the small brewery community.

The May 2008 board meeting, the first I attended, was held in Washington, DC, during the joint legislative conference of the BI and the National Beer Wholesalers Association (NBWA). I took my seat next to August Busch IV; Tom Long, CEO of Miller Brewing Company and the joint venture MillerCoors; Peter Swinburne, CEO of Coors Brewing Company, who was accompanied by Peter Coors, the Coors chair; Don Blaustein of Heineken USA; and Carlos Fernandez of Modelo Brewing Co. It was an honor to be sitting at the same table with men whose beers I had drunk for many of my early years and whose ads I had seen and heard my whole life.

That charmed moment did not last long. The big were about to get bigger, with serious implications for the entire industry. A few months later AB was sold to the Belgian-based, Brazilian-controlled megabrewer InBev, forming AB InBev. Miller and Coors had combined in a joint venture to become

MillerCoors in 2007. At the next meeting I attended, August Busch IV was gone, Peter Coors was gone, and it occurred to me that Brooklyn Brewery was the only wholly American-owned brewery at the table. I resisted the urge to point this out. Busch had been replaced by Dave Peacock, a man well known in the industry as a close aide to August Busch IV. Long was the sole representative of MillerCoors. The Brazilians had achieved a breathtaking conquest with their takeover of AB. And they quickly let it be known that the lavish executive style of the Busch family was a thing of the past. They gutted the executive offices in St. Louis, packing a few hundred people onto a floor that had once held just a handful of AB executives. About 2,500 people were laid off, and the entire AB sales force was instructed to hand in their Blackberries. The new owners announced that traveling executives would stay at budget hotels and rent inexpensive cars. The Brazilians sold most of the company's corporate jets.

In the days of August Busch III, AB distributors lived in fear of his unannounced white-glove inspections and rapid-fire questions. But at least he was familiar. In Europe and South America, where InBev operated, no three-tier system protected distributors from brewer control. AB already had complete ownership of distributors in some important US cities, where state laws allowed it. The new AB InBev empire, many feared, would be unstoppable.

Many AB distributors in the United States were multimillionaires; some had private jets and several homes. They were able to accumulate this wealth because their businesses covered a lot of territory. Since the 1970s American beer distributors had slowly and steadily consolidated. According to Joe Thompson, a distribution consultant, the United States had 5,180 distributors in 1970; by 2013 it had about 1,000.[1] Many of those left standing were very large.

In my observation, once you reach a critical mass of business, a beer distributorship is a license to print money. In unguarded moments some AB InBev executives have expressed a desire to expand the brewery's ownership of distributors so it could take advantage of both the brewer's margin and the distributor's margin. At annual conferences sponsored by *Beer Marketer's Insights,* the industry's most authoritative newsletter, industry analysts have spoken of the billions of dollars in margin that the distributors are harvesting. Now I wondered when this issue would come to the fore. Wouldn't the new owners of AB regard the distributor profits as excessive? If AB InBev executives were keeping a careful rein on expenses, it seemed logical that they soon would ask their distributors to do the same.

Both AB InBev and MillerCoors encouraged their distributors to continue consolidating, as quickly as possible. The large brewers felt the United States simply had too many distributors. Some states had twenty-five to thirty distributors. The large brewers saw this system as inefficient and costly.

Naturally the distributors saw it differently. Almost all were happy with their little kingdoms. These were family businesses—in many cases second or third generation. They were living well. Why should they sell? Also, most regulation of alcoholic beverages is at the state level. In most states franchise laws protect distributors from the predations of large brewers. Brewers cannot terminate contracts with distributors unless the brewers have good cause. If a distributor is doing its job, it has nothing to fear from a brewer, small or large.

But after the AB InBev and MillerCoors mergers, the distributors began to get nervous. Other business and government trends exacerbated their concerns. Some small winemakers were selling their wines directly to consumers, across state lines, in violation of the three-tier system. In other words, instead of selling to a distributor, who then sold to a retailer, vintners were beginning to sell directly to the consumer, often over the Internet, with the help of UPS or FedEx.

The three-tier system is not strictly observed in many states. For instance, in New York, a brewer can self-distribute, and a brewery can sell directly to the public at a restaurant on its brewery premises. Marc Sorini of McDermott, Will & Emory, who is counsel for the BA, said the three-tier system developed slowly, state-by-state, after Prohibition ended.

"Many architects of post-Prohibition regulation of alcohol supported the concept of a two-tier system, with tied-house laws separating retailers from either wholesalers or producers," he said. "But I have seen no evidence that the early post-Prohibition regulatory regimes prohibited brewers from selling directly to retailers and/or owning their own wholesalers. Indeed, even today a substantial number of states still allow one or both."[2]

But when retailers objected, small winemakers countered that they could not get their wines distributed in some states because distributors did not want to handle small quantities. Federal courts ruled that laws limiting a winemaker's ability to sell in some states were an unlawful restraint of trade, a violation of the dormant commerce clause of the US Constitution.

The most prominent case was *Granholm v. Heald* (2005). The US Supreme Court ruled 5–4 that laws in New York and Michigan permitting in-state wineries to sell and ship wine directly to consumers—but prohibiting out-of-state wineries from doing so—were unconstitutional. The case pitted the so-called dormant commerce clause (implied by the commerce clause of the Constitution) against section 2 of the Twenty-first Amendment—the amendment that ended Prohibition and granted the states great powers to regulate alcoholic beverages.

Section 2 says: "The transportation or importation into any State, Territory, or possession of the United States for delivery or use therein of intoxicating liquors, in violation of the laws thereof, is hereby prohibited."

The plaintiffs claimed that this section clashed with the commerce clause, article I, section 8, of the Constitution, which grants Congress the power "to regulate Commerce with foreign Nations, and among the several States, and with the Indian Tribes."

The dormant commerce clause, implied by the Constitution and its historical context, basically holds that a state may not enact laws that favor in-state producers of alcoholic beverages over out-of-state producers.[3] The *Wall Street Journal* took up the cause of the small winemakers, arguing that it was wrong to bar a winemaker in, say, Oregon from shipping a fine, small-growth pinot noir to New York City.

In later articles, the *Journal* quoted the conservative think tank Competitive Enterprise Institute as saying "the existence of legally protected middlemen drives up consumer costs and threatens the vibrancy of the craft beer industry by making it harder for microbrewers to sell their beer directly to bars or retail stores."[4]

In a later article, reporter Harry Graver said beer distributors "have this kind of protected role in something called the three-tier system" that prevents a small brewer from delivering a six-pack of beer to a customer just across the street from the brewery. Under three-tier, the distributor must deliver the beer, thus driving up the price, he said. He added that the Michigan Beer and Wine Wholesalers Association assured its protected status with $3 million in campaign contributions over a decade, compared to craft brewers who had difficulty scraping $10,000 together.[5]

In March 2004 Costco, the big-box retailer and big-volume beer seller, sued Washington State saying Costco should have the right to negotiate discounts for buying beer, wine, and hard liquor in bulk. In Washington every case of beer costs the retailer the same no matter how many cases it buys. So Costco pays $25 a case for, say, Deschutes Mirror Pond Pale Ale, whether it buys 1 case or 1,000 cases. Costco claimed the distributor, who makes probably 30 percent of that case price, is reaping an unfair profit on a delivery of 1,000 cases.

In 2006 a federal district court ruled in Costco's favor on many of the issues, allowing brewers to sell directly to Costco in Washington State. But the Ninth Circuit Court of Appeals overturned the rulings in 2008, and Costco declined to appeal to the Supreme Court. It was a big victory for beer distributors because it restored state rules requiring uniform pricing, bans on credit, bans on quantity discounts, retail to retail sales, and central warehousing by retailers.[6]

Distributors in America have powerful lobbies in their home states, and since most regulation of alcoholic beverages is at the state level, the rules regarding distribution and excise taxes vary from state to state. Through their state associations distributors have advanced legislation favorable to them. The franchise laws are the best example. Historically the NBWA has been a brewer's best friend—lobbying to keep federal beer excise taxes low, the federal government from limiting brewers' ability to advertise, the Occupational Safety and Health Administration from enacting stringent protections for workers, and to hold other federal regulations to a minimum. The NBWA has also lobbied for low estate taxes because most of its members are family-run enterprises, and their owners want to pass their businesses on to their children.

Since 1990 the NBWA and the BI had held a joint legislative conference in Washington, DC, every spring. More than a thousand distributors and representatives of the nation's breweries swarm Capitol Hill to take their message to Congress.

But the nation's beer wholesalers were getting nervous about direct shipping by small winemakers and the decisions in the Costco case and *Granholm*. In a survey of its members the NBWA found that an overwhelming number believed their legislative clout in Washington should be focused squarely on distributor issues, not brewers' issues. Something had to be done about the perceived erosion of the three-tier system.

The result of this finding was a bill, introduced in Congress on April 15, 2010, called the Comprehensive Alcohol Regulatory Effectiveness Act (CARE).

If enacted the CARE Act would effectively neuter the commerce clause and relegate regulation of alcoholic beverages to the states, where distributors have strong influence over legislatures. The bill's "burden of proof" section would require the federal government to prove that a state law has discriminated against other states, and the "strong presumption of validity" accorded to state laws would have made that very difficult.

The CARE Act was, in effect, a declaration of war by distributors against producers of beer, wine, and spirits. The threat it posed brought winemakers, distillers, and brewers together in unprecedented ways.

Little did I realize what I was getting into when I agreed to become a member of the BI board of directors.

For small brewers several issues loomed large and put us in lockstep with the large brewers. The right to self-distribution was, and remains, critical. Companies like mine probably would never have been able to get a foothold in New York City if we had been unable to exercise the right to distribute our own beer, at least until we could attract a big distributor. Also, we were working hard to obtain an exemption to the state franchise laws. Most small brewers lack the money to challenge their distributor's performance in court. If the CARE Act became law, distributors in many states probably would seek to outlaw self-distribution and remove any chance of a state's granting small brewers exemptions from the franchise law.

As a board member, I sat in on a dozen meetings in which the BI board tried to reach some sort of compromise on the CARE Act with the leading board members of the NBWA. The sessions were grueling and fruitless. It seemed the new owners of AB InBev did not understand our wariness of the distributors. The weekend before one BI–NBWA meeting in Chicago, a British publication quoted Carlos Brito, AB InBev's CEO, as saying AB InBev could theoretically own half its distribution in the United States. This aroused the distributors and flummoxed Dave Peacock, president of AB In-Bev North America, who was representing AB InBev in the Chicago talks. Peacock spent much of that meeting trying to control the damage Brito's statements had caused.

If you were a distributor, would you believe the CEO or the regional president?

About a month before the NBWA's CARE bill was introduced in Congress in the spring of 2010, the House Judiciary Committee's Subcommittee on Courts and Competition held a hearing to consider the issues the measure was raising. Long, chair of the BI's board, asked me to represent the BI at the hearing. Why do you think the BI wanted me to testify? I represented not only the national beer industry as a BI board member, but also small business, free enterprise, entrepreneurship, Mom, and apple pie. Mine was the face the industry wanted. I had no problem testifying against the distributors on this issue because I genuinely believed the CARE Act would be a disaster for small brewers. The hearing was held in the Judiciary Committee's chambers, the same room where it had pondered the impeachment of Richard Nixon in the early 1970s. On the walls were oil paintings of former chairs, including Peter Rodino of New Jersey, the chair during the impeachment trial. Among the sixty or seventy lobbyists in the gallery behind me were representatives of the beer, wine, and liquor industries. I have never seen so many lobbyists. Some were people I had spotted at the BI and other gatherings in Washington, DC, without knowing who they were. It was a powerful demonstration of the political might of the alcoholic beverage industry. My presentation was preceded by a couple of members of Congress from California who said they were concerned about the rights of the state's 4,000 winery owners.

My testimony focused on the concerns of small brewers. "In an effort to get products not available through the three-tier system, some wineries and consumers have brought suit, challenging state alcohol laws that mandate that alcohol beverages be sold through the three-tier system," I said. "A small number of state laws have been struck down as discriminatory, but most have been upheld. The cost of defending these lawsuits, and the threat of more litigation to erode the three-tier system, has raised concern among some members of the beer industry.

"We understand these concerns, but we do not see any need for a drastic change in the balance between state and federal authorities that has served the public for many years. There has been talk of ceding federal control of alcohol beverage regulation to the states. That would be a disaster for small brewers."[7]

Testifying on behalf of the NBWA was Michigan's chief of alcohol beverage regulation, Nida Samona. *Granholm* had struck down Michigan's ban on out of state wineries shipping into the state. Samona argued that *Granholm* and similar cases placed an expensive burden on Michigan to defend its alcohol control laws. "State regulatory systems are under siege, and these lawsuits are gutting out the effective state regulation that we are asking Congress to come in an to address," she testified.[8]

Another witness for the NBWA was Pamela S. Erickson, CEO of Public Action Management of Scottsdale, Arizona, an expert who spoke about how the deregulation of the alcoholic beverage industry in Britain had led to many social problems like underage drinking. The title of her testimony was "The Danger of Alcohol Deregulation: The United Kingdom Experience." She painted a grim picture of modern Britain and warned that the same state of affairs could develop in America if alcoholic beverages were deregulated.

She predicted a dark future for the nation if the CARE Act did not become law. "The U.S. has serious problems with alcohol—particularly with underage drinking, but it has not reached the point of an epidemic," she said. The beer distributors seemed to be trying to cast themselves as the only safeguard against alcohol-inspired anarchy on the streets of the United States.[9]

After US Representative William Delahunt, a Massachusetts Democrat, and 152 cosponsors introduced H.R. 5034, lobbyists and principals on both sides went to war in the halls of Congress. Brewers refused to participate in the BI–NBWA joint legislative conference for the first time in eighteen years. Instead the distributors trooped up to Capitol Hill to promote H.R. 5034 and the brewers met separately with key representatives to make the case against the measure. I was always impressed by the large brewers' access to key leaders in Congress. When you were with the BI, you met with such powerful people as the then–House Minority Leader John Boehner and the Senate majority leader, Harry Reid. The large brewers had long-term relationships with these politicians.

NBWA's campaign for the CARE Act played out over a two-year period. The association often enlisted people like Erickson and organizations that are long-time opponents of the alcoholic beverage industry, including the Center for Science in the Public Interest. It seemed to me to be a hopeless effort on the part of the NBWA, so long as the beer, wine, and liquor industries remained united. But Craig Purser, the NBWA president, and his chief lobbyist, Mike Johnson, persisted. The next year US Representative Jason Chaffetz, a Utah Republican, and 122 cosponsors introduced a new version of the CARE Act, H.R. 1161. Its new name was the Community Alcohol Regulatory Effectiveness Act of 2011 (instead of the *Comprehensive* Alcohol Regulatory Effectiveness Act). They shortened the content of the bill, but its potential was the same. Rich Doyle of Harpoon Brewery had succeeded me on the BI board by then, and he testified at a second congressional hearing.

The brewers and distributors fought to a standoff. In 2012 the leaders of the BI and the NBWA reached the tacit understanding that the distributors would not pursue the CARE Act, although Purser insisted that the campaign had done much to educate Congress about the need to preserve the three-tier system and prevent large brewers from owning and/or controlling their distributors.

"The CARE Act provided a great opportunity to educate policymakers and the public about the need for effective alcohol regulation by the states," Purser said. "It raised a new awareness about the distinctions between suppliers, distributors, and retailers and also generated a greater understanding of the value of a strong independent three-tier system."[10]

The war over the CARE Act was an important learning experience for the BA. Here was an initiative that could have profoundly changed the nature of alcoholic beverage regulation in the United States. It could have had a devastating effect on the ability of small brewers to take their beers to market and to develop productive, respectful partnerships with distributors. It was a great example of the power that a unified industry could have on the course of legislation in Washington.

Throughout this ordeal the BA maintained good communication and close relationships with the leadership of the NBWA. The leaders of the two groups met regularly and discussed issues important to small brewers, such as self-distribution and franchise law reform. The NBWA never blamed the BA for its opposition to the CARE Act and held no grudge when the bill went nowhere.

Distributors and small brewers have always had a sense of common interest. Both are, to a certain extent, concerned about the power of the large international brewers. For the most part, both represent relatively small local businesses that play important roles in their communities. Still, most distributors are not in favor of small brewers gaining the right to self-distribute, and most distributors are dead set against small brewers gaining any flexibility within the franchise laws.

Nonetheless the New York State BA was able to get a law passed and signed by Governor Andrew Cuomo in 2012 that reformed the state's franchise law. The new law asserts that any brewer who represents less than 3 percent of a distributor's business and who produces fewer than 300,000 barrels of beer annually has the right to move to a different distributor if the brewer pays fair market value for the loss of business. This means that small brewers who feel they are not getting adequate attention from a wholesaler may move to another wholesaler without a costly lawsuit. Several small brewers have already taken advantage of the new law. By 2013 at least one lawsuit was underway, focused on the question of how the 3 percent is to be measured.

The craft beer revolution has given many distributors, especially AB InBev distributors, a new sense of independence and ownership of their companies. They no longer live in fear of a surprise visit by August Busch III or one of the other large brewery CEOs. I believe that relations between distributors and small brewers will be key to the future of the craft beer revolution.

NOT LONG AFTER THE TWO ORGANIZATIONS REACHED AGREEMENT ON THE CARE ACT, small and large brewers locked horns over federal beer excise taxes and the question of who deserves to be called a craft brewer.

You may recall the BA persuaded the BI to include a tax break for small brewers in its proposed legislation to roll back the 1991 doubling of the federal excise tax on beer. The proposed legislation is known as the BEER Act (the Brewers Excise and Economic Relief Act). The BI added a clause that would cut the excise tax on the first 60,000 barrels of production in half, from $7 a barrel to $3.50 a barrel. That break would go only to brewers of fewer than 2 million barrels of production annually. The BA regarded this as a small victory.

In 2009, Kevin Brady, a Republican Texan, and Richie Neal, a Democrat from Massachussets, introduced a tax measure that would extend the tax break for brewers of less than 2 million barrels to those brewers who produced fewer than 6 million barrels a year and decrease the excise tax from $18 per barrel to $16 per barrel on the first 2 million barrels. This came to be known as the Small BREW Act, (the Small Brewers Reinvestment and Expanding Workforce Act). That would save four brewing companies, Boston Beer, D.G. Yuengling & Son, Pabst, and North American Breweries, a lot of money if they grew to produce more than 2 million barrels annually. Koch's bill was sponsored by US Representatives Jim Neal, a Massachusetts Democrat, and Jim Gerlach, a Pennsylvania Republican.

Given the economic turmoil that was unleashed in 2008, and the resulting recession, the measure seemed to have little chance of passing. But the BA leadership decided to back Koch's bill in the unlikely event that it was enacted. With the help of Charles Rangel, the New York Democrat who then chaired the House Ways and Means Committee, a group of us met with Neal's tax counsel and made the case for cutting the excise tax for brewers of fewer than 60,000 barrels from $7 per barrel to $3.50 per barrel. The BI was not happy with the proposed bill because it did nothing for breweries making more than 6 million barrels annually, but it vowed not to actively oppose it.

The BA board, at its November 2010 meeting, voted to change the definition of craft brewer to be consistent with the 6 million barrel ceiling in the proposed excise tax bill. This led to loud opposition from some BA members, particularly August Schell, which had been excluded from the craft brewer designation because its main beer is not an all-malt product, and Larry Bell of Bell's, who complained that the benefit to Boston Beer Company was disproportionate to the benefit to the BA's smaller members. Bell urged Michigan Representative Dave Camp, then chair of the House Ways and Means Committee, to block the bill.

At BA members' meetings in 2011, 2012, and 2013, the overwhelming majority backed the bill, despite opposition from a vocal minority. The new version of the bill, known as the Small BREW Act, was presented as a job-creating measure on December 10, 2009, at a time when Congress was looking for inexpensive ways to create jobs. A study conducted by the Brewing Industry Production Survey (BIPS) found that the craft brewing industry had already created more than 100,000 jobs, compared to 40,000 in the large brewers' industry, and that passage of the Small BREW Act would create 5,000 new jobs the first year and many more after that.[11] The BI was not happy with the measure because it revealed that brewers were divided. Having two wings of the beer industry promoting different excise tax measures would be confusing to members of Congress, but the two organizations nonetheless continue to pursue their own versions.

In the 2009–2010 congressional session 132 representatives and 27 senators signed the Small BREW Act. Representative Peter DeFazio of Oregon agreed to chair a House Small Brewers Caucas similar to the House Wine Caucus. In the Senate, Senator Max Baucus of Montana, chair of the Senate Finance Committee, agreed to chair the Senate Brewers Caucus. Both caucuses worked to support small brewers. When the BA re-introduced the act in the 2011–2012 congressional session, 175 representatives and 43 senators signed. In the 2013–2014 congressional session the current tally is 110 representatives and 31 senators, and growing.[12]

The BA was clearly getting some traction in Washington with its tax bill. BI lobbyists, however, insisted that neither the BEER Act nor the Small BREW Act had a snowball's chance in hell. Some lobbyists hinted darkly that they could use their longstanding relationships with the leadership of the House and Senate to kill the Small BREW Act and leave no fingerprints. I was reminded of the gaggle of industry lobbyists that had showed up to support the BI when I testified against the CARE Act in the House Judiciary Committee chambers.[13] There is no question that the large brewers and the BI have a lot of clout in Washington.

In April 2013 BI spokesman Chris Thorne announced that the large brewers were going to "actively oppose" the Small BREW Act.[14] There was a flurry of stories in the press about a "beer war," but the BI and the BA struggled to keep the story from expanding.[15]

The friction between large and small brewers was aggravated by two other developments that had nothing to do with the excise tax bills. In late 2012 the editorial page editor of the *St. Louis Post-Dispatch* contacted Dan Kopman of Schlafly Beer and asked him to write an op-ed piece discussing small brewers' unhappiness with the large brewers' craft-like beers, Blue Moon and Shock Top.

The resulting op-ed, signed by Charlie Papazian as president of the BA, the BA's COO Bob Pease, and Kopman, took the large brewers to task for not identifying themselves as the brewers of Blue Moon and Shock Top and using instead the trade names Blue Moon Brewing Company and Shock Top Brewing Co.[16] This sort of criticism is not unknown in the history of brewing in the United States. In the 1970s AB made much of Miller Brewing Company's brewing of Germany's Lowenbrau beer in the United States.

Unfortunately the op-ed piece also made much of the BA's definition of *craft brewer*, and the BA staff posted a list of noncraft brewers on its website. This brought withering criticism from the August Schell Brewing Company, one of the oldest breweries in America. Schell is excluded from claiming to be a craft brewer because its flagship beer, Grain Belt, is a lager made with a corn syrup. The objections of Schell and other critics of the craft brewer definition briefly overshadowed the main point of the op-ed piece, which was that the large brewers were not owning up to their ownership of Blue Moon and Shock Top.

The op-ed bore the catchy headline "Craft vs. Crafty," and the large brewers took offense at being characterized as crafty. Tom Long, the Miller-Coors President and CCO, responded with an op-ed piece published at cnn. com suggesting that the quality of the beer is the important issue, not who is brewing it. Let the consumer decide who makes the best beer, he argued.[17]

The other irritant was AB InBev's 2012 proposed purchase of Mexico's Modelo Brewery. I wrote an op-ed piece published at cnn.com expressing opposition on the grounds that AB InBev and MillerCoors already had unfair advantages in their control of shelf placements of beer in supermarkets and their control of beer taps at sports venues.[18] Other small brewers opposed the deal in private conversations with the Justice Department's Anti-Trust Division, which had to approve the deal. As it turned out, the small brewers' objections probably had no bearing on the Justice Department's deliberations, but the small brewers' participation angered some of the large brewers.

The DOJ allowed the purchase to proceed but required AB InBev to sell a large Mexican brewery to the importer of Corona Beer, Crown Imports Inc., which now brews and sells Corona in the United States.

The large brewers privately expressed their anger at what they saw as the wholesale denigration of their beers and companies by small brewers. I was reappointed to the BI board in 2010, and was still holding the seat at the table. It was becoming a hot seat.

CHAPTER TWELVE

THE THIRD GENERATION

MANY MODELS EMERGE

2000: *1,509 craft breweries*

29 noncraft regional and national breweries

AB InBev and MillerCoors: 81 percent share

2013: *2,594 craft breweries*

10 noncraft regional and national breweries

AB InBev and MillerCoors: 74 percent share

WITH 1,500 NEW BREWERIES IN PLANNING STAGES, AND A BREWERY OPENING EV-ery day across America, there has been much talk once again of a craft-brewing bubble and an impending shakeout. Part of the reason for the perhaps irrational exuberance is the industry's astounding success. Fifty percent of all brewpubs ever started, and 70 percent of production breweries, are still in business, whereas the majority of other small businesses don't make it past their first year. I don't know how many of those breweries are actually profitable, but they've certainly shown staying power. In following the various new players I see several different strategies emerging.

The first is to stay small.

Whenever anyone asks me how big Brooklyn Brewery can get, I say my goal is to be twice as big as I am now. I think most brewers of my generation and the second generation look at their business that way. But the next wave of craft brewers may have different expectations. Many seem to be satisfied with the intangible rewards of brewing—making great beer, creating community, being the go-to beer guy or gal in their circles. Many are happy to run a brewpub, although, as the Class of '88 demonstrated, many brewpubs become large production breweries.

I call this the "back to the future" dream. It recalls a time when all brewing was local, when you bought your beer from the guy down the street who made it. Of course, that was back in the 1860s, when the United States had 1,269 breweries serving a total national population of about 30 million. In *Brewing Battles,* author Amy Mittelman reports the state of New York was home to 220 breweries that employed a handful of people each at the end of the nineteenth century. Brooklyn alone had forty-five breweries in 1898.[1]

Maybe the new Brooklyn is Bend, Oregon, where Gary Fish decided to locate his Deschutes Brewery Bend Public House in 1988. At that time the population of bucolic Bend was 15,000. Today the city's population has grown to 85,000, and sixteen breweries are located within the city and five more are nearby. One, Crux Fermentation Project, was started in 2012 by Larry Sidor, Fish's former brewmaster and a veteran brewer who worked for Olympia Brewing Co. His partners are Dave Wilson, a former Deschutes sales manager, and Paul Evers, who also has a background in the brewing business.[2]

Sidor, 63, has worked in the brewing industry for 40 years. He joined Deschutes in 2004. He has a unique perspective on the craft brewing revolution. "The beers that I made when I started my career would be considered craft beers today," he said. "But they dumbed down those beers to the point of mediocrity. . . . A famous quote from a marketing-branding guy who will remain nameless was 'Larry, make the beer as close to water as you possibly can, because I can sell it if you do that.'"

The words of the water lover are echoed in the reminiscences of Brooklyn Brewery's first brewmaster, William M. Moeller, who was in the brewing industry for more than forty years. I recall Moeller's saying the only guidance he ever got from his bosses was to make the beer lighter and do it less expensively. His experience with Brooklyn was the first time anyone asked him "to make the best damn beer I could make."

Sidor said he felt craft brewers were a real challenge to the large brewers, who could not promote flavor in beer lest they undercut their big flavorless brands. Sidor said he was not worried about the proliferation of small brewers. "Four thousand breweries might be conservative; it might be 8,000," he said. "One of the big changes I saw when I was at Deschutes, and now

Larry Sidor of Crux Fermentation Project.

at Crux, is the local aspect of beer production is really gaining. People want local. I am not surprised, but I am taken aback. I learned at Deschutes how educated and informed the consumer is about beer."

Sidor said when he started brewing in the 1970s, the Pacific Northwest had about 7.5 million barrels of production capacity. Since then a number of regional breweries have closed, the region's production capacity today is 2.2 million barrels, and it has more than 200 breweries. "Can we support 400 breweries and go to 4.4 million? Absolutely," he said.

Sidor said he is now running a brewpub, but he plans to develop a production brewery that can brew 15,000 to 20,000 barrels annually. "My concept is to expand the brewery so I can support my family and my partners' families and the families of our employees," he said.

"Ours is a brewery that happens to have a pub, as opposed to a pub that happens to have a brewery somewhere off in the corner. When you come in here, you are totally involved in the aromas, the sounds, the looks, the whole deal of a brewery. You are definitely in a brewery. The brewery is in the back half of the building, and the tasting room is toward the front, and guess where everybody likes to sit? Next to the brewery. People want the smell and look."

Sidor barely conceals his delight in owning Crux. "It's been the best thing I have done in my life so far," he said. "I've been having a ball."[3]

ANOTHER BREWER WHO IS LIVING THE "BACK TO THE FUTURE" AND "SMALL IS beautiful" dream is Ben Millstein, founder and president of the Kodiak Island Brewing Company in Alaska. Kodiak is draft only and serves five year-round beers at all times, beers like Beyond the Pale, Snowshoe Pale, Wing-Nut Brown Ale, and Sarah Pale, and four specialty and seasonal choices. Millstein came to the island of 14,000 inhabitants with his wife, Karen Kincheloe, in 1994. They met at a folk music festival in Homer, Alaska, on the mainland. She was a physician's assistant with college loans to pay off, and Kodiak was a place in need of her skills. They figured they would stay for a few years, pay off the loans, and head back to the mainland. But then they had two daughters, bought a house, and started a brewery.

"I was a carpenter, and I enjoyed being a carpenter, but I didn't feel I was contributing to my community in a unique way," Millstein said. "I was also a homebrewer, and I watched other people start breweries in Alaska, and I thought I could do it, too. I wrote a business plan and it wasn't so good, but I worked on it and I got there. It took time and persistence." He started with a ten-barrel system because he wasn't sure he could attract help. He figured he would brew once a week and spend the rest of the time selling the beer. At that time Alaska law prevented Millstein and Kincheloe from selling beer at their brewery. The original brewery was in an 1,800-square-foot building with a hundred square feet of retail space where Millstein filled growlers for walk-in customers. The law changed a few years ago, allowing them to serve as much as thirty-six ounces per visitor in a tasting room. Millstein limits visitors to two pints. His new brewery is 9,000 square feet with a tasting room of 2,500 square feet. This year, he expects to sell 900 to 950 barrels of beer. He employs five people. He sells pints and growlers at the brewery and delivers to some bars and restaurants, including kegs, in his Subaru Baha. His most distant customer is a bar ten miles from the brewery.[4]

Millstein was born in California and grew up in Delaware and Pennsylvania. After getting an environmental science degree from the University of California, Santa Cruz, he traveled the world, spending a year in Israel and time in Nepal and India. He made his first homebrew in Crested Butte, Colorado, where he worked as a ski bum for a couple of winters. He likes Kodiak because of the community, the wilderness, and the wide-open spaces.

Founder Ben Milstein and brewer Mike Trussell of Kodiak Island. Photograph courtesy of Kodiak Island Brewing Co.

He said Kodiak is famous for the biggest grizzly bears in the world. The main employer is the Coast Guard base, and the biggest industry is hunting and fishing tourism. Millstein makes a living at the brewery.

"It's been a pretty good living," he said, "depending on how you define pretty good. I think most of us getting into brewing are not expecting great wealth. I like being a part of the community and contributing to that community. I felt like there was a need for a brewery in Kodiak. . . . We are a very small brewery with an outsized footprint in our town. People use our brewery for social meetings and for business meetings. Even if they have had a bad day, they walk into the brewery and they are happy to see us. It's not like being a car mechanic where people are bringing you their problems."[5]

I met Millstein at a Brewers Association (BA) meeting with the Senate Democratic Caucus in Washington, DC. The meeting was chaired by Senator Mark Begich of Alaska, who heaped praise on Millstein for his contributions to Kodiak and Alaska. Begich had visited the brewery on Memorial Day weekend. Senator Lisa Markowski, an Alaska Republican, also had visited in May. How many businesses in America can say that both of their state's senators have visited them? During the caucus meeting Millstein said the scale of his brewery could lead to a nation "with a brewery on every corner."

Many other small brewers are working on nanobreweries, one- and two-barrel systems that are not much different than the system cobbled together by Jack McAuliffe forty years ago.

EVAN KLEIN, FOUNDER OF BARRIER BREWING CO. IN OCEANSIDE, NEW YORK, started out in June 2010 as a nanobrewer with a 1.5 barrel system. He was brewing twelve times a week on a three-day schedule and then selling and delivering his own beer. A homebrewer with a degree in environmental science, he interned at Sixpoint Brewery in Brooklyn before starting Barrier on the south shore of New York's Long Island. The head brewer at Sixpoint, Craig Frymark, joined Klein, and they upgraded to a five-barrel system in June 2012. Klein, his wife Melissa, and her father funded the company.[6]

Klein said his nanobrewery, brewers yielding one barrel per brew, was not sustainable. When you start as a nanobrewer, "you have to realize it is not the end goal. You can't maintain it. We know a couple of people who are starting that way, and we told them we would help, but we don't recommend it." It is simply not profitable.

Barrier now brews twenty different beers a year, using four or five different yeasts, and it services more than 125 accounts, most of them in Manhattan

Evan Klein of Barrier Brewing Co. showing where the waters of Superstorm Sandy crested.

and Brooklyn. Thursday is delivery day. Klein and Frymark deliver kegs in a yellow box truck bearing the Barrier logo.

"Small batch, variety, it's working for us," Klein said. "We're obviously a very small operation. We don't have a flagship. We do have some beers that sell better than others. It seems that our accounts appreciate it. When they get our inventory list, they round out their own draft towers, like, I don't have an ESB (Extra Special Bitter), I'll take that. Middle of July, no one has a stout. Barrier probably has one. It keeps it fun for us as brewers, too."

Before they got the box truck, they delivered kegs with their own pickup trucks, Klein's Ford Ranger and Frymark's Toyota Tacoma. Klein's pickup was destroyed when Superstorm Sandy surged into the industrial enclave where Barrier is located, but that was not the worst of their losses. Its keg filler, glycol chiller, mill, grain, and hops—not to mention all the pumps and electrical systems—were destroyed, along with a leased electric forklift, the only insured piece of equipment. Barrier was out of business for three months, until they got help from Ommegang Brewery in Cooperstown, New York. Simon Thorpe, Ommegang's CEO, collaborated with Barrier on a new IPA called Mare Undarium (Latin for Sea of Tides), named for a crater on the moon and brewed with a Belgian yeast. Ommegang sold the beer and shared the profit with Barrier to help fill its cratered bottom line. A group of Long Island breweries also brewed a new ale called Surge Protector to benefit Barrier and charities helping other Sandy victims.

Klein said he is making a living with Barrier, but Melissa, a lab manager at a local hospital, is the big family breadwinner. He expects to sell 1,500 barrels of beer in 2013. Besides Frymark, he has one other full-time employee. He is building a tasting room to augment the growler sales he now does.

"I'd like to grow the business to a healthy size," he said. "The idea of staying local in New York is appealing, making it a destination brand . . . so people who come from out of state are excited to try some Barrier. The main goal is to be happy, and support the family and lead a good life and have some free time—which there is none of now."[7]

Some nanobrewers are trying to sell their beer the way small farmers sell their produce—through a "community-supported agriculture' model. Brewer Robby Crafton at Big Alice Brewing in Long Island City, New York, is charging 90 subscribers $200 each to get two 750-milliliter bottles of beer per month for six months. The clients also get two Big Alice-branded glasses. "Every beer we make is a one-off creation, so we still have a large number of beers available every month," he told *BeerAdvocate*.

RYAN SOROKA AND HIS PARTNERS RAISED $500,000 AND OPENED THE 8TH WONDER
Brewery in downtown Houston in February 2013. The brewery's name pays homage to the Astrodome (which bills itself as the "Eighth Wonder of the World"), and the brewery is only a few blocks away from the Houston Astros' MLB stadium, the Houston Rockets NBA arena, and Houston Dynamo Major League Soccer stadium. A perfect spot for a brewery and pub, but the quirky alcohol beverage laws of Texas so far prohibit Soroka and his partners from selling beer to the public. "However, there is a bill on the governor's desk, just waiting to be signed, that would allow us to sell on-premise," Soroka said.

Soroka majored in finance and marketing at Tulane University, then worked as a financial consultant until he was laid off in 2008. He then went to hospitality school at the University of Houston and earned an MBA. During the summer of 2010 a high school friend, Alex Vassilakidis, called him with the idea of starting a gourmet food truck. They partnered with their childhood friend, Matt Marcus, a chef who trained at the Culinary Institute of America.

Aaron Corsi, Ryan Soroka, Matt Marcus, Alex Vassilakidis of Eatsie Boys and 8th Wonder Brewery. Photograph courtesy of Eatsie Boys and 8th Wonder Brewery.

They called themselves the Eatsie Boys, after the Beastie Boys, and became part of the first wave of high-end food truck operators in the city. The press loved them from the outset. A homebrewer, Soroka had drawn up a business plan for a brewpub while in graduate school. After researching the Texas alcohol laws he rewrote the plan to make the business a production brewery. The success of the Eatsie Boys food truck helped recruit investors for 8th Wonder. They then partnered with Aaron Corsi, a brewmaster who teaches fermentation studies at the University of Houston, and 8th Wonder Brewery was born.

In Texas just as production breweries cannot sell beer on the premises, brewpubs cannot sell beer off their premises, so the partners devised their own "nontraditional brewpub" by parking the Eatsie Boys truck in front of the brewery. They also own Eatsie Boys Cafe, but it cannot serve beer. They do encourage guests to bring 8th Wonder brews to the cafe. Soroka hopes to get the laws changed so they can serve food at the brewery and beer at the cafe. "It's a long road to integrate the two businesses, but when the dust settles on the current legislative push, we will try to move forward," he says.[8]

Soroka said he expects to sell 1,200 barrels of beer in 2013, but he dreams of growing the company to be ten or twenty times larger. He sees 8th Wonder as part of a second wave of breweries in Houston. Saint Arnold Brewing Company, which was started in the mid-1990s, was the only successful brewery for many years. Soroka said Brock Wagner, founder of St. Arnold, was helpful to him. "We're excited to be part of the local beerscape; we want our businesses to be iconic landmarks in the culinary world of Houston," Soroka said. "I'm a food and beverage guy. I found my niche. It took a long time, but I know this is what I want to do. I like making good food, and I like making good beer and sharing it with people."[9]

IN WISCONSIN, HUSBAND-AND-WIFE TEAM DAN CAREY, BREWMASTER, AND DEB Carey, CEO, run the New Glarus Brewing Co. and they sell 100 percent of their 140,000 barrels in their home state. They employ seventy-eight people and their flagship beer, Spotted Cow, is a pilsner that accounts for 65 percent of their production. They opened for business in 1993, but Dan has had a long career in the brewing business, starting with a microbrewery called Kessler in Montana in 1982, then with brewery fabricator JVNW, then an apprenticeship with the Ayinger Brewery in Bavaria and three years at the AB brewery in Fort Collins, Colorado.

*Dan and Deb Carey of New Glarus. Photograph
courtesy of Sue Moen, New Glarus Brewing Company.*

He said New Glarus started out with a focus on Wisconsin but also shipped its Wisconsin Belgian Red, made with Wisconsin cherries, to Oregon, New York, and Illinois. But demand in Wisconsin squeezed its capacity, and he ran into some problems with distributor consolidation in the out-of-state markets. "The problem of selling in New York and Oregon is you need to have a presence there—either advertising or salesmanship. We were really concentrating completely on manufacturing. It was important for us to have a really strong relationship with our wholesalers, so geography meant it was just easier to stay local," Dan Carey said.

He said Wisconsin is loyal to locally produced brands. "You can go around the country, and you find expat Wisconsin bars where people go and they eat Wisconsin food, unique Wisconsin food, which is sort of what you might call German American—bratwurst and those sorts of things. And they watch Badger and Packer games. And so there is a very strong parochial sense in the state. . . . We're part of the Wisconsin scenery, and I think if we were to change that, we would probably lose that cachet."

Carey is confident the craft brewing revolution will continue. "The post–World War I industrialization of the brewing industry is more an anomaly than the norm," he said. "The idea of the huge megashippers is not the norm. That was the deviation. We are not the deviation."[10]

A FEW OF THE FIRST- AND SECOND-GENERATION CRAFT BREWERS ARE EXPLORING yet another strategy—the national brewery.

Boston Beer Company was the first and most successful of this breed of company. Samuel Adams Boston Lager was available in all fifty states ten years after the company opened. Founder Jim Koch raced to sign up distributors all across the country. Many credited him with creating the craft beer revolution. Jack Joyce, founder of Rogue Ales of Oregon, said, "We all played a part in the revolution, but Jim Koch financed the revolution with his marketing and advertising." Call me jealous, or a curmudgeon, but I always thought Koch's goal was to dominate—to own—the craft brewing revolution. I think he saw Samuel Adams lager as a brand that could be number one in every state in the nation. For a few years it did seem possible.

But the proliferation of local craft brewers in every state is eating away at Boston Beer's presence. Koch originally tried to address this problem with Oregon Ale, but he gave that venture up years ago. In recent years Boston Beer Company's beer portfolio has not been growing as rapidly as the other portfolios in the craft brewing industry. Koch now is expanding his company into other segments of the alcohol beverage industry by producing flavored malt beverages like Twisted Tea and Angry Orchard Hard Cider. He also has developed a dizzying array of specialty and seasonal beers. Boston Beer Company continues to invest heavily in radio and television advertising.

Koch also has started a subsidiary, Alchemy & Science, and hired a founder of Magic Hat, Alan Newman, to run it. A&S has purchased a small brewery in Los Angeles and more recently the Coney Island Lager brands in Brooklyn, New York, formerly owned by Jeremy Cohen of Shmaltz Brewing Company.

It is important to remember that nearly every member of the Class of '88 started out with a brewpub, and many evolved into regional breweries. Sometimes intentions change. The hottest hand in the craft brewing industry is being played by Tony Magee, the voluble founder of the Lagunitas Brewing Company, who started out planning to do private-label beers for bars and restaurants. He had no intention of developing a national brand. His Lagunitas IPA has propelled him to 40 percent growth in recent years. He is building a large production brewery in Chicago and clearly believes his can be a national brand. He has predicted that his IPA will be the next megabrand in America, replacing the light lager beers of the giants. In his book, *Lagunitas Brewing Company: The Story*, he writes, "When I first set out on this trip in 1993, I wanted to do only local draught beers made 12 kegs at a time and hand-sold into the bars and restaurants of West Marin under their own individual names. I suppose I hoped that word would sneak out about this small brewer in the back of an old grocery store, but that was secondary."[11]

Ken Grossman of Sierra Nevada Brewing Co., also a national brewer, is building a new brewery in Asheville, North Carolina, that will be coming on line in 2014. Grossman is creator of the largest single craft beer brand, Sierra Nevada Pale Ale, but in recent years he too has released an array of specialty, seasonal, and collaboration beers. Grossman built his brand on word-of-mouth marketing, and he told me he had no intention of ever doing television advertising.[12]

Kim Jordan gave up control of New Belgium Brewing Company to an employee stock ownership plan in 2012, the same year she announced plans to build a new brewery to serve the eastern United States. Like Grossman, she chose Asheville. New Belgium's Fat Tire Amber Ale seemed to be leading a charge toward national distribution, but in 2013 the company announced an expansion of its Fort Collins plant and a delay in the construction of the North Carolina brewery. And Dale Katechis of Oskar Blues Brewing Co. has already built a brewery in North Carolina and is producing 56,000 barrels and sells kegs and cans in the East.

The other big national player is the Craft Brewers Alliance (CBA), the partnership of Redhook, the Widmer Brothers Brewing Company, and Kona Brewing Co. in which AB InBev owns a 32.5 percent stake. AB InBev distributors handle distribution of the alliance's beers across the country. This growth of this venture also has lagged behind that of the craft brewing industry as a whole. CBA is now ably led by Andy Thomas, former CEO of Heineken USA. But one wonders about the commitment of AB InBev to developing CBA brands. AB InBev developed its Shock Top brand to counter MillerCoors' Blue Moon Belgian-Style Wheat Ale, but the proliferation of Shock Top seems to have damaged Widmer Brother's, a CBA member, main brand Widmer Hefeweizen.

A number of craft brewers are pursuing an international strategy. Boston Beer, Sierra Nevada, and Brooklyn Brewery are all exporting significant volumes of American craft beer and finding eager foreign markets. The BA has helped many small brewers export their beer. The BA says that craft beer exports grew by 72 percent in 2012. Stone Brewing announced their intention to build a brewery in Europe. Brooklyn expects to open a brewery in Stockholm in 2014 in partnership with Carlsberg. Becoming an international brand is an exciting prospect, and one with plenty of precedent. Heineken, the third-largest brewer in the world, and Carlsberg, the fourth, both are sold primarily outside their small home countries' markets.

CONTRACT BREWING IS ANOTHER STRATEGY THAT SOME EXPERIENCED PLAYERS ARE developing. When I started Brooklyn Brewery, contract brewing was not seen by the industry as real brewing. It was derided by many craft brewers who had done the hard work of building a brewery from scratch. Brooklyn Brewery was exclusively a contract brewer until we built our brewery in Brooklyn in 1996, but we never hid our relationship with Matt Brewing Company and our claim on our labels, "Brewed and bottled by the Brooklyn Brewery, Utica, New York," is true. We hold a brewer's license in Utica. We buy all the ingredients and packaging and have a brewmaster on site.

Today contract brewing has a new moniker: gypsy brewing. The term sounds more romantic than contract brewing, and gypsy breweries don't hide their relationship to the company making their beer. For instance, Pretty Things Beer and Ale Project was started by a husband-and-wife team, Dann Paquette and Martha Holley-Paquette. They make their beers at Buzzard's Bay Brewing. At a recent Brewbound conference in Boston, they explained that they draw their own labels and devise their own recipes. They have two employees, one to coordinate events and one to represent their brand. Martha Holley-Paquette said they are "big on authenticity" and don't allow anyone who isn't a Paquette to touch the beer. And Dann Paquette declared that, when they have completed their project, Pretty Things will be finished.[13]

A couple of new ventures are seeking to capitalize on the gypsy brewing phenomenon by building breweries solely for contract production. Two Roads Brewing Co. raised $15 million to build a brewery in Stratford, Connecticut, to develop its own brand and contract brew for other brewers. Brad Hittle, CEO of Two Roads, is a beer industry veteran, having worked

Phil Markowski, Brad Hittle, Clem Pellani, and Peter Doering of Two Roads.

for Labatt's, Rolling Rock, and Pabst. The idea for Two Roads came out of his efforts to establish a high-end brand at Pabst. He said, "When I was at Pabst, the Pabst portfolio was sorely missing the high end, and I knew Phil Markowski [brewer at Southampton Publick House in New York], and we attempted through a strategic alliance with them to sell and market Southampton beers because we had such confidence in Phil and their products."

He could not find a contract brewer to produce Markowski's beers. The available contact brewers were too big or too small or too busy, lacked quality control, or were unwilling to use Southampton's yeasts. Hittle eventually left Pabst with a yen to get into brewing for himself. "I didn't want to just open a brewery like the 1,500 other people who are working on that," he said. "That is a tough row to hoe. And I knew there was this pent-up demand of people looking for a brewery that could deliver a hundred-barrel batch of beer.

"My idea was to build a highly efficient brewery and attract the best customers who needed capacity and would be long-term players," he said. "By bringing in contract players, that absorbs costs and enables me to build my own brand and not feel compelled to over distribute it and let it sit on the vine and suffer, like so many other brands have in the past. And it also enables me to invest in selling and marketing, which in the distributor world is a nice advantage to have when you are trying to break through the thousands of other brands that are coming on—that was the premise of Two Roads and the name Two Roads has to do with my affinity for the poem by Robert Frost."[14]

I visited Hittle at Two Roads in June 2013, eight months after he started brewing. He was overseeing the installation of ten 300-barrel fermenters from Rolec, the German fabricator that has supplied breweries to many American craft brewers, including Brooklyn Beer. Hittle expects to double his goal of 2,500 barrels of Two Roads' proprietary brands in the first year in business. And he expects to do 30,000 barrels of contract production for ten contracts, including Evil Twin Brewing, Stillwater Artisanal Ales, Fire Island Beer Company, and City Steam Brewery Cafe and Restaurant. He said he still gets calls every day from potential contractors, or gypsy brewers.

Two Roads can brew and package beer in kegs, bottles, or cans. The brewery is in a lovely old industrial building in a blue-collar town that has been down on its luck. The community has embraced Two Roads, the most positive development in manufacturing in decades. Markowski did a rye-barrel–aged imperial stout called Igor's Dream to commemorate Igor Sikorsky, the famous inventor of the helicopter and founder of the company that still makes Blackhawks. A thousand bottles sold out in three hours. Two days before I visited, rain forced the postponement of the Stratford mayor's golf outing. He brought a gaggle of golfers to the brewery for beers instead.

The new fermenters will bring the outside capacity of Two Roads to 120,000 barrels. Hittle figures the actual capacity will be 90,000 to 100,000 barrels because of the many beers brewed at Two Roads. He feels he has an advantage over Brew Hub, the contract brewing operation that a group of former AB executives has announced, because he started before them. They have raised $100 million and are planning to build contract breweries in several locations around the country. The first is a 75,000-barrel brewery in Lakeland, Florida.[15]

"It's not a complicated model," Hittle said. "I know others can do it, but it is good to have the first mover advantage."[16]

These contract-production breweries will open up new possibilities for contract-brewed brands and for private label brands for restaurant chains and big-box retailers like Costco, Walmart, Whole Foods, and others. Hittle said he has no interest in private label brands.

The Brew Hub venture in Florida by the former AB executives points to another interesting dynamic of the craft beer revolution. Thousands of highly trained AB and MillerCoors employees have been let go as the two big brewers reap the benefits of their enormous size. Many of these career brewers, sales reps, production workers, and marketing executives have migrated to the craft brewing industry. At Brooklyn Brewery we employ Mary Wiles, a former AB brewmaster; Terry Matthews, a former AB chain sales manager; and John Boegel, a former MillerCoors sales manager. Joe Lazarra, a former AB production guru, is helping us plan future expansions. Steve Jones, once an AB sales manager, is completing construction of a ten-barrel brewery—Solid Rock Brewing—outside Austin. He knows of two other former AB colleagues working for craft brewers.

Kent Taylor of Blackstone Brewpub & Brewery in Nashville has a former MillerCoors packaging manager anchoring his packaging lines. Randy Mosher at 5 Rabbits Cerveceria hired two brewers from the AB-owned Goose Island. Dogfish's brewmaster and brewing supervisor are both former MillerCoors employees. Steve Dunkerken of Ritual Brewing Co., hired Ed Heethuis, a former AB sales manager, to handle sales and distributor management. Schlafly Brewing hired Alastair Pringle, a former AB brewer, and his former colleagues have found work with many other small brewers. As the craft beer industry grows, I have no doubt that more and more former employees of AB and MillerCoors will work their way into key roles.

Craft brewers are developing many new production strategies and business models. I don't think any single strategy is right for the future of craft brewing.

Sam Calagione of Dogfish Head believes all these categories will see successes and failures. "There are going to be awesome success models at every scale," he said. "There are going to be local breweries that do awesome local beer that cannot travel. There will be awesome regionals, and there will be awesome nationals, and internationals. The cream will rise to the top."

But one thing is certain: you must brew consistent quality beer. "In the era when Dogfish was born, they would forgive you because you were a local option," he said. "Delawareans were drinking Dogfish not because they wanted the hoppiest beer made with continual hopping or a Randall, but because they wanted to support a local company. Now every community has more than one local option. If you are not brewing consistent quality beer, you are not going to make it."[17]

Some people believe the large international brewers will continue to build their craft brands, acquire existing craft brewers, and eventually tame the revolution. Jim Koch told me he believes the large brewers could steal the revolution by producing craft-like beers at a lower price point. They could use their scale advantages—lower costs for raw materials and lower production costs—to overwhelm the craft brewing revolution.[18]

J. B. Shireman, an industry consultant who once was a sales rep for New Belgium, disagrees. "I don't think there is any way they are stopping [the revolution]," he said. "It is so deep and so widespread, but more to the point, it is so completely out of their hands. It has so been given over to the consumer and societal trends that have to do with farm to table, and variety and newness, and upgrades that have to do with music and technology and all these things that are favorable to our movement that there is no way they are turning it around."

Shireman recalled sitting behind the industry analyst Bob Weinberg at a conference in 2003 when Shireman's then boss, Kim Jordan, predicted that craft beer would become 10 percent of the US beer market. At the time, it was 3.3 percent.

"I am literally sitting right behind him, and you know they are talking about the ten share, and everybody is applauding, and there is all this energy in the room, and Bob leans over to someone he is sitting next to and he says: 'Wonderful speech—not possible.' And I remember puffing my chest out and thinking, 'You're, like, the smartest guy in the room, and you are wrong! Cause we are going to do this! We so are going to do this, and you older guys just don't see it coming.' And I don't think any of the big brewers ever saw this. They were myopic. They were very inwardly focused on their own stuff, their own domestic beer and their competitors like Strohs and Pabst and Miller and Coors and AB, and they didn't see what was going on in the beverage world, much less in society."[19]

One huge issue looming for the older craft brewers is succession. How will those companies make the transition from their founders to a new generation? Fritz Maytag sold his company to former Skyy Vodka owners Keith Greggor and Tony Foglio. Paul Shipman has entrusted Redhook to the Craft Brewers Alliance, run by Andy Thomas, to which the Widmer brothers have entrusted their brewery, and Mattson Davis has entrusted Kona Brewing Co.

Ken Grossman at Sierra Nevada is planning to turn that company over to his son Brian. AB InBev has purchased Goose Island. The Ottaway family now controls Brooklyn Brewery, though Garrett Oliver and I still hold a minority share of common stock. Robin and Eric Ottaway are the next generation at Brooklyn. New Belgium is 100 percent employee owned, as is Full Sail. Gary Fish at Deschutes has tiptoed into employee ownership, selling 8 percent of his company to the employees. Boston Beer is publicly traded, but

Jim Koch controls its voting stock. Koch has said he needs no succession plan because he plans to live forever. The large brewers, both foreign and domestic, have made it clear they are interested in buying any craft brewer who wants to sell. The Moortgat family in Belgium, brewers of Duvel Ale, bought Boulevard Brewing Co. in October.

If you date the craft beer revolution to 1965, when Maytag bought Anchor Brewing Company, then the revolution is forty-eight years old.

The next forty-eight years are going to be very interesting.

EPILOGUE

2014 MARKED THE FIFTH STRAIGHT YEAR OF DOUBLE-DIGIT GROWTH FOR AMERICA'S craft brewers. Perhaps not surprisingly, 2014 also saw the long-simmering rift between the large brewers and the small brewers explode into open warfare. In a letter to Congress, Jim McGreevy, the new president of the Beer Institute (BI), issued a strong statement of opposition to the Brewers Association's tax bill, the Small BREW Act. McGreevy, a former lobbyist for the soft-drink industry, is no stranger to interindustry conflict. Remember Coke vs. Pepsi?

The letter zeroed in on the Small BREW Act's revision of the federal definition of a small brewer from 2 million barrels produced to 6 million. The letter said, in part, " . . . such a change would significantly expand the already-generous market advantages enjoyed by just a handful of players in the brewing sector, potentially affect state laws governing the structure of the industry."

The National Beer Wholesalers Association (NBWA) also wrote a letter to Congress opposing the Small BREW Act. (Relations between the BA and the NBWA have been strained since the BA published an op-ed in the *New York Times* in March 2014 titled "Free Craft Beer!," which challenged the fairness of franchise laws to small brewers.)

This means that in the new Congress, legislators will be forced to choose between supporting the BA bill or honoring the requests of the BI and NBWA. As if that were not potent enough opposition, in early 2015 the 1.4-million-member Teamsters Union weighed in on behalf of the large brewers.

Earlier in the year, the Beer Institute appointed Rogue Ales president Brett Joyce to its board, replacing me. The BI pointedly chose a small brewer who is not a member of the BA board. The BI claims to represent the entire beer industry, but its membership consists of only 50 small brewers. The BA has 2,400 small brewer members. Some prominent small brewers like Boston

Beer, Sierra Nevada and Deschutes have canceled their BI memberships in response to the BI's opposition to the Small BREW Act. More may follow.

It seems unlikely that the Small BREW Act, in its present form, can overcome the opposition of these two powerful industry trade groups plus the Teamsters. As you may recall, the NBWA's CARE Act failed in Congress because of the united opposition of the BI and the BA.

The BA's "Craft or Crafty?" op-ed, which appeared in the *St. Louis Post-Dispatch* in December 2012 and called out the megabrewers for their craft-like beers Blue Moon and Shock Top, also continues to reverberate with the media, further aggravating the BA–BI split. And the large brewers continue to lose volume and market share to the small brewers. With the economy rebounding, there were some signs of a tiny revival of the big brewers' brands, but they've lost close to 20 million barrels of volume in the past five years.

The BA amended its definition of *craft brewer* in 2014 in a way that allowed Yuengling and August Schell to become voting members. That assured that the BA's market share would jump to 11 percent. The BA has set a goal of 20 percent market share by 2020. I would not be surprised to see it reach 30 percent in the next couple of decades.

The BA grows stronger every year. Its budget for 2015 is $24 million. The organization bought a new headquarters building in Boulder, Colorado, and established an office and lobbyist in Washington in 2015. Close to 10,000 people attended the Craft Brewers Conference in Denver in 2014, and more are expected this year. The American Homebrewers Association has nearly 39,000 members. There are now state brewers associations in all 50 states.

In late 2014 McGreevy told me the BI would be introducing new tax relief legislation in 2015, based on a proposed compromise between the BI and the BA in mid-2014. This bill would extend tax relief to all brewers and importers. It would drop the idea of rolling back the beer excise tax to 1991 levels. Brewers that produce less than 2 million barrels would benefit significantly. The benefit for those that produce over 2 million would be capped at $4 million.

The BA ultimately rejected the compromise because it would have extended the tax break to foreign importers, but McGreevy told me he still hoped that the BA and the BI could come together on a joint bill.

The BI's insistence on extending the tax benefit to importers was based on the fact that some view the exclusion of imported beers as a violation of international trade rules. Indeed, I recall Fritz Maytag worrying about the BA's effort to garner tax advantages because it could trigger opposition based on World Trade Organization rules. Maytag feared that such efforts could result in American small brewers losing their tax break for production below 60,000 barrels. But that tax break has been in effect for almost 40 years with no opposition.

In an effort to reduce tensions with BI, the BA agreed to try to restrain its members from denigrating the megabrewers' products as "fizzy yellow beer," but it is virtually impossible to stay the tongues of 3,500 individual entrepreneurs. The spirit of revolution is at the heart of the craft beer revolution, as expressed in Garrett Oliver's story of the Beer Gods and Megaliths, Jerome Chicvara's 1997 *Star Wars* speech, and Jim Koch's first radio ads that first appeared 28 years ago.

Some craft brewers believe the large brewers could still co-opt the craft beer revolution by buying up small brewers and using their control of the distribution networks to push their "crafty" brands. These brewers believe that Blue Moon and Shock Top (the craft-like brews of MillerCoors and Anheuser-Busch InBev, respectively) are threats to the craft beer revolution. In 2014, AB InBev bought three more craft breweries, Blue Point Brewing Company in Long Island, New York; 10 Barrel Brewing Co. in Bend, Oregon; and Elysian Brewing in Seattle. These breweries joined Goose Island as arms of the AB InBev empire. AB InBev also owns 32.5 percent of the Craft Brew Alliance, which includes Redhook, Widmer Brothers, and Kona.

AB InBev continues to buy wholesalers where possible. In 2014, the Belgian-based conglomerate bought distribution operations in Oregon and Kentucky.

Jim Koch is the most eloquent and persuasive of the craft brewers on this subject. At a conference sponsored by *Beer Marketer's Insights* in May 2013, Koch credited AB InBev and MillerCoors with making quality beer, but went on to explain the importance of craft brewers' distinguishing themselves from the large brewers to create a "meaningful point of differentiation" that "creates a price premium, drives volume and engages consumers in a way that the beer industry has never done before." Without this, he said, craft brewers are unlikely to survive. He said the large brewers have greater access to ingredients and raw materials, and they can buy them at a much lower cost than craft brewers. Jim is the champion of the 6 million barrel legislation. His volume, which includes cider and the malt beverage "Twisted Tea," is well over 4 million barrels annually.

I think there are limits to the effectiveness of the craft beer revolutionary creed. I do not believe that the Small BREW Act, in its current form, has a chance of passing over the opposition of the BI, the NBWA and the Teamsters. I believe this unnecessary battle will cost both small brewers and large brewers much political capital in Washington, D.C., just as the CARE Act did a couple of years ago.

Craft brewers are winning the battle for market share. Why aggravate the big guys? The craft beer revolution is returning beer to its traditional, artisanal, local roots after decades of industrialization and mass production. Once you embrace the wonderful rainbow of beer styles of the craft beer revolution, it is impossible to return to the monotony of light lager beer. Blue Moon and Shock Top are not challenges to the craft beer revolution, but rather an admission by the large brewers that craft beer is here to stay. They are gateway beers that will introduce more and more consumers to real craft beer, to beer with flavor.

In used to think that sooner or later, the craft beer revolution was going to have to shelve its revolutionary spirit and begin to work with the large brewers and take responsibility for the overall health of the beer industry. But hope for cooperation is dimming as positions harden on the tax issue. In spite of the turmoil in 2014, the BA and BI worked together in 2015 to thwart a Food and Drug Administration proposal to further regulate the handling of spent grain. The two organizations also collaborated on a policy toward dietary guidelines.

The enemies of the beer industry favor higher taxes, more stringent regulation, and restrictions on the industry's right to promote its products. These enemies do not differentiate between craft brewers and large brewers. And the boundaries between large brewers and craft brewers are not always going to be clear. Private equity investors are swarming over the craft beer industry today. The new money is reminiscent of the IPO storm of the mid-1990s. Boston Beer's market capitalization is in excess of $3 billion, and Sierra Nevada and New Belgium are not far behind. That is good news for all brewers, because the value of the industry leaders is indicative of the value of all.

Industry divisions are not limited to large and small brewers. Some members of the new generation of craft brewers regard the nationally distributed craft brands as their main competition. Many self-distribute in a hyper-local territory and do not understand the conflict over franchise laws. Such divisions make the entire industry more vulnerable to its enemies.

No one should forget that Congress doubled the beer excise tax in 1991, and some organizations, like Mothers Against Drunk Driving and the Center for Science in the Public Interest, would like to see it doubled again. The large brewers could endure such a cataclysmic event, but I am not sure how many small brewers could. The BA and BI are squabbling over competing tax bills at a time when Congress and the White House are looking for ways to pay down the huge national debt. This lack of unity could not come at a worse time, since history shows that legislative bodies often rally around so-called "sin taxes" in times of need.

Craft brewers have banded together to create a powerful trade association with a smart and dedicated staff. Thanks to term limits, the BA board is transitioning from the first generation of craft brewers to the second and third. The future of the craft beer revolution depends on the wisdom and foresight of these new leaders.

—Steve Hindy
Brooklyn, New York, April 2015

APPENDIX A

A CHRONOLOGY OF LARGE BREWER EFFORTS TO ESTABLISH CRAFT-STYLE BRANDS

1985   Adolph Coors Company, Molson Brewery, and Kaltenberg Castle Brewery
       of Germany announce plans to build the Masters Brewing Co. in Chicago to
       produce super-premium beers.

1986   Miller Brewing Company (MBC) introduces Gettelman, a double-hopped lager
       named for a brewery acquired by Miller in 1961.

1987   Adolph Coors Company announces it is considering building on the site of
       the former Simon Pure Brewery in Buffalo, New York. Gary Truitt, Coors vice
       president of sales, says: "A small company in a land of giant breweries must be
       innovative. Microbreweries are the sign of the future."

       Anheuser-Busch (AB) launches Anheuser Marzen in Manchester, New
       Hampshire, and Anheuser Pilsner in Phoenix, Arizona.

       MBC purchases Jacob Leinenkugel Brewing Company of Chippewa Falls,
       Wisconsin.

1990   MBC launches its first all-malt beer, Miller Reserve, a 100 percent barley
       draft packaged in a 20-sided bottle and high-sided six pack. "We started with
       the most expensive brewing ingredient, barley, and used it exclusively," said
       new product category director David Krishock. "We then combine it with a
       costlier brewing process to produce a beer that represents the utmost in brewing
       quality."

1991   AB releases Michelob Golden Draft and Michelob Golden Draft Light.

1993   MBC introduces Leinenkugel's Red Lager and Miller Reserve Amber Ale.

Coors says it will expand its seasonal line and releases Coors Eisbock.

Miller releases Miller Reserve Velvet Stout.

1994   AB introduces Elk Mountain Amber Ale and Red Wolf Lager Beer.

AB buys 25 percent of Redhook Brewery of Seattle and announces a strategic distribution alliance.

MBC introduces Red Dog under the Plank Road Brewery name.

Coors introduces a summer seasonal weizenbier.

1995   Coors opens the Sandlot Brewery at Coors field in Denver.

Redhook establishes strategic alliance with Anheuser-Busch and announces they will build a $30 million brewery in Portsmouth, New Hampshire.

Coors introduces Blue Moon Brewing Company with three beers, Honey Blonde Ale, Nut Brown Ale, and Belgian White, all brewed at Matt Brewing Company in Utica, New York.

Miller's American Specialty Beer Co. buys stakes in the Celis Brewery in Austin, Texas, and the Shipyard Brewing Company in Portland, Maine.

1996   MBC releases Leinenkugel's Auburn Ale, the first top-fermented beer in its 128-year history.

AB releases Faust in a 16-ounce swing-top bottle. The beer is part of AB's American Originals series, based on a beer once brewed for the owner of a St. Louis oyster house.

MBC introduces Leinenkugel's Big Butt Doppelbock, Lowenbrau Pils, and Lowenbrau Marzen.

AB introduces American Hop Ale, Michelob Hefeweizen, and Winter's Bourbon Cask Ale.

1997   AB introduces Pacific Ridge Pale Ale, Michelob Honey Lager, Michelob Golden Pilsner, Michelob Pale Ale, and Michelob Porter. AB announces and then postpones Budweiser American Ale.

1998   AB introduces Michelob Maple Brown.

At the AB hop farm in Bonners Ferry, Idaho, samples of a sweet stout, a dry stout, a lager, and a 70-IBU IPA are poured. "We as brewers can make anything," says Terry Guriel from the Fort Collins, Colorado, brewery. "We've just got to convince the marketing department to sell it."

MBC announces Leinenkugel's Creamy Draft, a nitro-charged pale ale.

Shipyard buys back Miller's ownership stake.

2001   MBC closes the Celis Brewery in Austin and sells the brands to the Michigan Brewing Co.

2003   AB brings back Anheuser Marzen, a beer first released in the late 1980s. AB introduces World Select, a continental pilsner formulated by brewmasters from 10 countries.

2005   Miller and Coors agree to a joint venture, MillerCoors (MC).

AB announces Tilt, a beer with caffeine, guarana, and ginseng.

2006   MC announces Mickey's Stinger to compete with Tilt and Leinenkugel Sunset Wheat.

AB introduces Beach Bum Blonde Ale, described as "wonderfully crisp and easily drinkable" by brewmaster Florian Kuplent, as part of a series that will include Jack's Pumpkin Spice Ale, Winter Bourbon Cask Ale, and Spring Heat Spiced Wheat. Spring Heat Spiced Wheat was a forerunner to Shock Top. AB also releases Michelob Ultra Amber; Wild Blue, a blueberry beer; and Fresh Hop Ale.

2007   AB introduces Spring Heat Spiced Wheat, Amber Bock, Michelob Bavarian Wheat, and Michelob Cherry Celebrate, in an aluminum bottle shaped like a 155mm artillery shell. AB introduces Michelob Ultra pomegranate, raspberry, lime cactus, Tuscan orange grapefruit. AB also releases Red Bridge, a gluten-free sorghum beer.

MC announces a Henry Weinhard's New Original Amber Ale. MC releases Leinenkugel Berry Weisse and Honey Weisse. MC announces it is developing a Miller Craft Lite selection of beers, a wheat, amber and a blonde ale. MC introduces AC Golden Brewing Co. to make specialty beers like the Herman Joseph line, Winterfest and Colorado Native.

2008   MC kills the Miller Craft Lite line. MC announces Leinenkugel Summer Shandy.

AB announces the Michelob Brewing Company, "a huge growth opportunity in the craft beer segment." This includes a Michelob specialty line: amber, porter, pale ale, maerzen, Irish red, and dunkelweizen. AB introduces Michelob Winter's Bourbon Cask Ale. AB introduces Budweiser Amber Ale.

2009   AB introduces Michelob Hop Hound, Amber Wheat, and Honey Wheat. AB releases Bud Light Gold Wheat.

MC brings back Leinenkugel's first craft style beer, a lager.

2010   MC introduces Batch 19 in 12-ounce bottles and half gallon growlers. MC introduces Colorado Native, made with 100 percent Colorado ingredients.

AB introduces Michelob Ginger Wheat Beer. Coors Golden also launches a "Hidden Barrel" line, with a Peche, Apricot, Sour and Brett beers.

2011   AB acquires Goose Island Brewing Co and introduces Shock Top Raspberry Wheat Ale, Belgian Wheat, and Pumpkin Wheat.

2012   AB introduces Shock Top Lemon Shandy, Shock Top IPA, and Ultra Light Tea and Lemonade. AB announces Project 12, versions of Budweiser from the 12 AB breweries across America, each identified by its Zip Code.

MC announces Big Eddy Wee Heavy Scotch Ale and releases Third Shift, an amber lager.

2013   MillerCoors' Blue Moon Brewing Company releases a Vintage Ale Collection that features ales with the juice of red or white wine grapes. The whites are called Proximity and Golden Knot and the reds are Impulse and Crimson Crossing. Also under the Blue Moon brand are an Expressionist Collection featuring Short Straw Farmhouse Red Ale and Rounder Belgian-style Pale; a Graffiti Collection that includes Pine in the Neck and Tongue Thai-ed; a Seasonal Collection of Valencia Grove Amber, Agave Nectar Ale, Harvest Pumpkin Ale, and Mountain Abbey Ale; and Specialty Releases Sunshine Citrus Blonde, Blackberry Tart Ale, Caramel Apple Spiced Ale, Gingerbread Spiced Ale, and Raspberry Cream Ale.

AB's Shock Top brand releases limited edition beers Campfire Wheat—tastes like s'mores—and Ghost Pepper Wheat.

APPENDIX B

TOP 50 US BREWERS AND
TOP 10 US BREWERS AND IMPORTERS

TOP 50 US BREWERS (BY BARRELS SOLD)

Rank	Company	2012 Beer Sales by volume
1	Anheuser-Busch Inc.	99,200,000
2	MillerCoors	58,950,000
3	Pabst Brewing Co.	5,400,000
4	D. G. Yuengling and Son Inc.	2,789,736
5	Boston Beer Co.	2,125,000
6	North American Breweries	NA
7	Sierra Nevada Brewing Co.	966,007
8	New Belgium Brewing Co.	764,741
9	Craft Brew Alliance, Inc.	650,000
10	The Gambrinus Co.	605,896
11	Minhas Craft Brewery	258,000
12	Deschutes Brewery	255,093
13	Lagunitas Brewing Co.	244,420
14	Bell's Brewery, Inc.	216,316
15	Matt Brewing Co.	207,900
16	Harpoon Brewery	193,000
17	Stone Brewing Co.	177,199
18	Brooklyn Brewery	176,000
19	Boulevard Brewing Co.	173,793
20	Dogfish Head Craft Brewery	172,333
21	Abita Brewing Co.	151,000
22	World Brews/Winery Exchange	145,000
23	Shipyard Brewing Co.	140,000
24	Alaskan Brewing Co.	139,930
25	August Schell Brewing Co.	131,900
26	New Glarus Brewing Co.	126,727

27	Long Trail Brewing Co.	125,000
28	Great Lakes Brewing Co.	119,624
29	Firestone Walker Brewing Co.	118,564
30	Anchor Brewing Co.	117,000
31	Rogue Ales Brewery	113,209
32	Summit Brewing Co.	112,451
33	Full Sail Brewery	110,000
34	SweetWater Brewing Co.	110,000
35	Victory Brewing Co.	93,196
36	Oskar Blues Brewery	87,750
37	Pittsburgh Brewing Co.	85,000
38	Mendocino Brewing Co.	84,000
39	Cold Spring Brewing Co./Third Street Brewhouse	76,140
40	Flying Dog Brewery	NA
41	Founders Brewing Co.	71,000
42	Ninkasi Brewing Co.	68,427
43	CraftWorks	67,890
44	Odell Brewing Co.	67,194
45	Bear Republic Brewing Co.	65,314
46	Stevens Point Brewery Co.	63,600
47	Blue Point Brewing Co.	63,000
48	Southern Tier Brewing Co.	61,618
49	Lost Coast Brewery and Cafe	59,100
50	Karl Strauss Brewing Co.	58,700

TOP 10 US BREWERS AND IMPORTERS (BY BARRELS SOLD)

Rank	Company	2012 Beer Sales by volume
1	Anheuser-Busch InBev	99,200,000
2	MillerCoors	58,950,000
3	Crown Imports LLC	12,300,000
4	Heineken USA	8,460,000
5	Pabst Brewing Co.	5,950,000
6	D.G. Yuengling & Son	2,790,000
7	Boston Beer Company	2,727,000
8	North American Breweries	2,715,000
9	Diageo/Guinness	2,580,000
10	Mark Anthony Group	1,425,000

NOTES

PROLOGUE

1. Ray Daniels, "Cicerone Program Hits 30,000 Certified Beer Servers," *Craft Business Daily,* December 11, 2013.

CHAPTER ONE: THE PIONEERS

1. Manfred Friedrich and Donald Bull, *The Register of United States Breweries 1876–1976* (Donald Bull, 1976). There were 126 national and regional brewing companies who owned 182 breweries between them; All chapter opening statistics have been provided by the following two sources: Paul Gatza, Director of the Brewers Association, email to author, November 14, 2013; Pete Reid, Publisher of *Modern Brewery Age,* email to author, November 13, 2013.
2. The Brewers Association's Paul Gatza, interview with author, August 15, 2013.
3. Fritz Maytag and Ken Grossman, transcript of conversation at Craft Brewers Conference, May, 2012, San Diego, from Brewers Association tape recording transcribed by author.
4. Ibid.
5. Amy Mittelman, *Brewing Battles: A History of American Beer* (New York: Algora, 2008), 129.
6. Maytag and Grossman, Craft Brewers' Conference 2012.
7. Charley Ryan, interview by author, July 1, 2013, Brooklyn, New York.
8. Benj Steinman, publisher of *Beer Marketer's Insights,* interview with author, October 12, 2013.
9. Ken Grossman, *Beyond the Pale* (New York: Wiley, 2013), 36.
10. William Ristow and Michael E. Miller, "Brewing 'Real Ale' Is a Yeasty Business; An Obsession for 'Real Ale' That Led to a Business," *Washington Post,* July 9, 1978.
11. Suzanne Denison, telephone interview by author, July 8, 2013.
12. Ristow and Miller, "Brewing 'Real Ale.'"
13. John Holl, editor of *All About Beer* magazine, "The Man Who Started a Revolution," www.craftbeer.com, June 9, 2010.
14. Denison interview, July 8, 2013.
15. Jack McAuliffe, unpublished interview by John Holl, from the personal files of John Holl.
16. Don Barkeley talk at 1984 Microbrewery Conference, Denver, published in *New Brewer,* March–April 1985.
17. Jim Koch, interview by author, January 29, 2013, Craft Brewers Conference, San Antonio, Texas.
18. William Newman, interview by Greg Gorgio, *New Brewer,* July–August 1991, 35.
19. Peter Krebs, *Redhook: Beer Pioneer* (New York: Four Walls Eight Windows, 1998), 41.
20. Ibid., 80–81.
21. Ibid., 115.
22. Ibid., 116, 117.
23. Ibid., 128.
24. Ibid., 120.
25. Garret Oliver, ed., *Oxford Companion to Beer* (New York: Oxford University Press, 2012), 569; Matthew Reich, interview by author, November 17, 2012, Hastings-on-Hudson, New York.

26. F. X. Matt, interview by author, March 1988, Utica, New York.
27. Reich interview, November 17, 2012.
28. Ibid.
29. Ibid.
30. Krebs, *Redhook,* 7.
31. Reich interview, November 17, 2012.
32. Koch interview, January 29, 2013.
33. Reich interview, November 17, 2012.
34. Greg Giorgio, "Brewers School of Hard Knocks," *New Brewer,* July–August 1991, 36.
35. Ibid., 37.

CHAPTER TWO: POLITICS, WRITERS, TEACHERS, AND COMMUNITY BUILDERS

1. Nick Matt, telephone interview by author, July 11, 2013.
2. Ken Grossman, interview by author, February 26, 2013, Boulder, Colorado;
3. Amy Mittelman, *Brewing Battles: A History of American Beer* (New York: Algora, 2008).
4. Henry King, speech for the Craft Brewers Conference, April 25, 1995, in Austin, Texas, "How Small Brewers Got Their Tax Differential," *The New Brewer,* March–April 1996, 58-60.
5. Ibid.
6. The break did little to interrupt the downward spiral of many of these regional breweries. Their real problem was they had surrendered whatever local character there was in their products, and instead were making light lager beer like that produced by the national giants. They could not compete with AB and Miller in the price of their products or in television and radio marketing. The giants could buy hops, malt, corn, rice and packaging much cheaper than the regionals. Their situation was hopeless. The regionals may have been snickering at Fritz Maytag and his effort to revive Anchor Brewing Co., but they should have paid attention to him. Years later, some did.
7. Grossman interview, February 26, 2013.
8. Ibid.
9. King speech for the Craft Brewers Conference, April 25, 1995.
10. Charlie Papazian, introduction to *The Complete Joy of Homebrewing,* New York, Avon Books, 1984, 1.
11. Charlie Papazian, interview by author, February 27, 2013, Boulder, Colorado.
12. Papazian interview, February 27, 2013,
13. Ibid.
14. Ibid. Papazian recalls that Helmut Keininger, a professor at the prestigious German brewing school, the Weihenstephan Center of Life and Food Sciences, also attended an early BAA conference. Keininger committed suicide in 1986 after being jailed for adding chemicals to his beer, a violation of the German Purity Law, the Reinheitsgebot. The vaunted Reinheitsgebot was overturned by the European Court a year later as a restraint of trade among the European states.
15. John Holl, "The Man Who Started a Revolution," www.craftbeer.com, June 9, 2010.
16. Ken Grossman, *Beyond the Pale* (New York: Wiley, 2013), 53-54.
17. Michael Jackson, *The Simon & Schuster Pocket Guide to Beer* (New York: Fireside, 1986) 100.
18. Michael Jackson, *The World Guide to Beer* (Philadelphia: Running Press, 1977), 215.
19. Charlie Finkel, interview by author, June 15, 2012, Seattle, Washington.
20. Garrett Oliver, notes for Michael Jackson eulogy, 2007, from the personal files of Garrett Oliver.
21. Tommy Chou, interview by author, March 12, 2013, New York, New York.

CHAPTER 3: THE FIRST GENERATION

1. Alan Dikty, "Hanging From the Rafters," *New Brewer,* July–August 1984, 2.
2. Jim Koch, interview by author, January 29, 2013, Craft Brewers Conference, San Antonio, Texas.
3. Jim Koch, recording of Boston Beer radio ad circa 1986, transcribed by author.
4. Mark Stark, "Beer Wars, Round Two: A Boston brewer takes on his German rivals," *Newsweek,* June 8, 1996.

5.   Philip Van Munching, *Beer Blast* (New York: Random House, 1998), 149.

6.   Ibid., 154.

7.   Jim Koch, telephone interview by author, November 13, 2013.

8.   Ibid., 153.

9.   Ibid., 166.

10.   Koch interview, January 29, 2013.

11.   Virginia Thomas, "America's Beer Awards," *New Brewer,* July–August 1987, 8.

12.   Kurt Widmer, phone interview by the author, July 15, 2013.

13.   Daniel Bradford, interview by author, March 29, 2013, Washington, DC.

14.   Jeff Mendel, telephone interview by author, August 26, 2013.

15.   Bradford interview, March 29, 2013; Mendel interview, August 26, 2013.

16.   Daniel Bradford, "Contract Brewing: The Thorny Issue," *New Brewer,* November–December 1986, 29.

17.   Ibid.

18.   Bert Grant and Jim Koch, "Brewers Go Head to Head Over Beer Ads," *Wall Street Journal,* December 31, 1993.

19.   Papazian, interview by author, February 27, 2013, Boulder. Colorado.

20.   Virginia Thomas, "GABF Works for Resolve: Great American Beer Festival and Boston Beer Co. reach agreement," *New Brewer,* January–February 1994, 48.

21.   Ibid.

22.   Ibid.

CHAPTER FOUR: THE CLASS OF '88

1.   John Hickenlooper, email to author, October 15, 2013.

2.   David Bruce, e-mail to author, April 23, 2013.

3.   Stan Hieronymus, "The Class of '88," *All About Beer,* February 1998.

4.   John Hickenlooper, phone interview by author, April 24, 2013.

5.   Bruce email, April 23, 2013.

6.   Charlie Papazian, interview by author, February 27, 2013, Boulder, Colorado.

7.   Ibid.; Hickenlooper interview, April 24, 2013.

8.   Marty Jones, email to author, July 8, 2013.

9.   Karen Kane, interview of Greg Noonan, *Yankee Brew News,* January 1996.

10.   Janet Essman Franz, "Tap Dancing," *Business People—Vermont,* February 2007.

11.   Ibid.

12.   Ibid.

13.   Ibid.

14.   Ibid.

15.   Ibid.

16.   Ibid.

17.   Random House Webster's College Dictionary (New York: Random House, 2000), 1143.

18.   "About Us: Rogue Ales: The Creation," *Rogue,* n.d., http://rogue.com/about/about.php.

19.   Jack Joyce, telephone interview by author, February 21, 2013.

20.   Ibid.

21.   Nick Matt, telephone interview by author, July 11, 2013.

22.   Ibid.

23.   Ibid.

24.   Ibid.

25.   Mark Ruedrich, telephone interview by author, April 5, 2013.

26.   Richard Pfeffer, interview by author, March 27, 2013, Washington, DC.

27.   Ibid.

28.   Kathy Ames Carr, "Growth on Tap at Great Lakes Brewing Co.," *Crain's Cleveland Business,* September 27, 2010.

29.   Marianne Eppig, "Great Lakes Brewing: A Cleveland Ecosystem," *Renovating the Rust Belt* (blog), October 1, 2009, http://renovatingtherustbelt.wordpress.com/?s=pat+conway+great+lakes+brewing&submit=Search.

30. Ibid.; "Sustainability: Burning River Foundation," *Great Lakes Brewing*, n.d., http://www.greatlakesbrewing.com/sustainability/burning-river-foundation.
31. Carr, "Growth on Tap at Great Lakes Brewing Co."; The brewery has an Environmental Programs Director who will send you an annual Sustainability Report if you visit the company website.
32. Ibid.
33. Eppig, "Great Lakes Brewing."
34. Dan Gordon, email to author, August 22, 2013.
35. Ed Dinger, "Gordon-Biersch Restaurant Group Inc.,"*Gale Directory of Company Histories*, www.answers.com.
36. Charles Holloway and Andrea Higuera, "Gordon Biersch: New Challenges and Opportunities," Dan Gordan, interviewed for Stanford Business School case study of Gordon Biersch, case no. E-122, 2002, revised February 14, 2011.
37. Ibid.
38. Julie Johnson, "Full Pints-Pull Up a Stool with Greg Hall," *All About Beer*, September 2010.
39. Ibid.
40. John Hall, phone interview by author May 5, 2013.
41. Ibid.
42. "Q&A: Gary Fish, Founder and CEO, Deschutes Brewery," *Oregon Business*, October 1, 2008.
43. Ibid.
44. Ibid.
45. "McMenamins Pubs," McMenamins, www.mcmenamins.com/pubs (accessed November 19, 2013).
46. Gary Fish, interview by author, March 25, 2013, Washington, DC.
47. Ibid.
48. "Brooklyn Brewery Advertisement," *Ale Street News*, September–October 1995, back page.

CHAPTER FIVE: BIG MONEY MEETS CRAFT BREWING
1. Sallie L. Gaines, "Under Probe, Busch Defends Its Marketing," *Chicago Tribune*, October 3, 1997.
2. Marc E. Sorini, "Legal Monitor: Antitrust and Fair Trade," *The New Brewer*, November–December 1997, 81.
3. Fred Bowman, interview by author, March 30, 2013, Brooklyn, New York.
4. Paul Shipman, "Looking to the Future", *New Brewer*, July–August 1997.
5. Anonymous Ten Springs Executive, interview with author.
6. Jeffrey Coons, "Look Here, Wall Street! Four Specialty Brewers Went Public in 1995," *New Brewer*, January–February 1996.
7. Paul Shipman, "The Beginning of the End for Imports; The End of the Beginning for Micros," *New Brewer*, January–February 1992.
8. *New Brewer*, annual industry reviews, May–June 1997, 56; May–June 2013.
9. Greg Kitsock, "Flavor Reigns in Seattle," *New Brewer*, May–June 1997.
10. Jim Koch, interview with author, January 29, 2013, Craft Brewers Conference, San Antonio, Texas.
11. Ibid.
12. Stone Philips, "Brew HaHa," *Dateline NBC*, October, 13, 1996
13. Ibid.
14. Greg Kitsock, "BREW NEWS: Put Up Your Dukes," *New Brewer*, January–February 1997, 98.
15. Pete Slosberg, *Beer for Pete's Sake* (Boulder, CO: Siris Books, 1998), 62-64.
16. Ibid., 66-67.
17. Ibid., 68-71.
18. Ibid., 135
19. Ibid., 137
20. Pete Slosberg, interview by author, March 26, 2013, Craft Brewers Conference, Washington, DC.
21. Ibid., 66; Coons, "Look Here, Wall Street! Four Specialty Brewers Went Public in 1995."
22. George Hancock, interview by author, April 15, 2013, Phoenix, Arizona.

23. The irrepressible Belgian had revived the white beer style by resurrecting the Hoegaarden brand of his native land. Years earlier, Celis sold Hoegaarden to the Belgian giant InBev and embraced his new life in America.

24. Aaron Smith, "Shipyard Sails Into Union with Miller," *Bangor Daily News,* November 24, 1995; interview with Shipyard President Fred Forsley, October 26, 2012, www.journeytothe beerstore.blogspot.com.

25. Scott Sunde, "Microbrewery Pioneer Bert Grant Led Northwest Beer Revolution," *Seattle Post Intelligencer,* August 1, 2001.

26. Greg Kitsock, "Flavor Reigns in Seattle, May–June 1997, *The New Brewer,* 72.

27. Jerome Chicvara, "If You Build It, They Will Come," speech to Craft Brewers Conference, March 24, 1997, Seattle, Washington, transcribed by author from tape recording.

28. Ibid.

29. *Star Wars Episode IV: A New Hope,* directed by George Lucas, Los Angeles, California, 20th Century Fox Pictures, 1977.

30. Ibid.

31. Chicvara, "If You Build It, They Will Come."

32. Greg Kitsock, "The 1998 Craft-Brewers Conference and Trade Show," quoting keynote speaker Fritz Maytag, *New Brewer,* July–August 1998, 47.

33. David Geary, speech to 1996 Craft Brewers Conference, Boston, Massachusetts, transcribed in *Modern Brewery Age,* May 20, 1996, 7.

34. Jerome Chicvara, e-mail to author, February 11, 2013.

35. Ibid.

36. Koch interview, January 29, 2013. Koch later joined the board of directors of the Brewers Association as an at-large member and played an important role in the development of the organization. Thirteen brewers are elected to the board by the BA membership. Two members are appointed by the board as at-large members.

37. Helen Stapinski, "3100 Gallons of Good Beer Down a Drain," *The New York Times,*" May 7, 1997; Alex Fryer, "Redhook: Craft Beer Shakeout Due," *The Seattle Times,*" May 22, 1997; David Sharp, "Specialty Beers Still Too Special to Become a Market Force," *The Associated Press,* Portland, Maine, May 21, 2000; Tom Acitelli, "The Great Shakeout, 1996-2000," *The Audacity of Hops,* (Chicago: Chicago Review Press, 2013).

38. *Webster's Encyclopedic Unabridged Dictionary;* David Edgar, "1998 Industry in Review," *New Brewer,* May–June 1998, 18-19.

39. Rifka Rosenwein, "OBIT: Why Catamount Brewery Closed," *Inc.,* October 1, 2000.

40. Helene Stapinski, "3,100 Gallons of Good Beer Down a Drain: Microbrews Are Giving Way to Cans of Cheap Beer," *New York Times,* May 7, 1997.

CHAPTER SIX: THE SECOND GENERATION

1. Daniel Bradford, interview by author, March 29, 2013, Washington, DC.

2. *Brettanomyces,* or brett, as it is called, is considered a threat to quality in most breweries and wineries.

3. Tomme Arthur, "Inventing Styles for a Brave New World," *New Brewer,* January–February 2000.

4. Kim Jordan, telephone interview by author, February 12, 2013. Knight of Belgian Beer is an honorary title bestowed by the Belgian Brewers Guild.

5. Ibid.

6. Ibid.

7. J. B. Shireman, interview by author, May 7, 2013, Brooklyn, New York.

8. Ibid.

9. Ibid.

10. Ibid.

11. Arthur, "Inventing Styles."

12. Rob Tod, telephone interview by author, May 30, 2013.

13. Ibid.

14. Ibid.

15. Vinnie Cilurzo, e-mail to author, May 24, 2013.

16. Ibid.
17. Ibid.
18. Ibid.
19. Paul Gatza, email to author, November 5, 2013.
20. Greg Koch and Steve Wagner, with Randy Clemens, *The Craft of Stone Brewing Co.: Liquid Lore, Epic Recipes, and Unabashed Arrogance* (Berkeley: Ten Speed Press, 2011), 43.
21. Sam Calagione, telephone interview by author, May 30, 2013.
22. Ibid.
23. Ibid.
24. Ibid.
25. Garrett Oliver, interview by author, June 13, 2013, Brooklyn, New York.
26. Ibid.
27. Ibid.
28. Ibid.
29. Utopias, "Every Craft Beer Has a Story," Samuel Adams website, www.samueladams.com /craft/utopias (accessed November 4, 2013).
30. Dale Katechis, telephone interview by author, May 30, 2013.
31. Ibid.
32. The state government in North Carolina has aggressively courted small brewers, attracting New Belgium and Sierra Nevada as well as Oskar Blues.
33. Ibid.
34. Larry Bell, telephone interview by author, June 11, 2013. Two-row barley is considered to be the highest quality barley available.
35. Ibid.

CHAPTER SEVEN: BEER AND THE MEDIA

1. Daniel Bradford, interview by author, March 29, 2013, Washington, DC.
2. Rob Tod, telephone interview by author, May 30, 2013.
3. www.beeradvocate.com.
4. Todd and Jason Alstrom, telephone interview by author, April 25, 2013.
5. Ibid.
6. Ibid.
7. Ibid.
8. Ibid.
9. Ibid.
10. Joe Tucker, telephone interview by author, May 7, 2013.
11. Ibid.
12. Daniel Bradford, telephone interview by author, April 27, 2013.
13. Ibid.
14. Ibid.
15. Tom Dalldorf, telephone interview by author, May 10, 2013.
16. Ibid.
17. Tony Forder, telephone interview by author, May 8, 2013.
18. Scott Metzger, telephone interview by author, August 10, 2013.
19. Benj Steinman, e-mail to author, August 28, 2013.
20. Harry Schuhmacher, telephone interview by author, September 10, 2013.

CHAPTER 8: CRAFT BREWERS RESUSCITATE THE BREWERS' ASSOCIATION OF AMERICA

1. Obituary for William-Pflaumer, *New York Times,* May 29, 2010. Pflaumer, who also owned the Schmidt Brewery in Philadelphia, was forced to sell it after being convicted of tax evasion.
2. David Edgar, "Legislative Alert," *New Brewer,* July–August 1995, 7.
3. Kim Jordan, telephone interview by author, May 10, 2013.
4. Jack Joyce, telephone interview by author, February 21, 2013.
5. Ken Grossman, interview by author, February 26, 2013, Boulder, Colorado.
6. Rich Doyle, telephone interview by author, May 15, 2013.

7.   Gary Fish, interview by author, March 25, 2013, Washington, DC; Joyce interview, February 21, 2013.

8.   Joyce interview, February 21, 2013; Fish interview, March 25, 2013; Jordan interview, May 10, 2013.

9.   George Hancock, interview by author, April 15, 2013, Phoenix, Arizona.

10.   Jordan interview, May 10, 2013; Doyle interview, May 15, 2013.

11.   Doyle interview, May 15, 2013.

12.   "BAA Position on Miller Contract," adopted on December 22, 1998, Brewers Association of America archive, Brewers Association, Boulder, Colorado.

13.   Ibid.

14.   "BAA Position on Franchise Laws: Draft for Board Consideration," adopted on October 24, 1999, Brewers Association of America Archive, Brewers Association, Boulder, Colorado.

15.   Daniel Bradford, phone interview by author, April 28, 2013.

CHAPTER NINE: JAILBREAK

1.   Lomuscio was famous in Brooklyn for shooting his brother during a gunfight in their warehouse. The brother was not seriously wounded.

2.   Jerry Sheehan, interview by author, March 28, 2013, Washington, DC.

3.   Daniel Bradford, telephone interview by author, April 28, 2013

4.   Sheehan interview, March 28, 2013.

5.   Ibid.

6.   Liz Oliphant, *Ben E. Keith: The First 100 Years,1906-2006,* (Austin: Eakin Press, 2006), 32.

7.   Ibid., 135-152.

8.   Howard Hallam, telephone interview by author, May 24, 2013.

9.   Ibid.

10.   "AB 'Alignment' Comments Create Cracks in Nascent Big Brewer-Small Brewer-Distributor Unity," *Beer Marketer's Insights,* November 11, 2011.

11.   Benj Steinman, Beer Marketer's Insights conference, New York City, November 11, 2013.

12.   Robert Weinberg, phone interview with author, August 2, 2013.

13.   Jimmy Reyes, telephone interview by author, June 5, 2013.

14.   Ibid.

15.   Benj Steinman, e-mail to author, August 28, 2013.

16.   Ibid.

CHAPTER TEN: THE BREWERS' ASSOCIATION OF AMERICA AND THE ASSOCIATION OF BREWERS MERGE

1.   Bob Pease, e-mail to author, May 12, 2013.

2.   Steve Hindy, "One Voice for Craft Brewers: The Story Behind the Brewers Association," *New Brewer,* May–June 2006.

3.   Ibid.

4.   John Hickenlooper, telephone interview by author, April 24, 2013.

5.   Kim Jordan, telephone interview by author, May 10, 2013.

6.   Hickenlooper interview, April 24, 2013.

7.   Steve Hindy, "One Voice for Craft Brewers."

8.   Jack Joyce, telephone interview by author, February 21, 2013.

9.   Daniel Bradford, interview by author, March 29, 2013.

10.   Kim Jordan, telephone interview, May 10, 2013.

11.   Ibid.

12.   Steve Hindy, "One Voice for Craft Brewers."

13.   Ibid.

14.   Jordan interview, May 10, 2013.

15.   Steve Hindy, "One Voice for Craft Brewers."

16.   Ibid.

17.   Jordan interview, May 10, 2013.

CHAPTER ELEVEN: A SEAT AT THE TABLE

1.   Joe Thompson, e-mail to author, September 12, 2013.

2. Marc Sorini, email to author, October 28, 2013.

3. Adam Sasiadek, "What Is the Dormant Commerce Clause?" Constitutionland.com, http://constitutionland.com/Dormant_Commerce_Clause.html.

4. Joseph B. White, "Beer Distributors Say Yes to Middlemen," *The Wall Street Journal*, January 17, 2013.

5. Henry Graver, "Opinion: Set Michigan Craft Brewers Free," *The Wall Street Journal* online, August 9, 2013.

6. "Costco Reversed (Mostly)! Are Distribs, State Regs Regaining Traction in Fed Courts?" *Beer Marketer's Insights*, Volume 39, Number 3, February 11, 2008.

7. Testimony of Steve Hindy, Chairman and President, Brooklyn Brewery, Committee on the Judiciary of the House of Representatives, Subcommittee on Courts and Competition Policy, 112th Congress, March 18, 2010,

8. Testimony of Nida Samona, "Legal Issues Concerning State Alcohol Regulation," Committee on the Judiciary of the House of Representatives, Subcommittee on Courts and Competition Policy, 112th Congress, March 18, 2010, 38.

9. Testimony of Pamela S. Erikson, CEO of Public Action Management, "The Danger of Alcohol Deregulation: The United Kingdom Experience," Committee on the Judiciary of the House of Representatives, Subcommittee on Courts and Competition Policy, 112th Congress, March 18, 2010, 54-55.

10. Craig Purser, email to author, August 9, 2013.

11. John N. Friedman, "Economic Impact of the Small Brewers Reinvestment and Expanding Workforce Act (H.R. 494)," unpublished research paper sponsored by the Brewers Association, March 19, 2013.

12. Bob Pease, email to the author, August 29, 2013.

13. Anonymous sources in the Beer Institute, interview with the author.

14. Kevin Bogardus, "Beer Fight Brewing Over Taxes," *The Hill*, March 27, 2013.

15. Joan Voight, "Craft Wars: How the world's biggest brewers developed a taste for the artisanal—and indie beer brands fought back," *Adweek*, April 1-7, 2013.

16. Charlie Papazian, Bob Pease, and Dan Kopman, "Craft or Crafty: Consumers Deserve to Know the Truth," *St. Louis Post Dispatch*, December 13, 2013, http://www.stltoday.com/news/opinion/columns/craft-or-crafty-consumers-deserve-to-know-the-truth/article_e34ce949-d34a-5b0f-ba92-9e6db5a3ed99.html.

17. Tom Long, "For Brewers, It's Not the Size That Counts," CNN.com, December 21, 2012, http://eatocracy.cnn.com/2012/12/21/opinion-for-breweries-its-not-the-size-that-counts/.

18. Steve Hindy, "Opinion: Don't Let Big Brewers Win Beer Wars," CNN.com, December 10, 2012, http://eatocracy.cnn.com/2012/12/12/hindy-beer-wars/index.html/.

CHAPTER TWELVE: THE THIRD GENERATION

1. Amy Mittelman, *Brewing Battles: A History of American Beer* (New York: Algora, 2008), 55; Will Anderson, *The Breweries of Brooklyn* (New York: Anderson,1976).

2. Larry Sidon, telephone interview by author, June 21, 2013.

3. Ibid.

4. Ben Millstein, telephone interview by author, May 28, 2013.

5. Ibid.

6. Evan Klein, interview by author, June 4, 2013, Hempstead, New York.

7. Ibid.

8. Ryan Soroka, telephone interview by author, June 3, 2013.

9. Ibid.

10. Dan Carey, telephone interview by author, June 12, 2013.

11. Tony Magee, *Lagunitas Brewing Company: The Story* (Sonoma, California: Charles Pinot Press, 2012), 90.

12. Ken Grossman, interview by author, March 28, 2013.

13. Dann Holley-Paquette and Martha Holley-Paquette, interviewed at Brewbound Conference, May 2, 2013, Boston MA, www.brewbound.com%2fnews%2fbrewbound-session-showcases-the-many-identities-of-craft-brewers.

14. Brad Hittle, interview by author, June 6, 2013, Stratford, CT.

15. "Brew Hub Announces Plans for First Brewery in Lakeland, Florida," Market Watch, March 19, 2013, http://www.marketwatch.com/story/brew-hub-announces-plans-for-first-brewery -in-lakeland-florida-2013-03-19.
16. Hittle interview, June 6, 2013.
17. Sam Calagione, telephone interview by author, May 30, 2013.
18. Jim Koch, interview by author, January 29, 2013, San Antonio, TX.
19. J. B. Shireman, interview by author, May 7, 2013, Brooklyn, New York.

INDEX

AB-InBev. *see* Anheuser-Busch (AB)
Adolph Coors Company. *see* Coors
Ale Street News, 87, 151–152
ale yeast vs. lager yeast, 36
All About Beer (magazine), 14, 60, 80, 144, 148–149, 164, 176, 191
Allagash Brewing Company, 122–125
Allen, Tom, 70–72
American Homebrewer's Association (AHA), 33–35, 58, 147, 189–193, 227
American Hop Ale, 232
Anchor Brewing Company, 6–14, 18, 20, 22, 24, 27, 33, 40, 41, 51, 139, 226, 236
Anchor Steam Beer, 9–12, 18, 22, 24
Anheuser-Busch (AB)
    dispute with Miller over use of additives in their beers, 11
    distributors that have following Sheehan's lead, 181–183
    and Gussie Busch II, 178–179
    100 percent share of mind policy," 90–91, 104–105, 156, 164–165, 175–176, 194
    and Shock Top, 206, 220, 228, 233, 234
    and TV ads, 143–144
    versus Koch, 90
    see also Budweiser; Goose Island
Arrogant Bastard Ale, 128–130
Arthur, Tomme, 114–115, 122, 126
artisanal brewer(s). *see* craft brewer(s)/breweries
Association of Brewers (AOB)
    the merger of the BAA and the AOB, 83, 187–194
    versus the BAA, in government affairs/politics, 91
August Schell Brewing Company, 10, 30, 40, 67, 95
    beer sales by volume in 2012, 235
    as a member of the BAA, 161
    objection to the BA's definition of craft beer, 193, 204–206

Austin, Peter, 16, 74
the bard of beer. *see* Jackson, Michael

Barkley, Don, 15, 71, 91
Becker, Jeff, 160, 165–169, 195
Beck's
    AB acquires, 181
    Koch attacks, 45–47
    as popular tap beer in NY, 21
Bell, James, 109
Bell, Larry, 54, 139–140, 162–163, 205
Bell's Brewery, 139–140
beer
    festivals, 32–35, 48–56, 60, 97, 110, 117, 139, 146, 148, 149, 152, 154, 157, 161, 164, 166, 188–190, 193
    imported, 21, 46, 47, 68, 87, 90, 124, 148, 171, 172
    and IPA without the bitterness, 132
    lambic, 40, 116, 122
    and the media, 143–154
    and the old three-pint rule, 141
    preservatives in, 45
    recipes are like poetry, 115
    war(s), 46, 52–54, 104–106, 205–206
    see also craft brewer(s)/breweries; individual breweries/brewers names
Beer Advocate, 132, 133, 136, 144–146, 154, 215
Beer Blast (Van Munching), 46
Beer Business Daily, 153–154, 176
Beer for Pete's Sake (Slosberg), 99
The Beer Hunter (TV series), 37
Beer Institute (BI), 158, 187, 195, 229
Beer Marketer's Insights, 153, 184, 196, 228
Beer School: Bottling Success at the Brooklyn Brewery (Hindy and Potter), 88
Beer Wholesaler, 22
Berger, Don, 52
Bernadette, Andy, 22, 51
Beyond the Pale (Grossman), 13

Biersch, Dean, 78–80
Big Book of Brewing (Line), 13, 29, 70
The Blind Pig, 125
Boulder Beer Company, 5, 33, 35, 49, 50
bottle conditioning, 29, 136
Boston Beer Company. *see* Koch, Jim; Sam Adams
Boston Consulting Group (BCG), 24, 45, 108
Boston Globe, 53, 55, 98
Boukhart, Peter, 126
Bowker, Gordon, 18–19, 36
Bowman, Fred, 90, 96, 108, 161, 164
Bradford, Daniel, 48–50, 113, 144, 148–150, 164, 166–167, 176, 188–191
Brewers Association (BA), 157
    and the BEER Act, 205, 229
    and definition of craft brewer, 82, 204–206
    evolution of, 3
    executive board, 191
    exports of craft beer, 221
    and Fish, 85
    fosters the creation of state brewers associations, 227
    founders of, 3
    gets a seat on the voting board of the Beer Institute (BI), 195–207
    meets with August Busch IV, 193–194
    membership, 227
    and the merger of the BAA and the AOB, 83, 187–194
    and the NBWA, 203
    New York State, 203
    and post-Prohibition regulation, 197
    and the small BREW act, 205, 229
    statistics, 1, 57, 211
    and tax break for small brewers, 204
Brewer's Association of America (BAA)
    beginnings of, 9, 27
    convention(s), 8–9